The Glyph and the Gramophone

S0-ANE-394

NEW DIRECTIONS IN RELIGION AND LITERATURE

This series aims to showcase new work at the forefront of religion and literature through short studies written by leading and rising scholars in the field. Books will pursue a variety of theoretical approaches as they engage with writing from different religious and literary traditions. Collectively, the series will offer a timely critical intervention to the interdisciplinary crossover between religion and literature, speaking to wider contemporary interests and mapping out new directions for the field in the early twenty-first century.

Also Available From Bloomsbury:

Blake. Wordsworth. Religion. Jonathan Roberts
Do the Gods Wear Capes?, Ben Saunders
England's Secular Scripture, Jo Carruthers
John Cage and Buddhist Ecopoetics, Peter Jaeger
Late Walter Benjamin, John Schad
The New Atheist Novel, Arthur Bradley and Andrew Tate
Victorian Parables, Susan E. Colón

Forthcoming:

Faithful Reading, Mark Knight and Emma Mason
Rewriting the Old Testament in Anglo-Saxon Verse,
Samantha Zacher

The Glyph and the Gramophone

D. H. Lawrence's Religion

LUKE FERRETTER

New Directions in Religion and
Literature

B L O O M S B U R Y

LONDON · NEW DELHI · NEW YORK · SYDNEY

Bloomsbury Academic

An imprint of Bloomsbury Publishing Plc

50 Bedford Square
London
WC1B 3DP
UK

1385 Broadway
New York
NY 10018
USA

www.bloomsbury.com

Bloomsbury is a registered trade mark of Bloomsbury Publishing Plc

First published 2013

© Luke Ferretter, 2013

Luke Ferretter has asserted his right under the Copyright, Designs and
Patents Act, 1988, to be identified as Author of this work.

All rights reserved. No part of this publication may be reproduced or transmitted in any
form or by any means, electronic or mechanical, including photocopying, recording, or
any information storage or retrieval system, without prior
permission in writing from the publishers.

No responsibility for loss caused to any individual or organization acting on or
refraining from action as a result of the material in this publication can
be accepted by Bloomsbury or the author.

British Library Cataloguing-in-Publication Data
A catalogue record for this book is available from the British Library.

ISBN: HB: 978-1-4411-3258-1
PB: 978-1-4411-2295-7
ePDF: 978-1-4411-2435-7
ePub: 978-1-4411-1939-1

Library of Congress Cataloging-in-Publication Data
Ferretter, Luke, 1970–
The glyph and the gramophone: D. H. Lawrence's religion/Luke Ferretter.
pages cm. – (New Directions in Religion and Literature)
Includes bibliographical references and index.
ISBN 978-1-4411-2295-7 (pbk.) – ISBN 978-1-4411-3258-1 (hardcover) –
ISBN 978-1-4411-2435-7 (pdf) – ISBN 978-1-4411-1939-1 (epub)
1. Lawrence, D. H. (David Herbert), 1885–1930 – Religion. I. Title.
PR6023.A93Z62837 2013
823'.912–dc23
2013008912

Typeset by Deanta Global Publishing Services, Chennai, India
Printed and bound in Great Britain

In Memoriam Donley H. Johnson, 1946–2005

Contents

Acknowledgements ix
Abbreviations x

Introduction 1

1 'Beyond these gods of today': The war years 11

Rananim 11
The dialogue with Russell 15
'The Crown' 20
Theosophy 27
Women in Love 40

2 'The cultured animist': Native American religion 51

First essays, 1922–23 52
Essays on Native American religion, 1924 54
Lawrence and the Hopi 57
Pan in America 65
'The Woman Who Rode Away': The question of gender 67
Apophasis in *St Mawr* 76

3 'The dark God': From *Kangaroo* to *The Plumed Serpent* 81

Kangaroo 81
Mexican religion 88
Quetzalcoatl 98
The *Adelphi* articles 102
The Plumed Serpent: The morning star 104
The Plumed Serpent: Religion in society 106
The question of authority 112

4 'Being in touch': Last works 121

Lady Chatterley's Lover 121
The Escaped Cock 130
Sketches of Etruscan Places 136
Apocalypse 141
'The Last Poems Notebook' 147

Bibliography 159
Index 169

Acknowledgements

I would like to thank the College of Arts and Sciences at Baylor University for the awards of a Research Leave and a Summer Sabbatical, during which I worked on this book. Dr Dianna Vitanza chaired a department that supported my research and assisted me in every way. I am especially grateful for the funds to travel to the past four international D. H. Lawrence conferences.

These conferences have been a great source of intellectual companionship, and I would like to express my appreciation to Ginette Katz-Roy and Stephen Rowley for their superb organization of them. This book has benefitted enormously from the work and the conversation of Keith Cushman, Michael Bell, Ginette Katz-Roy, Sandra Gilbert, Bethan Jones, Andrew Harrison, Neil Roberts, Nathalya Reinhold, Marina Ragachewskaya, Howard Booth, the late Peter Preston, George Hyde, Sue Reid, Jane Costin, Carl Krockel, Laurence Steven, Jonathan Long and many others.

I would like to thank David Avital and Laura Murray at Bloomsbury for their exemplary work as editors. It has been their skill, support and patience that have seen this book through to its final form. I would also like to thank Mark Knight and Emma Mason for commissioning this book, and for their support throughout the entire project. Writing this book has been just one of the many ways from which I have benefitted from the work that they do in promoting the study of literature and religion.

I am grateful to Jim Nogalski for his help with my Hebrew, and for the talent and efficiency of two outstanding research assistants, Alisha Barker and Rachel de Smith. My thanks to Janet Sheets, Andrea Turner, Libby Shockley and Janet Jasek at Baylor University Libraries. I would like to thank my parents and my mother-in-law for their constant support throughout the time I spent working on this book. My greatest debt, as always, is to my beloved wife Jen.

Abbreviations

The following abbreviations have been used for works by D. H. Lawrence. Unless otherwise indicated, all references are to the Cambridge Edition of the Letters and Works of D. H. Lawrence, published by Cambridge University Press.

A   *Apocalypse and the Writings on Revelation*, ed. Mara Kalnins, 1980.

FSLC   *The First and Second Lady Chatterley Novels*, ed. Dieter Mehl and Christa Jansohn, 2001.

FWL   *The First Women in Love*, ed. John Worthen and Lindeth Vasey, 1998.

HRC   D. H. Lawrence Collection, Harry Ransom Center, University of Texas.

IR   *Introductions and Reviews*, ed. N. H. Reeve and John Worthen, 2005.

K   *Kangaroo*, ed. Bruce Steele, 1994.

L   *The Letters of D. H. Lawrence*, ed. James T. Boulton et al., 8 vols, 1979–2000.

LCL   *Lady Chatterley's Lover; A Propos of 'Lady Chatterley's Lover'*, ed. Michael Squires, 1993.

LEA   *Late Essays and Articles*, ed. James T. Boulton, 2004.

LBR   *Letters to Bertrand Russell*, ed. Harry T. Moore (New York: Gotham Book Mart, 1948)

MEH   *Movements in European History*, ed. Philip Crumpton, 1989.

MM   *Mornings in Mexico and Other Essays*, ed. Virginia Crosswhite Hyde, 2009.

P   *The Poems*, 2 vols., ed. Christopher Pollnitz, 2013.

PS   *The Plumed Serpent*, ed. L. D. Clark, 1987.

PPS   *The Plumed Serpent*, ed. L. D. Clark and Virginia Crosswhite Hyde (London: Penguin, 1995).

PUFU   *Psychoanalysis of the Unconscious and Fantasia of the Unconscious*, ed. Bruce Steele, 2004.

Q   *Quetzalcoatl*, ed. N. H. Reeve, 2011.

QM   *Quetzalcoatl*, ed. Louis L. Martz (New York: New Directions Books, 1995).

R   *The Rainbow*, ed. Mark Kinkead-Weekes, 1989.

RDP   *Reflections on the Death of a Porcupine and Other Essays*, ed. Michael Herbert, 1988.

SCAL   *Studies in Classic American Literature*, ed. Ezra Greenspan, Lindeth Vasey and John Worthen, 2003.

SEP   *Sketches of Etruscan Places and Other Italian Essays*, ed. Simonetta de Filippis, 1992.

SM   *St. Mawr and Other Stories*, ed. Brian Finney, 1983.

STH   *Study of Thomas Hardy and Other Essays*, ed. Bruce Steele, 1985.

TI   *Twilight in Italy and Other Essays*, ed. Paul Eggert, 1994.

VG   *The Virgin and the Gipsy and Other Stories*, ed. Michael Herbert, Bethan Jones and Lindeth Vasey, 2005.

WL   *Women in Love*, ed. David Farmer, Lindeth Vasey and John Worthen, 1987.

WRA   *The Woman Who Rode Away and Other Stories*, ed. Dieter Mehl and Christa Jansohn, 1995.

Introduction

D. H. Lawrence identified himself as a religious man throughout his life. At twenty-two, reflecting on his rejection of the Congregationalist Christianity in which he was brought up, he speaks of 'the rather deep religious faith' of his youth (*L* 1: 72). A year earlier, in December 1907, as he writes to his minister, Rev Robert Reid, explaining why he can no longer profess the Christian faith, he remains clear that he continues to hold religious beliefs of his own. 'I cannot be a materialist', he tells Reid, but 'a Cosmic God I can . . . believe in' and 'for the present my religion is the lessening, in some pitiful moiety, the great human discrepancies' (*L* 1: 40–1). He writes:

> A man gradually formulates his religion, be it what it may. A man has no religion who has not slowly and painfully gathered one together, adding to it, shaping it; and one's religion is never complete and final, it seems, but must always be undergoing modification. (40)

For the present, Lawrence concludes, 'there seems some hope in a religion which will not answer one with fiats and decrees' (41). At the same time as he finally expresses his rejection of Christianity, that is, Lawrence is clear that he continues to be developing religious beliefs of his own. Something similar occurs in 'Hymns in a Man's Life', written at the end of Lawrence's life. He reflects, 'By the time I was sixteen I had criticised and got over the christian dogma', but he continues to believe in 'the religious element inherent in all life', 'the *natural* religious sense' of wonder that all living creatures share, and which he himself learned in part from the hymns, despite the banality of their content, of his childhood (*LEA* 132).

From the time of his rejection of Christianity onwards, Lawrence continually professes religious beliefs of his own. In 1910, he writes,

'I have my own religion, which is to me the truth' (*L* 1: 215). By 1913, he can specify, 'My great religion is a belief in the blood, the flesh, as being wiser than the intellect' (*L* 1: 503), and in his review of Georgian poets, among whom he includes himself, he writes, 'Our religion is loving' (*IR* 204). In the same year, as he describes the development of his creative process, he writes, 'I always feel as if I stood naked for the fire of almighty God to go through me – and it's rather an awful feeling. One has to be so terribly religious, to be an artist' (*L* 1: 519). In 1914, he writes to his literary mentor Edward Garnett, concerning the novel that will become *The Rainbow*, 'Primarily I am a passionately religious man, and my novels must be written from the depths of my religious experience' (*L* 2: 165). In this book, I will expound this twofold claim of Lawrence's, which continues to be true for the rest of his writing life. I will trace the history, from 1915 to the end of his life, of Lawrence's developing religious thought and of his expressions of that thought in his literary work.

Lawrence rarely broaches a definition of religion. As we have seen, in writing to Rev Reid, he argues that a genuine religion is something that an individual develops and builds throughout his or her life, a process that lasts for the whole of an individual's life (*L* 1: 40). Lawrence reflects at greatest length on the nature of religion in an early version of *Apocalypse*, the study of the book of Revelation he wrote in the very last months of his life. In May 1919, he had asked his friend Samuel Koteliansky to send him a copy of William James' *The Varieties of Religious Experience* (*L* 3: 355–6; cf. Chambers 113), and in *Apocalypse* a decade later he follows James in arguing that religion consists primarily in emotional experience and only secondarily in theological reflections based on that experience. 'Religion is not a question of belief', he writes, 'it is a question of feeling. It is a question of a certain deep feeling which seems to soothe and reassure the whole soul' (*A* 154). As he goes on to describe art as a kind of religion, he adds, 'Whenever the soul is moved to a certain fullness of experience, that is religion. Every sincere and genuine feeling is a religious feeling' (155). In 'New Mexico', he says something similar: 'Religion is an experience, an uncontrollable, sensual experience even more so than love: I use sensual to mean an experience deep down in the senses, inexplicable and inscrutable' (*MM* 178). For Lawrence, religion consists first in experience, experience that is felt throughout the whole person and that is therefore not explicable in rational discourse. In 'The Risen Lord', he writes that 'the great religious images are only images of our own experience, or of our own state of mind or soul' (*LEA* 267), and in the first draft of his poem 'Demiurge', he emphasizes that it is when the whole person is involved, body and soul, that an experience is religious:

> Religion knows better than philosophy.
> Religion knows that Jesus was never Jesus
> till he was born from a womb, and ate soup and bread
> and grew up, and became, in the wonder of creation, Jesus,
> with a body and with needs, and a lovely spirit. (*P* 1270)

In *Apocalypse*, Lawrence specifies that 'everything that puts us into connection, into vivid touch, is religious' (155). In 'New Mexico', he adds, '[The] effort into sheer, naked contact, *without an intermediary or mediator*, is the real meaning of religion' (181). Religion consists for Lawrence in strong emotions that put the individual into contact with something that transcends his or her ordinary experience. A religious experience is one of 'linking up' or 'making a new connection' (*A* 156), which brings the person fully to life. In the early version of *Apocalypse*, he derives this definition from one of the etymologies of the word, the Latin *ligare*, 'to bind', with the prefix *re-*, 'back' or 'again'. He writes that 'the religious way of knowledge', as opposed to the scientific, is a 'linking up, binding back (religio) or referring back to a centre and a wholeness' (190). It is in this sense that the priestess of Isis in *The Escaped Cock* is a 'true priestess', because she sees in the face of the man who had died 'the other kind of beauty', 'the sheer stillness of the deeper life' (*VG* 147).

In speaking of Lawrence's 'religion' in this book, I will be using the term first in his own sense of the word. That is, I will mean that religion consists in emotions felt throughout the whole person, which put that person into relationship with something that transcends his or her known experience, and from which a sense of wholeness derives. In *The Varieties of Religious Experience*, William James argues that 'the word "religion" cannot stand for any single principle or essence', but proposes as a working definition, '*the feelings, acts and experiences of individual men in their solitude, so far as they apprehend themselves to*

William James

stand in relation to what they may consider the divine' (31). To account for atheistic religions such as Buddhism or that of Emerson, James means by 'divine' 'any object that is god*like*, whether it be a concrete deity or not' (34), and by 'god' he means first 'whatever . . . were most primal and enveloping and deeply true', or simply a 'primal truth' (34), and second, in order not to stretch the term too far beyond its ordinary use, 'only such a primal reality as the individual feels impelled to respond to solemnly and gravely' (38). This solemnity, James adds, always 'seems to contain a certain measure of its own opposite in solution', such that one can speak of a 'solemn joy', for example (48). Lawrence's letter to Frieda of May 1912 exemplifies the concept well: 'We can even wait a bit religiously for one another. My next coming to you is solemn, intrinsically – I am solemn over it – not sad, oh no – but it is my marriage after all, and a great thing' (*L* 1: 401). James concludes by 'summing up in the broadest possible way the characteristics of the religious life', which he finds to comprise the following beliefs:

1   That the visible world is part of a more spiritual universe from which it draws its chief significance;
2   That union or harmonious relation with that higher universe is our true end;
3   That prayer or inner communion with the spirit thereof – be that spirit 'God' or 'law' – is a process wherein work is really done, and spiritual energy flows in and produces effects, psychological or material, in the phenomenal world. (485)

These three beliefs are fundamental to Lawrence's thinking. In describing the thought of Lawrence's that I will be calling religious in the following pages, I will mean by that term, in addition to the senses Lawrence himself gives it, positions that can be reduced to one or more of these three related beliefs enumerated by James.

    The second scholar of religion on whose work I will draw in speaking of religion is Mircea Eliade. In *The Elementary Forms of Religious Life*, Émile Durkheim had argued that religious beliefs and practices are characterized by a division of the world into two absolutely heterogeneous worlds, that of the sacred and that of the profane:

All known religious beliefs, whether simple or complex, present a common quality: they presuppose a classification of things . . . into two classes, two opposite kinds, generally designated by two distinct terms effectively translated by the words *profane* and *sacred*. The division of the world into two comprehensive domains, one sacred, the other profane, is the hallmark of religious thought. (36)

In *The Sacred and the Profane*, Eliade develops this account of religion. Religious men and women live in a sacred rather than a profane world, he argues, where the sacred is the manifestation of a different, 'wholly other' world than the profane, non-sacred world, and which appears in and through the latter (11–12). Sacred and profane, indeed, are 'two modes of being in the world, two existential situations assumed by man in the course of his history' (14), and *homo religiosus* has always assumed and continues in the present to assume the former. Religion consists, throughout history and across different cultures, in 'a single type of behaviour', the 'modalities' of which Eliade sets out to describe (18). Religious man, he argues, lives in sacred space and sacred time, and he regards both the cosmos and human existence as sacred.

The sacred, for Eliade, constitutes the fullness of being, that which is really real. The profane, by contrast, seems to the religious man or woman disappointingly lacking in reality, a shadow, a sham form of existence in comparison to the sacred. Eliade writes, in a phrase that could serve as the motto of this investigation of Lawrence's thought, 'Religious man thirsts for *being*' (64). He has 'an ontological thirst', a 'will to take his stand at the very heart of the real', to be 'in short, precisely where he is *closest to the gods*' (64–5). 'If by some evil chance', Eliade writes, 'he strays into [the profane world], he feels emptied of his ontic substance, as if he were dissolving in Chaos, and he finally dies' (64). He sums up:

> *Homo religiosus* always believes that there is an absolute reality, the sacred, which transcends this world but which manifests itself in this world, thereby sanctifying it and making it real. He further believes that life has a sacred origin and that human existence realizes all of its potentialities in proportion as it is religious – that is, participates in reality. (202)

Lawrence is an example of Eliade's *homo religiosus* in these two senses. Lawrence's religious thought is an account first of that which is most real in the world, of that which most truly is, and second of that which therefore makes human life fully human. Those things that are, in Eliade's term, sacred to Lawrence are things in which the heart of reality itself, that which is most real, is revealed and experienced in the ordinary, 'profane' and, by contrast, less than truly real, modern world in which he lives.

A second significant aspect of Eliade's account of the sacred with respect to Lawrence is that religious men and women find the cosmos itself sacred: 'the cosmos as a whole is an organism at once *real*, *living* and *sacred*; it simultaneously reveals the modalities of being and of sacrality' (117). It is a fundamental principle of Lawrence's religion that the cosmos is alive, and that it is therefore sacred, that is fundamentally real. Eliade even goes on to argue that, as a result of the sacred nature of the cosmos, '[religious] man conceives of himself as a microcosm . . . in other words, he finds in himself the same sanctity that he recognises in the cosmos' (165), a view that Lawrence also espouses. Indeed, life itself is sacred, in Eliade's account: 'life is lived on a twofold plane; it takes its course as human existence and, at the same time, shares in a transhuman life, that of the cosmos or the gods' (167). Lawrence's very first position after his rejection of Christianity is what he calls a belief in life, which he has consciously substituted for the Christian faith:

> I lost my rather deep religious faith; I lost my idealism and my wistfulness . . . Now I have weaned myself from folks and God and my young dreams; . . . I believe in life. (*L* 1: 72)

In Eliade's sense, Lawrence's thought and practice is religious, in that he thinks of the world as divided into two worlds, the sacred and the profane, that the sacred appears in and through the profane, and that it constitutes the real world.

A final account of religion of importance to Lawrence is that of Herbert Spencer. In a letter to Rev Reid of October 1907, Lawrence writes, 'Reading of Darwin, Herbert Spencer, Renan, J. M. Robertson, Blatchford and Vivian . . . has seriously modified my religious beliefs' (*L* 1: 36). Not only did Lawrence's reading of Spencer contribute to his rejection of the Christianity in which he was brought up, but Spencer also provides him with certain fundamental principles of the religion that he comes to develop in its place. Spencer's first principle is what he calls a 'catholic' one, that 'majorities', while usually wrong, 'have not usually been *entirely* wrong' (4). Thus, of all the different claims to truth about a given subject in the world, only one of which can be true, Spencer believes that 'each of them contains truth more or less disguised by errors' (7). This 'catholic' principle allows him to find 'the soul of truth' not only in the conflicting claims of different religions but even in the conflicting claims of religion and of science. If there is any principle that underlies all the varieties of religious doctrine in the world, this principle not only is the essence of religion, for Spencer, but it also deserves to be considered true. In fact, he argues, there is one such principle:

> Religions diametrically opposed in their overt dogmas, are perfectly at one in the tacit conviction that the existence of the world with all it contains and all which surrounds it, is a mystery calling for interpretation. (36)

Despite what we know of the world, our knowledge is surrounded by mystery, by that which we do not know. The 'reality existing behind all appearances is, and must ever be, unknown' (55) – for Spencer, this is 'a truth underlying even the rudest beliefs' and is 'the vital element in all religions' (36). Every religion agrees that 'the Power which the Universe manifests to us is inscrutable', and since this is the point on which they all agree, Spencer argues that it can and should be considered true. Lawrence considers it to be true. There is a power in the universe, he believes, behind the phenomena that we understand; it is the power that Christianity, along with other monotheistic religions, has called 'God', and although Christianity's claim to speak truly about this power is mostly untrue, it is not entirely untrue. This Power, this Absolute, this 'X', as Lawrence calls it (*L* 5: 77), exists, and relationship to it is of the greatest importance in human life. This belief in an unknown God, with which Lawrence comes to replace the Christian theology of his youth, is a principle that he learns first from Spencer's account of religion. A corollary principle of Spencer's Lawrence also shares, namely that all religions have their own form of validity, their relative truth, in speaking about the Unknown. As Spencer puts it, 'Religions, even though no one of them be actually true, are yet all adumbrations of a truth', a view that Lawrence holds from the very earliest years after his rejection of

Christianity. As he tells his sister in 1911, comforting her in the loss of her own Christian faith:

> Whatever name one gives Him, in worship we all strive towards the same God, so we be generous hearted: – christians, Buddhists, Mrs Dax, me – we all stretch our hands in the same direction. What does it matter, the name we cry. (*L* 1: 256)

In his study of Lawrence's religious thought in his early works, Paul Poplawski writes, 'I believe that his basic religious outlook was established [by the time he had completed *The Rainbow*] and that it remained essentially unaltered thereafter, even though he continued to struggle and experiment with it' (41). Despite my debt to Poplawski's study, I do not agree with this claim. Lawrence's religious thought continues to develop, in fundamental and significant ways, after the completion of *The Rainbow*, as the war and its consequences begin to have a permanent effect on his sensibility, and in this book I will trace the history of this development. In Lawrence's early works, Poplawski argues, his religious thought is based on his concept of creativity (59). From 1915 onwards, I will argue in this book, if there is a thread that unites Lawrence's religious thought, it is that of the absolutely unknown nature, yet supreme importance in human life, of what, for want of a better word, he will still often call 'God'. This is the meaning of the title of this book, *The Glyph and the Gramophone*. In 'On Being Religious', Lawrence writes that the word 'God' is a 'glyph' (*RDP* 187). He also calls it 'a queer little word', 'an ejaculation' and 'just a noise and a shape, like pop! or Ra or Om' (187). Rudolf Otto describes theological accounts of religious experience as 'ideograms', because 'the consciousness of a "wholly other" evades precise formulation in words, and we have to employ symbolic phrases which seem sometimes sheer paradox' (59). For Lawrence too, the most fundamental theological term in Western tradition, 'God', cannot be given a rational meaning, because it refers to 'some undefinable pulse of life' in the person who uses it in faith (*RDP* 187). It is one of those 'words which represent deep emotional states in us, and are therefore incapable of definition' (*IR* 358). In 1907, Rev Reid had preached that 'faith . . . has relation not so much to things that cannot be known as to things that cannot be seen' (2). Lawrence came completely to disagree. In *Kangaroo*, Richard Somers speaks of 'the great living darkness which we represent by the glyph, God' (266). God, that is, or whatever 'more spiritual universe', in William James' language, one means by the term, is, for Lawrence a word whose meaning is absolutely unknown. A glyph (from the Greek *glyphē*) is a 'carving'. By describing the word 'God' as such, Lawrence means that, like a mere physical mark, it signifies nothing. It has the structure of signification – it appears to signify – but in fact does not do so. Both the sense and the reference of the word are absolutely 'dark', absolutely unknown, to us. We mean something when we say 'God', for Lawrence, but of what that thing is in itself we have absolutely no knowledge.

Having described God as dark in this way, Somers continues in *Kangaroo* to reflect on the supreme importance in life of relating to it. Although 'God', for want of a better word, is absolutely unknowable, Somers, like Lawrence himself, thinks and talks at length about it and about relationship to it. As the narrator says of Somers, 'He preached, and the record was taken down for this gramophone of a novel' (280). The gramophone in Lawrence's work is a symbol of the emptiness of modern speech, of modern culture and of the modern life of which it is an expression. He complained of his college professors, 'I might as well be taught by gramophones as by those men, for all the interest or sincerity they felt' (*L* 1: 72). In empty modern marriages, 'the marriage is made to music, the gramophone and the wireless orchestrate each small domestic act' (*LEA* 44). In 'Let us be men—', Lawrence says:

> For God's sake, let us be men
> not monkeys minding machines
> or sitting with tails curled
> while the machine amuses us, the radio or film or gramophone.
> (*P* 390)

The gramophone is a symbol of the emptiness of modern speech because of the emptiness of the modern lives that it expresses, for Lawrence. By calling *Kangaroo* a gramophone of a novel, he means that it is an inadequate expression of the ideas about the unknown God that he is trying to express in it. God cannot be known or truly spoken of, but he also must be spoken of, for Lawrence, even in the modern world, because of his supreme importance in human life, and so, like a negative theologian, Lawrence uses the language he has to speak of that of which language cannot speak, because language is all he has to do it with. This is the problematic in which I will argue that Lawrence's religious thinking and writing, from 1915 onwards, take place. I will discuss the history both of Lawrence's religious thought, as he expresses it directly in prose, and of his expressions of that thought in his literary works. We will see that his religious thinking and writing are continually developing, on the one hand, up until the very last weeks before his death, and that, on the other, this development constitutes a series of articulations of the dialectic of the glyph and the gramophone, of the 'God' who Lawrence believes cannot be known or spoken about and his constant and passionate effort to speak about it nevertheless.

1

'Beyond these gods of today': The war years

Rananim

Lawrence's religious thought develops in many ways in response to the 'nightmare' of the war (*K* 212). His first response is to think of the community of Rananim. Lawrence had dreamt of a small community of friends since adolescence (Chambers 49; Nehls III, 601–2), but the idea of a religious community was first conceived during Christmas 1914, at the Lawrences' party in Chesham (*L* 4: 165, 350). The name 'Rananim' comes from a Hebrew song, based on the text of Psalm 33:1, *rannĕnu saddîqîm bayhwâh*. In Kot's papers, the first line of the song is transcribed, *Ranani Zadikim Zadikim l'Adonoi* (*L* 2: 252). Frieda recalls him singing 'Ranani Sadekim Badonoi' at the Christmas party (81). The Hebrew verb *rānan*, from which the first word of the song comes, means 'to give a ringing cry'. It is used of cries of joy or exultation (Jer. 31:7; Isa. 12:6), of distress (Lam. 2:19), of the cry of summons or exhortation of Wisdom in Proverbs 1:20 and 8:3, and very frequently of cries or shouts of praise to God. The KJV translates Psalm 33:1 as 'Rejoice in the LORD, O ye righteous'; the NIV as 'Sing joyfully to the LORD, you righteous'. Although the plural noun *rĕnānîm* is used of a bird of 'piercing cries', an ostrich, at Job 39:13, Lawrence seems to have added the suffix '-im' to indicate a plural participle, with the sense 'those who rejoice in the Lord', who 'shout for joy to the Lord' and perhaps who are therefore 'righteous'. K. W. Grandsen suggests the word Rananim 'may also . . . be connected with the word Ra'annanim, meaning green, fresh or flourishing, an adjective (qualifying, again, sadikhim, the righteous) found in the fourteenth verse of Psalm 92)' (23). This is not the case etymologically, however. The adjective ra'ănān, 'luxuriant, fresh', from the verb רַעֲנָן (rā'an), 'to be or grow luxuriant, fresh, green', is unrelated to the verb רָנַן (rānan), 'to give a ringing cry'. Furthermore, the former word is frequently used in the formulaic phrase taḥaṯ kol-'ēṣ ra'ănān, 'under every green tree' (Jer. 2:20; 3:6; 3:13; Isa. 57:5: Ezk. 6:13, inter alia) to indicate a place of idolatrous worship, not at all the sense that Lawrence intends with his term. Had Kot mentioned to Lawrence the lexical clustering to which Grandsen points, it is unlikely that he would have mentioned the appearance of ra'ănān in Psalm 92:14 but not in the formulaic phrase in which it appears more frequently.

Lawrence seems to have chosen the name 'Rananim', therefore, to indicate that the community he envisaged during the war years would be founded on an active, joyful praise of God, which would be of a kind that, like the sound of a shout of praise, could in principle spread into society. He had been meditating on the concept of praise the previous month as he read Katherine Jenner's Christian Symbolism. He writes to Gordon Campbell on 20 December 1914, of the importance of grasping the 'Whole' of a system of thought and action, whether that of Celtic or Latin Christianity. In the latter, 'there is the Eternal God', 'surrounded by the Hierarchy of the Cherubim and Seraphim . . . and they are absorbed in praise eternally' (L 2: 249). Lawrence emphasizes the last phrase, and repeats this emphasis later in the letter:

> I cannot forget that the Cherubim who are nearest God and palpitate with his brightness are absorbed in praise. I don't know why, but the thought of the Great Bright Circle of Cherubim, Godly beyond measure, are absorbed forever in fiery praise. (250)

The idea of the absorption in praise of God of the Cherubim, which he has been reading about in Jenner, is one that has impressed itself upon Lawrence's sensibility. The praise of the community of Rananim, the term suggests, would constitute its righteousness, or right living before God.

In Lawrence's first description, the community has the aristocratic title 'Order of the Knights of Rananim', and its motto is the French 'Fier', i.e. proud, 'or the Latin equivalent' (L 2: 252). Lawrence draws a picture of the community's 'badge', which he says is 'an eagle, or phoenix argent, rising from a flaming nest of scarlet, on a black background' (253). The picture is copied from that of a medieval phoenix reproduced in Jenner's *Christian Symbolism*. As she expounds the meaning of the symbol, Jenner emphasizes its triumphant nature, speaking of the phoenix's 'triumph over death' and of its 'rising triumphantly from its flaming nest' (150). In blending the eagle and the phoenix in the badge of Rananim, Lawrence intends to symbolize both the concept of resurrection, of new life rising from the ruins of the old that the war has brought to its end, and a triumphant, aristocratic pride, into which the members of the community will rise.

Lawrence writes to Lady Ottoline Morrell that his new community is to be 'established upon the known, eternal good part in us,' and that forming it is 'the most sacred duty' (271–2). He writes, 'The ideal, the religion, must now be *lived, practised*. We will have no more *churches*. We will bring church and house and shop together', and he describes this not as a new religion but as starting to 'fulfil what religion we have' (272). Although, as George Zytaruk writes, 'Lawrence's utopia was constantly changing' (273), the core idea of a community founded on religious ideas and the practice of those ideas remains a constant vision for Lawrence throughout the war years. As he puts it to Lady Ottoline, 'The question now is how shall we fulfil our declaration "God is"', since contemporary life is based on the principle that 'God is not' (L 2: 272). In June 1915, he repeats precisely this conception, speaking of his intention to 'establish a little society or body around a *religious belief which leads to action*' (L 2: 359). Lawrence expounds, 'We must centre in the knowledge of the Infinite, of God. Then from this Centre each one of us must work to put the temporal things of our own natures . . . in accord with the Eternal God we know' (359).

Critics have emphasized the unrealistic nature of Lawrence's political and economic reflections on the 'sort of communism' (L 2: 259) he envisages as the material basis of Rananim. He tells Bertrand Russell in February 1915:

> There must be a revolution in the state . . . It shall begin by the nationalising of all industries and means of communication, and of the land . . . Which practically solves the whole economic question for the present. (*L* 2: 282)

Zytaruk describes this as 'an extreme form of daydreaming' (278); Daniel Schneider speaks of Lawrence's 'deep inclination to withdraw from the fray' (107); and Peter Fjågesund criticizes his 'escapism', writing that 'he signally refuses to act in this world, or, the moment he pretends to act for social and political change, he fails bitterly, because his interest is not primarily with the world at all' (60). Russell himself commented that Lawrence 'had no real wish to make the world better, but only to indulge in eloquent soliloquy about how bad it was' (*Autobiography* II, 12). As these criticisms make clear, the essence of Lawrence's vision of Rananim was not a material one. The economic basis of the community he imagined, whether on a remote island or in a socially transformed England, was not his primary concern. Rather, what matters to him is the foundation of the community upon the relationship of each member to what he calls 'the Whole', 'God', 'the Infinite' and 'the Eternal'. Lawrence's first response to the war, which he never entirely abandons, is the formation of a community of people whose lives together are based on the relationship of each to God. It is relationship to this unknown God, which Christianity once mediated but no longer does, that Lawrence seeks to revive during the war, and the community in which this religion will be revived, he believes, will be one of praise, joy and a kind of aristocratic disdain of the false religions on which contemporary society is based and which have led to the war.

This becomes increasingly clear as Lawrence thinks of living with John Middleton Murry and Katherine Mansfield at Zennor in early 1916. His vision of the couple living together with him and Frieda is explicitly described in terms of a monastic community. He tells Catherine Carswell in February 1916 that the couple will come to Zennor, and comments, 'It is always my idea, that a few people by being together should bring to pass a new earth and a new heaven' (*L* 2: 555). To Murry and Mansfield themselves he writes the following month that his hope is that, in living together with one or two others, 'we are like a little monastery'. Indeed, it will be 'our Rananim'

(*L* 2: 564). In January 1917, he is thinking of America in the same terms: he wants to 'live apart, away from the world', in California or the South Seas, and he hopes that 'we can be a little community, a monastery, a school – a little Hesperides of the soul and body' (*L* 3: 70).

The dialogue with Russell

The next form in which Lawrence's religious thought develops during the war is his dialogue with Bertrand Russell. Ottoline Morrell had introduced the two in February 1915 and in June, during one of Russell's visits to Greatham, they discussed a plan to give a series of public lectures together. Describing their discussion to Lady Ottoline, Lawrence criticizes what he sees to be Russell's overly practical, material political ideas: 'He *will* . . . be so temporal, so immediate. He won't let go, he won't act in the eternal things, when it comes to men and life' (*L* 2: 358). Lawrence wants Russell's thought to incorporate a more transcendental element, which he describes as 'Knowledge of the Absolute', 'Knowledge of Eternity'. Indeed, he tells Lady Ottoline that he has begun to convince Russell to think in these terms: 'Now he is changing. He is coming to have a real logical belief in Eternity, and upon this he can work: a belief in the absolute, an existence in the Infinite' (*L* 2: 358). The morning after his visit, Russell writes:

> We talked of a plan of lecturing in the autumn on his religion, politics in the light of religion, and so on. I believe something might be made of it. I could make a splendid course on political ideas: morality, the State, property, marriage, war, taking them to their roots in human nature, and showing how each is a prison for the infinite in us. (*Letters* 40)

The phrase 'how each is a prison for the infinite in us' reflects the discussions on the Infinite, the Absolute and the Eternal to which Lawrence referred the previous day, and represents the point in the dialogue between the two men in which both believed most closely in the possibility of some kind of common purpose in their response to the war. Lawrence's account of their discussion makes clear the way in which they would thereafter disagree. He tells Lady Ottoline:

> We think to have a lecture hall in London in the autumn, and give lectures: he on Ethics, I on Immortality: also to have meetings, to establish a little society or body around a *religious belief which leads to action*. We must centre in the knowledge of the Infinite, of God. Then from this Centre each one of us must work to put the temporal things of our own natures and of our own circumstances in accord with the Eternal God we know. (*L* 2: 359)

Lawrence can write the word 'God' in apposition to the phrase 'the Infinite', connoting the one by the other, which marks a point of departure from Russell's thought, who would not allow such a connotation. The same is true of Lawrence's phrase 'the Eternal God'. For all he believes that he has persuaded Russell to a 'logical belief in Eternity', there could be no question of Russell identifying that logical category with the theological one of God.

In July, Russell sent Lawrence the outline of his lectures, entitled 'Philosophy of Social Reconstruction', which Lawrence sent back to him with numerous critical notes and marginalia. The essence of this criticism he expresses to Lady Ottoline: 'As yet he stands too much on the shore of this existing world. He must get into a boat and preach from out of the waters of eternity, if he is going to do any good' (*L* 2: 362). In the lecture outline, Russell argues that the problem in contemporary society is 'disintegration', and that the remedy is 'cooperation not authority'. He traces the forms of authority at work in contemporary institutions, arguing that 'all [are] based on Power, not on Liberty and Love', and that 'all want fundamental reconstruction'. He looks for 'new political institutions' that will allow 'freedom for [the] impulse of growth and creation' and 'freedom to love' (*LBR* 79). The first institution for whose reconstruction he argues is the State. 'It involves an entirely artificial division of mankind and our duties towards them: towards one group we are bound by the law, towards the rest only by the prudence of highwaymen' (83). The State is 'based on Power', Russell argues, and in the political institutions of the future, 'the relationship of human beings should be based on mutual liberty, with Love' (91). Lawrence's response can be summed up in his insertion after Russell's point that one 'can't *worship* the State'. Lawrence writes, 'What can I worship?' (82). In a long passage in pencil, beneath Russell's typed section, he writes:

> We proceed to create our State according to our religious belief, our philosophical conception of life. The King represents God. The Ministers subject to the King are the Archangels subject to God. The metaphysical belief is no longer held. Therefore our State is a falsity.
> The State must represent the deepest philosophical or religious belief. (83–4)

This is the basis of Lawrence's political beliefs in his dialogue with Russell, that societies are the expression of a fundamental religious idea. There is no society of which this is not true, he argues, and so the question is only on which religious idea the society of the future will be based. Contemporary society, he writes in Russell's section on the Churches, 'all rests on the Christian metaphysic, which each man severally rejects, but to which we all subscribe as a State or Society' (85). What he wants Russell to articulate is a new metaphysic on which the better society for which they are looking will be based. Lawrence makes this point over and over again in his notes on Russell's typescript. In the section on the Churches, he writes, 'There is no living society possible but one which is held together by a great religious idea. We only need not be *subjectively* religious. But one and all we must act from a profound religious belief' (85).

When Lawrence and Russell met in London in early July 1915, Russell lent Lawrence John Burnet's *Early Greek Philosophy*. The following week Lawrence writes, 'I have been wrong, much too Christian, in my philosophy. These early Greeks have clarified my soul. I must drop all about God' (*L* 2: 364). He asserts, 'I am rid of all my christian religiosity' (365), and a few days later he writes, 'I shall write all my philosophy again. Last time I came out of the Christian Camp. This time I must come out of these early Greek philosophers' (*L* 2: 367). Critics who have traced the influence of Burnet's book on Lawrence have rightly emphasized Heraclitus' thought on the one and the many and on the flux of contraries (Kalnins; Montgomery 132–67; Schneider 101–3). We should add here that Lawrence also finds a relationship between religion and aristocratic politics in Heraclitus. He is impressed by Heraclitus' series of aristocratic fragments, two of which he copies out in his letter to Russell, and by Heraclitus' condemnation of popular religion, a fragment on which he also copies out:

> There must be an aristocracy of people who have wisdom, and there must be a Ruler: a Kaiser: no Presidents and democracies. I shall write out Herakleitos, on tablets of bronze.
> 'And it is law, too, to obey the counsel of one.'
> 'For what thought or wisdom have they? They follow the poets and take the crowd as their teacher, knowing not that there are many bad and few good . . .'
> 'They vainly purify themselves by defiling themselves with blood.' (*L* 2: 364–5)

Wisdom is a term Heraclitus associates closely with the divine. Fragment 65 reads, 'The wise is one only. It is unwilling and willing to be called by the name of Zeus'. Fragment 96 reads, 'The way of man has no wisdom, but that of God has' (Burnet, 2nd edn 151, 154). Burnet comments, 'With certain reservations, Herakleitos was prepared to call the one Wisdom by the name of Zeus . . . It is not, of course, to be pictured in the form of a man . . . This "god", if it is to be called so, is one . . . The one Wisdom ought to be worshipped in its integrity' (189). When Lawrence tells Russell, 'You must drop all your democracy . . . It must be a case of Wisdom, or Truth' (*L* 2: 364), it is Heraclitus' theology on which he is looking to base his aristocratic politics. Commenting on fragments of the kind that Lawrence copies out to Russell, Burnet writes, 'Heraclitus looks down . . . on the mass of men . . . He believed himself to have attained insight into some truth not hitherto recognised, though it was, as it were, staring men in the face' (157–8). Russell himself associated Lawrence's aristocratic politics with his reading of Heraclitus, saying in 1937 that 'Lawrence is one of a long line of people, beginning with Heraclitus and ending with Hitler, whose ruling motive is hatred derived from megalomania' (*Letters* 344).

Burnet repeatedly emphasizes the non-theological nature of pre-Socratic thought. He writes, 'The philosophers . . . departed altogether from the received usage of the word θεός [god, 'primarily an object of worship']. Empedokles called the Sphere and the Elements gods, though it is not to be supposed that he regarded them as objects of worship, and in the same way . . . Diogenes of Apollonia spoke of Air as a god . . . It was just this way of speaking that got philosophers the name of being ἄθεοι [godless]'. For Xenophanes, 'the god or gods he spoke of meant just the world or worlds' (74–5). It is in the light of such passages that Lawrence tells Russell, 'I have been wrong, much too Christian, in my philosophy . . . I must drop all about God' (*L* 2: 364). The most striking thing about this statement, however, is the extent to which Lawrence does not in fact do what he says he will, 'drop all about God' and get 'rid of all [his] christian religiosity'. In the very letter in which he makes these statements he also says, 'I am sure that, unless the new spirit comes, we shall be irrecoverably beaten' in the war. 'It is no longer a case for satire or gibe or criticism. It is for a new truth, a further belief' (*L* 2: 365). The concept of the 'new spirit', which governs all Lawrence's thinking, before and after reading the pre-Socratics, on how to respond to the war, is a profoundly non-pre-Socratic one. Burnet writes, 'There is no room for an immortal soul in any philosophy of this period' (91). Lawrence's apposition of 'truth' with 'belief' here is similarly non-pre-Socratic, suggesting as it does that the truth, like God, is an object of faith rather than of the kind of empirical investigation that Burnet argues characterizes pre-Socratic thought.

Throughout August 1915, Lawrence continues to express his belief in the 'spirit' (*L* 2: 379), the 'living spirit', 'the spirit of truth' and the 'faith' that moves mountains (381). By September, he is telling Lady Ottoline, 'There must be a new heaven and a new earth' (390), and Lady Cynthia Asquith, with respect to *Signature*, 'The light is beginning to shine for a new creation' (397). At the end of October, he writes, 'The fact of resurrection, in this life, is all to me now . . . If we could bring our souls through, to life' (420). The following month he tells Lady Cynthia, 'There must be a resurrection – resurrection: a resurrection with sound hands and feet and a whole body and a new soul: above all a new soul, a resurrection' (454). Lawrence has by no means got 'rid of all [his] christian religiosity' as he tells Russell that he has after reading Burnet, nor does he 'drop all about God'. From the very letter in which he makes these claims onwards, he continues to think in the heterodox Christian terms that he had been using in *The Rainbow* and the *Study of Thomas Hardy*, before his encounter with pre-Socratic philosophy. He draws especially on the Christian theology of resurrection, of regeneration and of the last things in insisting that the only hope, both for the individual and for society, after the disaster of the war, is a new and right relationship to God.

Even in his letters to Russell, which, after reading Burnet, focus primarily on the theory of the State, what Lawrence calls his christian religiosity is not entirely absent. In the letter of 16 July 1915, for example, in which he underlines the word 'must' fifteen times, in the phrase 'you *must* work out the idea of a new state', he criticizes Russell for focusing too completely on criticism of the contemporary State. He posits the kind of natural aristocracy he wants to see in place of contemporary democratic institutions, and concludes, 'The highest aim of the government is the highest good of the *soul* of the individual, the fulfilment in the Infinite, in the Absolute' (*L* 2: 366). In the original letter, the fifteen underlinings in 'You *must* work out the idea of a new state, not go on criticising the old one' dominate the page, as the next three lines are reduced to half lines. The final phrase on the highest aim of the government is squeezed in small handwriting into the space at the bottom of the page, which is not sufficient for handwriting of the size Lawrence uses in the rest of the letter (HRC Box 35, folder 3). Nevertheless, what Lawrence calls his 'christian religiosity' is not only not absent from his criticism of Russell's lecture on the State, but, even though it emerges only at the end of the letter, remains the basis of that criticism as well.

'The Crown'

Between 4 October and 1 November 1915, Lawrence, Murry and Mansfield brought out three issues of the periodical *Signature*, to which Lawrence's authorial contribution was 'The Crown'. His plans for this magazine are expressed in explicitly religious terms. He tells Lady Cynthia Asquith, 'I am going to do the preaching' in it, and that its subscribers must be 'people who care about the real living truth of things' (*L* 2: 386). To Russell he says that they must be people who 'really want a new world' (*L* 2: 387). Most fully, he tells Lady Cynthia:

It is really *something*: the seed, I hope, of a great change in life: the beginning of a new religious era, from my point. I hope to God the new religious era is starting into being also at other points, and that soon there will be a body of believers, in this howling desert of unbelief and sensation. (*L* 2: 399)

Of the essays that constitute 'The Crown', he says, 'I feel if only people, decent people, would read them, somehow a new era might set in' (405).

By 1907, Lawrence had read Herbert Spencer (*L* 1: 36; Chambers 113), as Paul Morel has in *Sons and Lovers* (251; cf. 240). Although Lawrence argues in the *Study of Thomas Hardy* that Spencer emphasizes the principle of evolution alone (98), it is precisely in his dualistic thought that Spencer's influence can be seen in 'The Crown'. In *First Principles*, Spencer seeks the universal truths that underlie all phenomena. He finds that one of these truths concerns the direction of motion, and asks the question, 'Are phenomena due to the variously conditioned workings of a single force, or are they due to the conflict of two forces?' (201). He answers that the latter is the case: 'matter cannot be conceived except as manifesting forces of attraction and repulsion' (201). These forces of attraction and repulsion pervade the entire universe, and as such are 'the forms by which the workings of the Unknowable', which religion calls God (19–37), 'are cognizable by us' (203). Spencer argues that these twin forces can be seen at work throughout the phenomenal world – in the solar system, in the fluctuations of the weather, in the natural world, in the principle of natural selection, in mental life, and in social and economic groups (205–18).

Burnet's book also influences 'The Crown'. The most fundamental principle of the cosmology of the pre-Socratic philosophers he expounds is that of the conflict of opposites. Anaximander's thought is based on 'the opposition and strife between the things which go to make up the world' (56). The changes of the seasons occur because 'the warm commits "injustice" in summer, the cold in winter' (60). This kind of conflict is at work in sleep and waking (171), in good and evil (187), in life and death (172), in the two sexes (282), in the life of plants (278–9), of the human body (242) and even of the gods (243). Furthermore, the pre-Socratics regarded balance between these opposing forces to constitute the perfect form of any given thing, such as the human body: 'Man was made up of the hot and the cold, the moist and the dry, and the rest of the opposites. Disease was just the "monarchy" of any one of these . . . while health was

the establishment in the body of a free government with equal laws'
(225–6). Lawrence will make use of both these views in 'The Crown',
that everything is made up of the conflict of opposing forces and that
balance between these forces is the source of goodness.

In expounding Anaximander's philosophy, Burnet writes, 'The
"opposites" are . . . at war with one another, and their strife is marked by
"unjust" encroachments on either side' (57). The pre-Socratics appeal
to Lawrence as he reads them during the war since many of them
articulate philosophies of war. This is true especially of Heraclitus:

(43) Homer was wrong in saying: 'Would that strife might perish
from among gods and men!' He did not see that he was praying
for the destruction of the universe; for if his prayer were heard, all
things would pass away.

(44) War is the father of all and the king of all . . .

(62) We must know that war is common to all and strife is
justice, and that all things come into being and pass away through
strife. (150–1)

It is Heraclitus' account of the conflict of opposites in particular on
which Lawrence draws in 'The Crown' since, just as Lawrence will
in the first chapter of his essay, Heraclitus sees war as an example
of the kind of conflict of which all life consists. The element of
Heraclitus' thought that influences 'The Crown' most strongly,
however, is his view that the conflict of opposing forces is the product
of a more fundamental unity and therefore, insofar as it reveals that
fundamental unity, good:

The 'strife of opposites' is really an 'attunement' (ἁρμονία) . . . The
world is at once one and many, and it is just the 'opposite tension'
of the Many that constitutes the unity of the One. (158–9)

Lawrence reads about the world consisting in the strife of opposite
forces throughout Burnet's account of the pre-Socratics, but it is in
Heraclitus that he reads that this strife is itself the product of a higher
unity that is also the highest good: 'Anaximander had treated the
strife of opposites as an "injustice", and what Herakleitos set himself
to show was that, on the contrary, it was the highest justice' (160).

In 'The Crown', Lawrence develops a series of abstract, symbolic
idioms in order to express the view that he had learnt from Spencer

and from Burnet, that everything in the universe is made up of opposite and conflicting forces. Michael Black describes 'The Crown' as 'uncompromisingly metaphorical', and suggests that 'it is as if Lawrence is saying that ordinary discursive conceptualisation will not serve' (330–1). I would add that the highly metaphorical discourse of the essay derives from Lawrence's desire to formulate the kind of non-empirical metaphysics he had learnt from the pre-Socratics. The universe, for many of them, was composed of forces moving in a circular motion. For Empedocles, 'There were two hemispheres, revolving round the earth, the one altogether composed of fire, the other of a mixture of air and a little fire' (273). For Heraclitus, 'the whole of reality is like an ever-flowing stream, and . . . nothing is ever at rest for a moment' (162). For Parmenides, 'there were crowns crossing one another and encircling one another, formed of the rare and the dense elements respectively, and . . . between these there were other mixed crowns made up of light and darkness' (215). It is this kind of metaphysical cosmology to which Lawrence intends to return in 'The Crown'. When he writes, for example, that 'the stream flows in opposite directions, back to the past, on to the future' (258), he is thinking in terms of Heraclitus' image of the stream, both upwards and downwards in direction, which reality constitutes (Burnet 162). When he writes, 'The motion of the eternities is dual: they flow together and they flow apart, they flow forever towards union, they start back forever in opposition' (300), he is thinking in the terms of Empedocles, for whom the two opposing forces which compose the universe are Love and Strife:

> They are what they are; but, running through one another, they become men and the tribes of beasts. At one time they are all brought together into one order by Love; at another, they are carried each in different directions by the repulsion of Strife. (Burnet 244)

Lawrence has many names for the opposing forces that make up everything in the universe. He calls them darkness and light, the beginning and the end, the flesh and the spirit, the pagan and the Christian eternity, and in *Twilight in Italy*, the Father and the Son (125). Perhaps most clearly, he describes them as the 'two natures of God' (*TI* 126). In the second chapter of 'The Crown', he associates God initially with the first of each of these pairs of terms. The human person is 'compound of two waves (265)', Lawrence writes, that of light and that of darkness.

The wave of light in a person seeks the darkness, which is to be found through the 'way of flesh', the 'road of the senses' (469). Down this road, 'I come to the Almighty God Who was in the beginning, is now, and ever shall be' (265). By going down the road of the flesh or of the senses, into the darkness where one meets the God who was in the Beginning, Lawrence means that 'I come to the woman in desire' (265), since 'she is the doorway, she is the dark eternity' (469). After this experience, which is an experience of becoming one with God, 'new-created' and 'new-born', 'I open my eyes to the light and know the goal, the end . . ., the everlasting day, the oneness of the spirit' (266). In *Twilight in Italy*, Lawrence emphasizes not so much the sexual act as any act whatever of self-assertion as the consummation of the flesh. He calls it 'the way of the tiger', thinking of Blake's image, in which 'in the sensual ecstasy, having drunk all blood and devoured all flesh, I am become again the eternal Fire, I am infinite' (*TI* 117).

Having gone all the way, through the flesh, into the darkness, which is the darkness of God who was in the Beginning, the good life is then completed, Lawrence argues in 'The Crown', by going all the way up from this experience, through the spirit, into the light which is the light of God who is at the End. He calls this 'travelling to the opposite eternity, to the infinite light of the Spirit, the consummation in the Spirit' (*RDP* 266). In *Twilight*, he specifies that this process consists in the Christian practice of giving oneself to the other. According to Christ's command to love your neighbour as yourself, 'God is that which is Not-Me. In realising the Not-Me, I am consummated, I become infinite . . . To achieve this consummation I love my neighbour as myself' (*TI* 120).

Because he sees himself to be living in an age in which the infinity of the spirit is privileged over against the infinity of the flesh, Lawrence's language clearly implies a preference for the consummation of the flesh, that is, for finding God in acts of assertion of the sensual self. Nevertheless, he insists that the God one meets in the flesh is only the first of the two 'natures of God' (*TI* 126), and that this experience must be complemented by the God one meets in the spirit, in the experience of giving oneself to the other, and consummated, if one is to authentically encounter God, in the relationship between his two natures. 'God is not the one infinite, nor the other, our immortality is not in the Original eternity, neither in the Ultimate eternity. God is the utter relation between the two eternities' (*RDP* 300). The 'relation which is established between the two Infinites, the two natures of God' is 'the Holy Ghost of the Christian Trinity', which 'relates the dual Infinites into One Whole' (*TI* 126). In the Holy Spirit, Lawrence writes, 'I know the Two Ways, the two Infinites, the two Consummations. And knowing the Two, I admit the Whole' (126). 'What is really Absolute is the mystic Reason which connects both Infinites, the Holy Ghost that relates both natures of God' (*TI* 148). Lawrence remains in 'The Crown' within the problematic of the letters he is writing at the same time, that of heterodox Christianity. He thinks at once in the language of Heraclitus and of the theology of the Trinity in order to express his sense in 'The Crown' that it is in the relationship between the opposite forces of which everything is made that God is to be encountered. Heraclitus had thought of the balance of these forces as the 'highest justice'; Lawrence calls it the Holy Ghost, meaning that in a world whose elements the pre-Socratic philosophers have rightly described, despite Burnet's insistence on the non-theological nature of their thought, God remains to be found.

Lawrence brings a new concept into his philosophy in the third chapter of 'The Crown', that of corruption. Having focused on the clash together of the two forces whose conflict constitutes life, Lawrence now reflects upon their ebb apart from each other. He calls this the 'flux of corruption' (272). When darkness tends only back towards darkness, rather than forward towards light, this is corruption, he writes, because it represents a refusal to come to the consummation that the clash of opposite forces constitutes. He learns this idea of corruption from Heraclitus, for whom 'the real rest is change . . . Rest in any other sense is tantamount to dissolution' (Burnet 173). If strife ceases, so will the world, for Heraclitus. The ethics of 'The Crown' derive from this principle. When people insist only on one of the two infinities that make up the world, as both the English and the Germans are doing in the war, this is evil. Nevertheless, such a tendency towards just one thing points out by its absence the possibility of good, that is the relationship between one opposite force and the other. For Lawrence, corruption in Heraclitus' sense can still be a way of coming to know God:

> The spirit of destruction is divine, when it breaks the ego and opens the soul to the heavens. In corruption there is divinity . . .,

there is the sign of the Godhead . . . Decay, corruption, destruction, breaking down is the opposite equivalent of creation. In infinite going-apart there is revealed again the pure absolute, the absolute relation. (292)

Since corruption makes the relationship between opposing forces manifest, then it too is a force in which the 'Godhead', the divine truth and fullness of the relationship between these two forces, dwells (293, 477).

The final essay of 'The Crown' is called in 1915, 'The Knowledge of God' which, as Black comments, 'crystallises the perception that all along "The Crown" has been a religious text' (388). The first place in which this knowledge is revealed, in the essay, is the human body. Since it is made, as the nature of the sexual act suggests, out of the conflict of the two opposing forces that make up the world, then, as 'the foam-burst of the two waves', it is 'a revelation of God' (301). The perfect idea of the body – and even the momentary perfection achieved by material bodies – represents, unlike the decaying mortal body, the perfect meeting-point of the two eternal forces that make up the body, and so reveals God, who consists in that consummated relationship. In its own way, therefore, Lawrence adds, great art also reveals God, in that it represents a perfect form attained from the consummation of these two forces. It may reveal the relationship of corruption between them, as they ebb away from one another, or it may reveal the relationship of creation between them, as they flow towards one another. Leonardo, for example, paints 'the spirit and the flesh departing each back to its separate infinity', and so is an artist of 'the divine corruption' (476). In either case, 'it is a revelation of God' (302). Despite writing at a period of his most intense anger and bitterness at the war, Lawrence continues to find God everywhere in 'The Crown'. Not only is the divine revealed in the Heraclitean balance between the opposing forces of the universe, but it is even revealed by its absence when one of those forces tends towards corruption, towards being in itself alone. It is this corruption, in both the English and the Germans, that has led to the disaster of the war, but even here, in 'The Crown', Lawrence continues to see God, true relationship to whom, he is certain, will both end the war and constitute the basis of any better society that is to come in the future.

Theosophy

Several scholars have pointed to an early acquaintance by Lawrence with theosophical ideas. Willie Hopkin's second wife Olive recalls that Lawrence went to the Theosophical Society in Nottingham (Cobau 133–4). He read the *New Age* regularly in 1908–09, which, as P. T. Whelan points out, was a regular publisher of articles and reviews on occult and esoteric subjects. As Whelan writes, 'theosophy and esotericism generally were in the air at the time, and . . . people who shared many of Lawrence's interests were attracted to it' (104). Lawrence's interest in theosophy was catalysed, however, in the summer of 1917, when Lawrence renewed his friendship with Philip Heseltine, who returned to Cornwall in the spring. As Émile Delavenay (*Man and His Work* 388, 458–9) and Mark Kinkead-Weekes (*Triumph to Exile* 386–7) have shown, Heseltine had a serious interest in the occult, and was reading esoteric books in Cornwall. Furthermore, Lawrence had become neighbours with the practising occultists Meredith Starr and his wife (*L* 3: 130), with whom he socialized (154), although he dismissed their practices as excessive (158). Nevertheless, as Kinkead-Weekes writes, '[Starr's] knowledge and books opened up ideas and images that Lawrence could use' (387). In July 1917, Lawrence writes:

> I am not a theosophist, though the esoteric doctrines are marvellously illuminating, historically. I hate the esoteric forms. Magic has also interested me a great deal. But it is all part of the past, and part of a past self in us: and it is no good going back, even to the wonderful things. (*L* 3: 143)

He insists, though, that 'there should be again a body of esoteric doctrine' (*L* 3: 143). The following month, he writes to his friend, the psychoanalyst David Eder:

> Have you read Blavatsky's *Secret Doctrine*? In many ways a bore, and not quite real. Yet one can glean a marvellous lot from it, enlarge the understanding immensely. Do you know the physical – physiological – interpretations of the esoteric doctrine? – the *chakras* and dualism in experience? The devils won't tell one

anything fully . . . Yet one can gather enough. Did you get Pryce's
Apocalypse Unsealed? (*L* 3: 150)

In November 1918, Lawrence refers also to having read Blavatsky's
Isis Unveiled (*L* 3: 298–9).

The theosophical work which influenced Lawrence most directly
is the book he refers to last in his letter to Eder, James Pryse's
Apocalypse Unsealed. Heseltine read this work, probably in Cornwall,
and recommended it in 1917 to friends (Kinkead-Weekes, *Triumph
to Exile* 386, 832). Pryse's argument is that the book of Revelation
is a coded expression of the 'esoteric' knowledge that constitutes
the core of all ancient science and religion (9). Since it is unlawful
to reveal esoteric doctrine except to the initiate, St John disguised
it in symbolic language (2–5). Pryse's first principle is that in all 'the
ancient religions, including that of early Christianity, . . . may be found
very clear intimations of a secret traditional lore, an arcane science,
handed down from times immemorial' (1). In Revelation, therefore,
St John has articulated 'the esoteric doctrine which underlies not only
Christianity but also all the religions of antiquity' (4).

As Lawrence's letter to Eder suggests, it is the physiology of Pryse's
system that interests him most. Pryse posits four 'principal life-centres'
in the body. These are: 1. the head, or brain, the organ of the 'higher
mind'. 2. 'The region of the heart, including all the organs above the
diaphragm', the seat of the 'lower mind'. 3. The region of the navel,
the centre of the 'passional nature'. 4. The genitals, the seat of 'the
vivifying forces on the lowest plane of existence' (14). There are two
nervous systems: the 'cerebro-spinal', consisting of the brain and spinal
cord, and the 'sympathetic or ganglionic' (15). The latter consists of
'a series of distinct nerve-centres, or ganglia . . . extending on each
side of the spinal column from the head to the coccyx' (15). In the
Upanishads, Pryse writes, these ganglia are called *chakras*. The seven
principal chakras are the sacral, the prostatic, the epigastric, the cardiac,
the pharyngeal, the cavernous and the conarium (16). Pryse gives the
Sanskrit terms for each of these ganglia and provides an anatomical
diagram of the body giving their location. At work within the body is
a force called, in Sanskrit, *kundalinî*, 'annular or ring-form force' and
in Greek *speirêma*, the 'serpent coil'. It is like 'a living, conscious
electricity, of incredible voltage' and it is symbolized in ancient myth

and religion as the 'good serpent' (11–12). Pryse even expresses this in the Trinitarian language that Lawrence had used in *Twilight in Italy*, identifying this force with the Holy Ghost (21), and calling the *speirêma* 'the *paraklêtos* in its active form' (122). In theosophical practice, when 'through the action of man's spiritual will', this previously coiled up force is aroused to activity, it passes from the lower through to the higher chakras. In doing so, 'it liberates and partakes of the quality peculiar to that centre, and it is then said to "conquer" the *chakra*' (16). This process leads to 'knowledge of spiritual realities . . . and it culminates in emancipation from physical existence through the "birth from above" ' (22). In Revelation, Pryse argues, St John has given a detailed account of precisely this process. In the drama of the opening of the seven seals, he describes the conquering of the seven *chakras*. The scroll sealed with the seven seals (Rev. 5:1), Pryse argues, is 'the human body, and its seals are [its] force-centres' (117). When St John writes that the scroll is 'written inside and on the back', he refers to the 'cerebro-spinal axis and the great sympathetic system', that is, he is giving a detailed esoteric account of the body and of the way to transcend bodily life. The opening of each of the seals represents the conquering of each of the chakras. For example, the sixth seal represents the sacral chakra, which 'lies at the base of the spinal cord and is the starting point of the central current' of *kundalinî* through the system:

> Upon the outpouring of this fiery electric force into the brain, the mind becomes blank and the novice is conscious only of blind terror; this is allegorized [in Rev. 6:12-16] as the darkening of the sun (the mind), the falling of the stars (the thoughts), the vanishing of the sky (the concept of space) and the panic of the earth-dwellers (the lower forces and faculties). (128–9)

Lawrence is persuaded by what he takes from Pryse. Six years later, he writes:

> The 'Apocalypse' is . . . a revelation of Initiation experience, and the clue is in the microcosm, in the human body itself . . . The Seals are ganglia of nerve-consciousness . . . The revelation is a conquest, one by one, of the lower affective centres by the mind. (*L* 4: 460)

However, Lawrence uses Pryse's work in a highly creative way, transforming Pryse's thought into his own, revisionary version of theosophical physiology and ethics. He later said of Pryse's work, 'It's not important. But it gave me the first clue' (Brewster 141–2). Lawrence initially expresses these revisionary theosophical ideas in the first version of the *Studies in Classic American Literature*, begun in the summer of 1917 and resumed between January and August 1918. In these essays, Lawrence asserts that before each child begins to think, 'the body is awake and alive, and in the body the great nerve centres are active'. He calls this kind of knowledge 'first-consciousness', and he locates it in 'the great nerve centres of the breast and the bowels, the cardiac plexus and the solar plexus' (192). Mental consciousness comes later, but our 'first-knowledge, root-knowledge' comes from the nerve centres in the upper and lower parts of the body (192).

Lawrence thus uses Pryse's physiology – two of his four divisions of the body, and two of his seven ganglia – to express the duality he perceives in human beings for which he had used pre-Socratic language in 'The Crown'. Pryse's theosophical language provides him with an account that is both religious and scientific, and so seems simply to be true, in whose terms to articulate this perception. The cardiac plexus, 'the great nerve centre in the breast', Lawrence thus identifies, in his revisionary system, as 'the centre of our dynamic spiritual consciousness', and the solar plexus, 'the great plexus in the bowels', as 'the centre of our dynamic sensual consciousness' (192). Selfless, spiritual love comes from the upper nerve centre of the breast, and sensual, selfish love comes from the lower nerve centre of the bowels. It is in the next step of his argument that Lawrence departs most completely from Pryse's theosophy. The goal of the sacred science, in Pryse's account, is the transcendence of bodily life into purely spiritual life. Lawrence values no such transcendence. Rather, the good life consists in 'the strange consummation into oneness, of the final understanding, which consummates the upper and the lower knowledge into one third pure state of wholeness' (192). Everyone has experienced, Lawrence argues, fulfilment in the spiritual or the sensual life. But the 'third and last state', in which one truly and alone becomes oneself, is 'when I am fulfilled in both the great dynamic ways of consciousness, and am free, a free being', because I need not compel myself in either direction, since both can fully express themselves in me (194).

In 'The Two Principles', Lawrence derives this physiology and its consequent ethics from a revisionary theosophical cosmology. In this essay, the influence of Helena Blavatsky, the founder of the theosophical movement, is dominant, particularly that of the first volume of her book *The Secret Doctrine*, on 'cosmogenesis'. It is a basic tenet of theosophy that the Bible, along with other ancient Scriptures, is true when interpreted according to its esoteric meaning. 'There is more wisdom concealed under the exoteric fables of Purânas and Bible than in all the exoteric facts and science in the literature of the world, and more OCCULT true Science, than there is of exact knowledge in all the academies' (Blavatsky i, 336). 'Without the help of symbology', Blavatsky writes, 'no ancient Scripture can ever be correctly understood' (i, 305). The Kabala has historically been 'the key that opens the secrets of the Bible' (344), but even it has been distorted by Christian mystics, and Blavatsky herself, like her disciple Pryse, has the task of reading the secret doctrine out of its symbolic expression in the world's Scriptures. With respect to cosmogony, it is particularly in the book of Genesis that this doctrine can be found. 'Read by the light of the Zohar, the initial four chapters of Genesis are the fragment of a highly philosophical page in the World's Cosmogony' (i, 10–11). *The Secret Doctrine* contains many expositions of the esoteric meaning of the Book of Genesis. In her account of the relationship between divine thought and primordial substance, with which Lawrence will wrestle in 'The Two Principles', Blavatsky expounds the secret doctrine in the form of an esoteric commentary on the first verses of the Book of Genesis:

> Let anyone read the first verses of chapter i of *Genesis* and reflect upon them. There 'God' commands to *another* 'god' *who does his bidding* . . .
> 'And the *Spirit* of GOD moved upon the face of the Waters' (v. 2), or the great Deep of the Infinite Space. And this Spirit is *Nara-yana*, or Vishnu.
> 'And God said, Let there be a firmament . . .' (v. 6), and 'God', the second, obeyed and '*made* the firmament' (v. 7). 'And God said, let there be light', and 'there was light'. Now the latter does not mean

light at all, but in the Kabala, the androgyne 'Adam Kadmon', or
Sephira (*Spiritual light*). (i, 336–7)

Although the content of his commentary revises the thought of
Blavatsky, Lawrence too begins his theosophical cosmogony in 'The
Two Principles' with precisely the kind of esoteric commentary on
the book of Genesis that he found in Blavatsky's cosmological work.

He begins, 'Following the obsolete language, we repeat that in
the beginning was the creative reality' (*SCAL* 260). The first phrase,
'Following the obsolete language', expresses the theosophical concept
of the 'exoteric' meaning of traditional religious discourse like that of
the Bible – what Blavatsky calls the 'dead letter of the Bible' (i, 305).
Lawrence means that, although the text can no longer be said literally to
be true, nevertheless there is a sense, the esoteric sense he will expound,
in which it does speak truly. The second phrase is much indebted to
Blavatsky's thought. She observes, 'The Initiates never use the epithet
"God" to designate the One and Secondless Principle in the Universe'
(ii, 555), and she practices this rule throughout *The Secret Doctrine*. With
a notable exception, which we will discuss below, Lawrence follows her
in this, and for the same reason – to distinguish his cosmology from
the exoteric, anthropomorphic theology of the Bible and of Christian
tradition. Hence he expounds the word 'God' of Gen. 1:1 to mean 'the
creative reality, living and substantial' (260). The God of whom he speaks
in 'The Two Principles' is not the God of Christian theology, he believes,
and it cannot be known by analogy to created things.

Blavatsky's cosmogony is highly complex. Its first principle is that
there exists, in simple language, an unknown and unknowable God,
'the unrevealed Deity' as she puts it early in *The Secret Doctrine*
(i, 2). The word 'God', however, is inadequate, since it connotes an
anthropomorphism beyond which Blavatsky thinks the first principle of
the universe. She prefers a series of more abstract terms or the terms
used for such a being in esoteric texts such as the Hindu Scriptures or
the Kabala. She defines it perhaps most systematically as follows:

An Omnipresent, Eternal, Boundless, and Immutable PRINCIPLE,
on which all speculation is impossible, since it transcends the
power of human conception and could only be dwarfed by any
human expression or similitude . . . [It] is the rootless root of 'all

that was, is, or ever shall be'. It is of course devoid of all attributes and is essentially without any relation to manifested, finite Being. It is 'Be-ness' rather than Being. (i, 14)

This absolute reality so transcends the universe that it cannot be thought of as entering into the relationship of creation with the universe (i, 7). Rather, 'in this ALL lies concealed its coeternal and coeval emanation or inherent radiation, which, upon becoming periodically Brahmâ . . . becomes or expands itself into the manifested Universe' (i, 7). All exoteric accounts of creator Gods refer esoterically to this process whereby the unrevealed Deity emanates the idea of the universe, which idea (exoterically called the creator god Brahmâ in Hinduism), acting upon the universal substance, which is identical to the unrevealed Deity, brings the universe into being. Blavatsky reads this doctrine from a text in the Upanishads:

'As a spider throws out and retracts its web,. . . so is the Universe derived from the undecaying one'. . . Brahmâ, as 'the germ of unknown Darkness', is the material from which all evolves and develops 'as the web from the spider . . .', etc. This is only graphic and true, if Brahmâ the 'Creator' is, as a term, derived from the root *brih*, to increase or expand. Brahmâ 'expands' and becomes the Universe woven out of his own substance. (i, 83)

As she puts it elsewhere, 'the whole Kosmos has sprung from the DIVINE THOUGHT. This thought impregnates matter, which is co-eternal with the ONE REALITY; and all that lives and breathes evolves from the emanations of the . . . eternal one-root' (i, 340).

Lawrence's esoteric reading of the first verses of Genesis in 'The Two Principles' is a revisionary version of this cosmology. For Lawrence, 'The living cosmos divided itself, and there was Heaven and Earth' (*SCAL* 260). He does not mean 'the sky and the terrestrial globe', since, as Gen. 1:2 says, the earth was still void and dark, but rather 'an inexplicable first duality, a division in the cosmos' (260). The idea of the living universe dividing itself into a primordial duality is Lawrence's revision of Blavatsky's divine idea acting upon the divine substance in order to bring forth the material universe. His ideas become increasingly revisionary as his commentary continues.

Gen. 1:2 reads, 'And the Spirit of God moved upon the face of the waters'. Lawrence expounds the esoteric sense of this verse as follows: 'The mystic Earth is the cosmic Waters, and the mystic Heaven the dark cosmic Fire' (261). Gen. 1:6-7 speaks of God's division of the waters with the firmament. Lawrence comments, 'If we conceive of the first division in Chaos', i.e. between primordial water and primordial fire, 'as being perpendicular . . ., then this next division, when the line of the firmament is drawn, we can consider as horizontal: thus we have the ⊕, the elements of the Rosy Cross' (261). The universe, as Genesis teaches esoterically, has the fourfold structure symbolized by the Rosy Cross, or the cross in the circle, being composed of the fire above and the fire below the firmament and of the water above and the water below the firmament.

Most commentators argue that this account of the universe as made out of the primal elements of fire and water is derived from Lawrence's reading of the pre-Socratic philosophers, and this is true to a certain extent. Burnet describes Heraclitus' account of summer and winter (174–5) and of day and night (186) as a product of the oscillation of fire and water. Lawrence himself writes, 'These strange unfathomable waters breathe back and forth, as the earliest Greek philosophers say, from one realm to the other' (SCAL 260). But this cosmology, although ultimately Lawrence's own, owes more to Blavatsky, who incorporates the thought of the pre-Socratics into her esoteric system: 'Herakleitos of Ephesus maintained that the one principle that underlies all phenomena in Nature is fire . . . And while Anaximenes said the same of air, and Thales of Miletus . . . of water, the Esoteric Doctrine reconciles all these philosophers by showing that though each was right the system of none was complete' (i, 77). Blavatsky's view of the elements is this:

Metaphysically and esoterically there is but ONE ELEMENT in nature, and at the root of it is the Deity; and the so-called *seven* elements, of which five have already manifested and asserted their existence, are the garment, *the veil, of that deity*. (i, 460)

By the five manifest elements she means the four 'spoken of in later antiquity', Fire, Air, Water and Earth, along with Æther, 'the synthesis of the rest', 'admitted only in philosophy' (i, 460). Lawrence follows her in her belief that the four elements are not to be identified with 'the passive, external form and matter of any object', but are rather 'the *noumenon* therein' (i, 461). In Plato and Aristotle, she writes, the elements were 'the *incorporeal principles* attached to the four great divisions of our Cosmic world', and it is increasingly exoteric thought that identifies these principles with gods, forces or, in the modern world, the chemical elements of the periodic table (i, 461). It is from this account that Lawrence derives his account of 'primordial' or 'cosmic' Water and Fire (*SCAL* 261), which are not to be identified with the material phenomena of water and fire, and from which everything else in the universe is made. Having learnt the concept of primal elements from Blavatsky, he develops his own belief that it is from the primal elements of fire and water in particular that the universe is made.

Lawrence argues that the universe, according to the esoteric sense of Genesis 1, has a fourfold structure, which is that of the ⊕, or the Rosy Cross. He learns the meaning of this symbol also from Blavatsky, who devotes a chapter of *The Secret Doctrine* to the symbol of the cross in the circle. She writes, 'The ideas of representing the *hidden* deity by the circumference of a Circle, and the Creative Power . . . by the diameter across it, is one the oldest symbols' (ii, 536). Lawrence revises this in writing, 'The simplest symbol, the divided circle ⊖, stands . . . for the first division in the living cosmos and for the two cosmic elements' (*SCAL* 267). 'When the diameter line is crossed by a vertical one ⊕', Blavatsky writes, 'it becomes the mundane cross' (i, 5). The cross, that is, symbolizes the worldly existence brought into being by the creative power of the divine thought. It symbolizes the four elements from which the world is made (ii, 562), the four quarters of the world (ii, 546), and even the four stages of human life – birth, life, death and immortality (ii, 557). Although the Rosicrucians call the cross within the circle 'the Union of the Rose and Cross' (i, 19), Blavatsky writes, in fact it symbolizes the universe as esoteric doctrine teaches it to be – the phenomenal world brought into being by the creative power of the unrevealed deity. This account is behind Lawrence's claim that 'the universe at the end of the Second Day of Creation is . . ., as the Rosy Cross, a fourfold division' (*SCAL* 261).

Lawrence believes that his revisionary theosophical cosmology is confirmed and perfected by contemporary science. Science is wrong, however, to exclude God from its cosmological discourse. 'In the beginning when the unthinkable living cosmos divided itself', Lawrence writes, 'God did not disappear' (*SCAL* 262), as contemporary empiricism would suggest. Rather, God must be considered in a radically non-anthropomorphic way. In Lawrence's words, 'If we try to conceive of God, in this instance, we must conceive some homogeneous rare *living* plasm, a *living* self-conscious ether, which filled the universe' (262). In the first *Studies in Classic American Literature*, Lawrence's thought, like Blavatsky's, is pantheistic. He has taken Blavatsky's concept of the divine substance out of which the universe is made by the divine thought, and which is co-extensive with the universe, and has conceived of God as the living, self-conscious substance out of which the universe is made by the process of self-division. He puts the case perhaps most clearly as follows:

> When life divides itself, there is no division in life. It is a new life-state, a new being which appears. So it is when an egg divides. There is no split in life. Only a new life- stage is created. (262)

We might note that the central image with which Lawrence expounds his concept of God here, that of an egg dividing in order to produce new life, recapitulates the symbol of the mundane egg, to which Blavatsky devotes a chapter of *The Secret Doctrine* as a symbol of the coming forth of the cosmos from the absolute. Lawrence conceives of God in the first *Studies* as the life itself of the living universe, which remains one and the same throughout the process of self-division by which it brings the universe into being.

The universe is fourfold, according to Lawrence's revisionary theosophy, as is all its creative activity (261–2, 266). This is also true, therefore, of the individual. In his essay on Crèvecoeur, Lawrence had written that the upper body is the source of spiritual consciousness, and the lower body the source of sensual consciousness. In 'The Two Principles', he adds that 'beyond the great centres of breast and bowels, there is a deeper and higher duality' (269). There are 'the wonderful plexuses of the face', which do not exist in Pryse's system, and which are the product of Lawrence's creative revision of this system, and the 'the great living plexus of the loins' (269). In the face, 'we pass in delight to our greater being, when we are one with all things'. These plexuses are the source of our self-transcendence, our sense of identification with others and with the universe. In the loins, 'we have our passionate self-possession, our unshakable and indomitable being' (270). This plexus is the source of our most fundamental sense of self, our difference from others and the universe and even our assimilation of others and the universe into our selves. Whereas the good life in the Crèvecoeur essay was a life in which the impulses of the breast and the belly were balanced, by the time Lawrence writes 'The Two Principles' it consists in a fourfold balance of the consciousness deriving from the cardiac and solar plexuses on the one hand and from the plexuses of the face and the loins on the other. Furthermore, Lawrence finds a second fourfold division in the body, developing a hint from Pryse. The latter had claimed that the scroll 'written inside and on the back' of Rev. 5:1 represented the human body, with its cerebro-spinal and ganglionic nervous systems (117), the systems posited by empirical science by esoteric religion respectively. Lawrence reads this distinction differently, however, and asserts, 'If we are divided horizontally at the diaphragm, we are divided also perpendicularly' (271). In Pryse, the sympathetic nervous system is the system of ganglia, as opposed to the neurological system of contemporary science (15). Lawrence, however, posits two sets of ganglia, one in the front and one in the back of the body, the first of which he calls sympathetic, the second spinal (270), altogether revising Pryse's terminology and thought. The four ganglia of the front of the body, which he has already described, are the sympathetic system, 'the great valve to the universe', from which the soul goes out of itself towards the other. Corresponding to these four, two upper and two lower, are two upper and two lower ganglia at the back of the body, which constitute the 'voluntary' system, from which 'the *will* acts in direct compulsion, outwards' (270), from which we attempt to force others and the universe into conformity with our will. Corresponding to the upper front ganglia of the breast and face, Lawrence writes, are the thoracic and the cervical ganglia (270). These are Lawrence's own terms, not part of Pryse's sevenfold system. From these ganglia 'go forth the motions and commands which force the external universe into that state which accords with the spiritual will-to-unification, the will for equality' (270). Corresponding to the lower front ganglia of the bowels and loins are the 'lumbar ganglion' and the 'sacral ganglion', only the latter of which is found in Pryse. From these plexuses go forth 'the great sensual will to dominion', 'the soul goes forth haughty and indomitable, seeking for mastery' (270). Lawrence has turned Pryse's system of seven ganglia into a fourfold system of eight ganglia, two at the upper front, two at the upper back, two at the lower front and two at the lower back of the body, and he has turned Pryse's ethics of conquering each chakra in a journey of increasingly spiritual self-transcendence into an ethics of balance between spiritual and sensual consciousness on the one hand and between self-giving sympathy and self-asserting will on the other. In this way, Lawrence believes, he has more accurately expounded the esoteric core of ancient religion and philosophy than his theosophical predecessors.

Lawrence continues to articulate theosophical ideas in *Psychoanalysis of the Unconscious*, written some eighteen months later in January 1920. In this book, he argues that his revisionary theosophical psychology constitutes a truer account of the unconscious than psychoanalysis. The unconscious posited by psychoanalysis, Lawrence argues, is 'the inverted reflection of our ideal consciousness' (*PUFU* 15). 'The true unconscious', by contrast, which Lawrence sets out to describe in *Psychoanalysis*, is 'that essential unique nature of every individual creature, which is, by its very nature, unanalysable, undefinable, inconceivable' (17). It is what Christian tradition calls the soul. 'Religion was right and science is wrong' on this issue, Lawrence writes, since every creature has a soul, a specific individual nature, which has been created out of nothing. Indeed, developing the new science of the unconscious will mean that 'science abandons its intellectualist position and embraces the old religious faculty' (18). Lawrence argues that the unconscious consists of the nerve-centres posited in his revisionary theosophy. He re-states in *Psychoanalysis* the fourfold system of nerve-centres articulated in the first Crèvecoeur essay, identifying them now with the unconscious. 'Having begun to explore the unconscious, we find we must go from centre to centre, chakra to chakra, to use an old esoteric word' (32). The unconscious consists of 'the nature of the consciousness manifested at each pole' of the theosophical system of nerve-centres (32).

　　Lawrence returned again to psychoanalysis another eighteen months later, in June 1921, with *Fantasia of the Unconscious*, to which he added the 'Introduction' and 'Epilogue' in October. In the 'Introduction', he deals with the very large number of negative reviews that *Psychoanalysis* received. He writes, in response to these reviews, 'I stick to the solar plexus' (62). He remains serious, that is, despite the lighter and even parodic tone of *Fantasia*, about his revisionary theosophy. He defends the central theosophical principle of a core of doctrine shared by all the philosophies and religions of the ancient world, even using the theosophical term 'esoteric' to describe this doctrine. He adds that Thomas Belt's account of the glacial period gives geographical support to this claim, showing that the world was once a much larger land-mass, where 'men wandered back and forth from Atlantis to the Polynesian Continent', and so were in 'one complete correspondence over all the earth' (63).

In *Fantasia*, Lawrence objects less to the psychoanalytic concept of the unconscious than to the Freudian concept of sex, specifically to the view that 'a sexual motive is to be attributed to all human activity' (66). Rather, what Lawrence calls 'the essentially religious or creative motive' is the ultimate source of human action. Sex, although a powerful motive, 'comes second' to the 'religious' desire, which Lawrence attributes to men in particular, to step out of oneself and create something new, or, as Lawrence puts it, to 'build a world' (67). In tracing this motive, in order to understand the human person better than orthodox psychoanalysis does, Lawrence re-states his belief in an unknown God. He begins by asserting that one cannot speak, as psychoanalysis does, of any first cause of human life. He has become more willing to allow the relative validity of theological language than during the war years, writing, 'If we want to talk about God, well, we can please ourselves. God has been talked about quite a lot, and He doesn't seem to mind' (68). In his own view, however, 'There's not a shadow of a doubt about it, the First Cause is just unknowable to us, and we'd be sorry if it wasn't. Whether it's God or the Atom' (68). Much more willing to allow the use of the concept of God than in the first *Studies in Classic American Literature*, Lawrence himself insists, in the apophatic way that he never abandons, that whatever we mean by 'God', or by any other term to denote the most fundamental reality of human life, we cannot in any sense know the meaning of that word. 'The business of every faith', as he puts it in *Fantasia*, 'is to declare its ignorance' of the nature of that which is believed (68).

Lawrence displays in his own discourse in *Fantasia* this greater willingness to allow the language of Christian tradition. He repeats his assertion in *Psychoanalysis* that each new individual is created from nothing, and that his or her individuality constitutes what Christian tradition has called the soul. He adds in *Fantasia* that this individuality, the deepest and unconscious self of a person, can be described as the Holy Ghost: 'The intrinsic truth of every individual is the new unit of unique individuality . . . This is the incalculable and intangible Holy Ghost each time – each individual his own Holy Ghost' (76). Indeed, he goes so far in appropriating the language of Christian tradition as to define the individual in Trinitarian terms, writing of each person's 'tripartite being' – 'the mother within him, the father within him, and the Holy Ghost, the self which he is supposed to consummate' (77). Later in the essay, he speaks of 'the voice of the self in its wholeness' as 'the Holy Ghost', 'our Holy Ghost within us' (155). This heterodox Christian language is used deliberately. Lawrence explicitly intends to use the concept of the soul in a theological sense. Contemporary science misunderstands the human body only as a highly complex mechanical system, since 'it is obvious that . . . you cannot keep such a machine running for one day without the most exact control' (95). 'There must', Lawrence argues, 'be a central god in the machine of each animate corpus', which is the soul. Even the universe, he argues, must have a similar soul governing it. If the human body is a complex machine like a bicycle, whose rider is the human soul, then the universe too is another larger complex machine, 'another bicycle riding full tilt' and 'we are bound to suppose a rider for that also' (97). Lawrence remains rigorously apophatic about this governing spiritual force of the universe – 'I shouldn't like, myself, to start guessing about the rider of the universe' (97). Nevertheless, he induces something structurally similar to the God of Christian tradition from his account, intended to correct those of psychoanalysis, of the soul. It is in *Fantasia*, as it has traditionally been, a theological category.

Women in Love

Women in Love has frequently been described as an apocalyptic work (Kermode 20; Wright, *Bible* 19). The characters' sense that they are living at the end of history is strong. On the second page of the novel, Gudrun complains to Ursula, 'Nothing materialises! Everything withers in the bud' (8). The miners are 'ghouls' (11). 'Not many people are anything at all', Birkin comments to Mrs Crich at the wedding party (25), and he sees the whole of humanity as corrupt, given over to death and about therefore to die:

> Humanity itself is dry-rotten really. There are myriads of human beings hanging on the bush – and they look very nice and rosy . . . But they are apples of Sodom, as a matter of fact, Dead Sea Fruit . . . their insides are full of bitter, corrupt ash. (126)

Keith Sagar compares Birkin to Dante in the *Inferno*, passing through milieux which are 'the levels of hell', in the sense that 'a hell is any way of life . . . cut off from the creative sources' (*Life into Art* 154). Gudrun describes the boys running in the mud after her Thames cruise as 'carrion creatures' whom 'no vulture or jackal could dream of approaching . . . for foulness', and Ursula adds that this is true of the entire population: 'It isn't the boys so much who are vermin; it's the people themselves, the whole body politic' (161).

In the final draft of the novel, this nihilism is subsumed, albeit in an understated way, into the negative religious claims articulated by Birkin. On many occasions, he sees the dissolution of the human race as a positive, progressive step in the history of the unknown creative force at work in the universe:

> What is mankind but just one expression of the incomprehensible? And if mankind passes away, it will only mean that this particular expression is completed and done . . . . There will be a new embodiment, in a new way. (59)

Birkin only uses the word 'God' once in the novel, to deny that such a being exists. Indeed, he derives his philosophy of marriage from this atheism, agreeing with Gerald that 'if there isn't the woman, there's nothing', 'seeing there's no God' (58). But only a page later, his concept of the 'incomprehensible', of which humanity is an 'expression', constitutes a kind of apophatic restatement of the Christian theology of divine creation. There is, in Birkin's view, something that is incomprehensible and creative, from which the human race has derived, and which will continue creating even after the human race has destroyed itself. Indeed, as he says that 'humanity doesn't embody the utterance of the incomprehensible any more', he suggests that the dissolution of the human race he sees all around him is precisely a result of its loss of a living relationship with the creative incomprehensible. Despite his atheism, that is, Birkin is a religious

thinker. As we have seen, for William James religious life includes the beliefs that 'the visible world is part of a more spiritual universe from which it draws its chief significance' and that 'union or harmonious relation with that higher universe is our true end' (485), and it is in just these senses that Birkin conceives the incomprehensible.

Birkin has a vision of a better world, from which the human race has been wiped out. Against Ursula's criticism, he tells her that he finds the idea of the world 'empty of people', with 'everybody in the world destroyed', a 'beautiful, clean thought', because 'then there would *never* be another foul humanity created, for a universal defilement' (127). 'Man is one of the mistakes of creation,' he argues, 'like the ichthyosauri' (128). If man were swept off the face of the earth, he repeats, 'creation would go on so marvellously, with a new start, non-human' (128). It is in the idea of something inhuman alone, something after humanity, after the corrupt human race of his day has destroyed itself or been destroyed, in which Birkin takes comfort and finds hope.

Ursula is initially critical of this idea. She asks Birkin, 'What *do* you believe in? . . . Simply in the end of the world and grass?' (129). She finds his idea of the world cleaned of humanity 'attractive', '*really* desirable', but she quickly reflects that it is 'only a pleasant fancy'. Furthermore, she questions whether Birkin really believes what he says. Along with his 'impatient fury' at humanity, she finds in him also a 'final tolerance', and it is this that she mistrusts. For all his professed belief in the non-human, 'she saw that, all the while, in spite of himself, he would have to be trying to save the world', and she hates this 'Salvator Mundi touch' (128). Four chapters later, however, in 'Sunday Evening', she has come to hold a view very similar to Birkin's. If the death of the human race was a positive for Birkin, so individual death becomes a positive for her, and for the same reason, that some new, better kind of experience must follow. She reflects that death is a 'great consummation', a 'development from life', saying to herself, 'Let us die, since the great experience is the one that follows now upon all the rest, death, which

needs Levenson

is the next great crisis in front of which we have arrived' (101). She
has been persuaded by Birkin's concept of the incomprehensible,
since she tells herself, 'To die is also a joy, a joy of submitting to that
which is greater than the known, namely the pure unknown' (192). Like
Birkin, Ursula thinks of death as a positive journey into the unknown,
positive because all that human beings know of themselves and the
world is corrupt, meaningless and unfulfilling. Death, as she puts it,
'compensates for all the bitterness of knowledge and the sordidness
of our humanity' (194). To be human has become 'shameful and
ignominious' and in the unknown, which death constitutes, one may
become new and better. 'To know is human', she reflects, 'and in death
we do not know, we are not human' (194). As she puts it most simply,
'One might come to fruit in death' (193).

Keith Sagar speaks of the 'progressive nature' of the final version
of *Women in Love* (*Life into Art* 190), and this is true of Ursula's
religious beliefs. She comes to share Birkin's religion of the non-
human. Reflecting on the falsity of anthropomorphic projections onto
nature, she concludes, 'The universe is non-human, thank God' (264).
By the end of the novel, she is arguing with Gudrun that a new and
better form of life can only occur through a complete rejection of
this one. To her sister's claim that 'a new world is a development
from this world' (437), Ursula responds, 'One has a sort of other self,
that belongs to a new planet, not to this. – You've got to hop off'
(438). She has come to agree with Birkin's claim that the good life
can only emerge through the complete destruction of contemporary
life. As the sisters argue about the place of love in their respective
worldviews, it becomes clear that Ursula has largely come to believe
in Birkin's religion of the unknown. She tells Gudrun:

> I believe in something inhuman, of which love is only a little part. I
> believe what we must fulfil comes out of the Unknown to us, and
> it is something infinitely more than love. (438)

It is this belief with which Birkin closes the novel, reflecting on
Gerald's death:

> God can do without man. God could do without the ichthyosauri
> and the mastodon. These monsters failed creatively to develop, so

God, the creative mystery, dispensed with them . . . The eternal creative mystery could dispose of man, and replace him with a finer created being: just as the horse has taken the place of the mastodon. (478–9)

The sense of Birkin's phrase 'God, the creative mystery' is that the new phrase 'creative mystery' is a better one, more accurately representing the object of his belief, than the old word 'God'. Throughout the rest of the paragraph, having as it were translated the word into this better language, he uses only the latter. This mystery is very like the Christian God: it is eternal and it creates mankind and the universe. Birkin insists on an apophatic relationship to it, however: it is not all that the Christian religion has said of it, as the slow death of the Christian Mr Crich in front of the reader's eyes makes clear. It is like God in some respects, but the truest thing one can say of it is that it is unknown. The fact that the unknown will continue to create better things than man is 'very consoling to Birkin' (479). He has a genuinely religious relationship to it. This is true in Lawrence's own sense of the term, 'a certain deep feeling which seems to soothe and reassure the whole soul' (A 154), and which 'puts us into connection, into vivid touch' (A 155). It is true in James' sense, as one of the 'feelings, acts and experiences of individual men . . . so far as they apprehend themselves to stand in relation to what they may consider the divine', where 'divine' means that which is 'most primal and enveloping and deeply true' and to which the individual responds 'solemnly and gravely' (James 31, 34, 38), and it is also true in Eliade's sense, expressing Birkin's 'will to take his stand at the very heart of the real' (Eliade 64).

Birkin derives an ethical principle from his belief in the unknown, concluding his reflection at the end of the novel with this principle: 'To have one's pulse beating direct from the mystery, this was perfection, unutterable satisfaction' (WL 479). William James argues that, in religious experience, 'union or harmonious relation with that higher universe [from which the visible universe draws its chief significance] is our true end' and that 'inner communion with the spirit thereof . . . is a process wherein work is really done' (James 485). This is the case in Birkin's thought. To be in touch with the eternal creative mystery, which has brought forth man and will bring forth 'new races and new species', is the basis of the good life, for Birkin. All his reflections on star-equilibrium and the desirability of a relationship with a woman and a relationship with another man, depend on this first and fundamental principle of his thought, that the good life is founded upon being in touch, at the level of the blood, with the unknown. The novel leaves us with the thought, towards which it has progressed, that the metaphysics of blood that Birkin has developed throughout it is ultimately founded on the religious principle of the creative mystery behind and from which has come the universe. This is why, in the 1919 Foreword, Lawrence speaks the overtly religious language of 'the God-mystery within us' in describing the fundamental concerns of the novel (485). T. R. Wright comments on the Foreword, '*Women in Love* presents itself as a radical but profoundly religious work' (129), and we need only add that it is absolutely right to do so.

The religious beliefs in *Women in Love* which have received most critical discussion are the early theosophical ideas that Lawrence wrote into the final version of the novel in 1917, expressed at greatest length in the chapter 'Excurse'. In a passage in which the Pussum's feelings towards Gerald are described, the November 1916 version reads:

> Her being suffused into his veins like a delirium, a lovely intoxicating maddening heat. (*FWL* 62)

In 1917, Lawrence revises this to:

> Her being suffused into his veins like a magnetic darkness, and concentrated at the base of his spine like a fearful source of power. (*WL* 72)

He also adds the sentence at the end of the paragraph, 'But the great centre of his force held steady, a magnificent pride to him, at the base of his spine' (73). He is putting to work in his novel, as he deals with the nature of the relationships between people, the theosophical physiology he has learned from Pryse. As we know, the *kundalinî*, or serpent force, is said to 'lie coiled up like a slumbering serpent' (Pryse 16), and in the initiate passes from the sacral ganglion, at the base of the spine, all the way up the spinal column to the conarium, or 'third eye', culminating in 'knowledge of spiritual realities' (22). Lawrence creatively draws on this body of doctrine in *Women in Love* to describe the ultimate significance of the nature of the passions felt by and between his characters. Gerald's feelings, in the final version of the novel, are of a universal, spiritual significance that was lacking before Lawrence was able to describe them in the language of theosophy.

The very creative way in which Lawrence uses Pryse's theosophy in the novel is made clear in a passage in 'Coal-Dust', added in 1917, in which Gudrun reflects on Gerald's earlier forcing of his horse to stand before the train. In the final version of the novel, Gudrun is 'as if numbed in her mind' by the sense of the 'strong, indomitable thighs of the blond man' forcing the horse under his control, by 'a sort of soft white magnetic domination from the loins and thighs and calves, enclosing and encompassing the mare heavily into unutterable subordination, soft blood-subordination' (113). In his essays, as we saw, Lawrence creatively revised the theosophy of Blavatsky and Pryse. He takes that creativity to a new level, however, in his fiction. Although there is a prostatic ganglion in Pryse's system, corresponding somewhat to the 'loins' of which Lawrence writes in this passage, the 'thighs' and the 'calves' through which the life-force pulses through Gerald are no part of Pryse's system. Nor is the kind of sexually magnificent power of domination which he uses this life-force to exercise. Pryse indeed emphasizes the necessity of celibacy for the initiate as he allows the *kundalinî* to conquer each chakra (21). Lawrence takes the concept of a powerful life-force, most comparable to physical forces like electricity and magnetism, from Pryse and transforms it into something entirely his own, the sexually impressive and spiritually significant force running through the body of a man, in which his deepest self, with which he can communicate truly with the deepest self of another, can be found.

This is done most powerfully in 'Excurse'. Ursula and Birkin achieve for a time the kind of star-equilibrium with which he is concerned, and Lawrence describes their achievement of this state in theosophical terms. As Ursula kneels in front of Birkin on the hearth-rug in The Saracen's Head, she begins 'tracing the back of his thighs, following some mysterious life-flow there' (313). Again, Lawrence is transforming the concept of *kundalinî* he found in Pryse into a revisionary theosophical metaphysic of his own. There is no sense in Pryse that one can physically or even spiritually feel the serpent force at work in the body, nor does it flow through the thighs, but rather upwards, from the base of the spine to the top of the head. Ursula, however, can feel 'the strange mystery of his life motion' 'at the back of the thighs' and 'down the flanks'. This life-force, in Lawrence's revisionary theosophy, is 'the very stuff of being'. In the 1917 revision of *Women in Love*, he uses this theosophical language along with the heterodox Biblical language of *The Rainbow*. He had used neither in the November 1916 text, but in 1917 uses Biblical language to describe the sacred nature of sexual relationships in conjunction with his revisionary theosophical physiology. So that as Ursula feels the life force flowing down the back of Birkin's thighs, 'she discovered him one of the Sons of God such as were in the beginning of the world' (313). In the final version of *Women in Love*, that is, Lawrence finds that theosophy allows him to express the sacred nature of human beings in relationship for which he had previously used Biblical language. As the 1919 Foreword to the novel also suggests, Lawrence's revisionary theosophical beliefs are now the way in which he can most accurately express his sense of the sacredness of authentic human being and of authentic human relationships.

   Critics have emphasized the extent to which *Women in Love*, and 'Excurse' in particular, are structured according to the progression of certain religious texts or rites. Thomas Miles sees the journey of the book of Revelation at work in the chapter, in its 'movement from death (Hermione) to a new birth in a dazzling body' (198). David Pitre sees the novel to express a series of Taoist concepts, arguing that 'many of the guiding principles of Taoism are found in Rupert Birkin's philosophy' (60). The most influential work on the religious structure of the novel and of the chapter is that of Gerald Doherty, whose work is cited by T. R. Wright (*Bible* 130) and Charles Burack (91, 177–8), and developed by Kyoko Kay Kondo. In 'The Salvator Mundi Touch', Doherty argues that there is a five-stage pattern in theosophical writing about teachers of esoteric doctrine, to which a five-stage pattern he discerns in *Women in Love* corresponds. In 'The Darkest Source', he argues that 'Excurse' is structured as an initiation ritual of Tantric yoga. The argument of the first essay I find unconvincing.

There is no such five-stage pattern clearly accessible in the work of
Blavatsky or Pryse. Certainly all five stages (early preaching, retreat,
instruction, initiation and the false prophet) can be found throughout
the works Doherty cites (although the fifth stage of the false prophet,
which corresponds neatly to the episodes involving Loerke at the
end of the novel, is found only in Pryse, because his commentary
on the book of Revelation, with its false prophet in 13:1-18, 16:13,
19:20 and 20:10, necessitates it). But the five-stage life of the initiate
that Doherty posits cannot be read out of the texts without a great
deal of hermeneutic effort, and it is unlikely that Lawrence did so in
such a way as to structure his novel according to this pattern. I am
also sceptical that Lawrence has used Tantrism in the deliberate way
that Doherty suggests in the second essay. Doherty is aware that
there is no evidence that Lawrence read any work of or on Tantrism,
and argues, 'Though Lawrence may not have read the treatises
themselves, for one who was so closely in touch with "esoteric" and
"occult" sources during this period it seems inconceivable that he
should have remained unaware of their content' ('Darkest' 213). This is
certainly a plausible claim. As Tindall (124–61), Delavenay (*Edwardian
Transition* 171; *Man and His Work* 388, 458–62), Whelan (104–8) and
Kinkead-Weekes (*Triumph to Exile* 386–7) have shown, Lawrence
had been reading esoteric and occultist books and periodicals since
1908. I would offer a counter-hypothesis to Doherty's, however, that,
had Lawrence been in a detailed or systematic way acquainted with
Tantrism, so congenial would he have found its association of sexual
and sacred experience that he would have read all that he could find
on the subject, and at least once have referred explicitly to having
done so.

In practice, the parallels Doherty draws between elements
of Tantric ritual and of 'Excurse' are sometimes convincing, and
sometimes not so. As an example of the latter case, I would point
to his claim that Birkin's offering of three rings to Ursula mirrors
'an essential aspect of the opening ceremonies in Tantric ritual',
the offering of jewels (215). The offering of the jewels, however,
Lawrence had put in the November 1916 version (*FWL* 277–8),
before he added the esoteric material based on his reading in 1917.
It is unlikely therefore that he intended the colour symbolism of the
rings, even if he re-thought the meaning of the original motif in 1917,

to have a Tantric significance, as Dohorty claims. Nor am I convinced by the claim that the sudden ending of the quarrel between Birkin and Ursula 'bears all the marks of a rite of passage' (215), since such changes in mood and the nature of the relationship between two people are a staple of Lawrence's fiction, as in 'Anna Victrix' in *The Rainbow*, for example. The most convincing parallel that Doherty draws is that Ursula touches Birkin as do the participants in Tantric initiation, where 'an elaborate rite of body stroking is practiced' in order to arouse the life force within the flesh (217). Here Doherty may be right. It may be that Lawrence had Ursula physically feel the life force running down Birkin's thighs and flanks because of some knowledge of Tantrism he had acquired through his occult reading. On the other hand, this may be Lawrence's creative invention, what Thomas Miles calls 'his own understanding of the kundalini energy' (195), the way in which he puts to work in imagining an authentic relationship between two lovers the theosophical physiology he has learnt and appropriated from Pryse.

2

'The cultured animist': Native American religion

Mabel Dodge Sterne saw in *Psychoanalysis and the Unconscious* 'allusions here and there that seemed to point to capacities' in Lawrence to 'understand the invisible but powerful spirit' of the Taos Valley (Luhan 12). After receiving her invitation to come and live in Taos, Lawrence wrote to Earl Brewster, 'The Indian, the Aztec, old Mexico – all that fascinates me and has fascinated me for years' (*L* 4: 125). To Mabel he writes, 'I . . . believe in Taos, without having seen it. I also believe in Indians' (*L* 4: 152). He specifies the nature of this belief to Thomas Seltzer, that 'in America one can catch up some kind of emotional impetus from the aboriginal Indian' that could lead to a 'new epoch' (*L* 4: 157). Lawrence came to Taos looking for a source of religious life in the native peoples of the American Southwest. As Charles Rossman puts it, he 'came to America on a religious pilgrimage' (187). Lawrence describes his ideas about American Indians as the product of a heart 'born in England and kindled with Fenimore Cooper' (*MM* 115), and throughout the first version of *Studies in Classic American Literature*, American and Mexican Indians had represented the sensual self, the blood, that part of the human soul in which men and women meet the 'life-mystery' (175), the 'Godhead' (182), and renew their lives in this encounter. As Lawrence puts it in the 1920 'Foreword', 'The black Demon of savage America . . . hides the Godhead which we seek' (384).

First essays, 1922–23

The most striking contrast between the real Apache and Pueblo Indians Lawrence describes and the Indians he had imagined in the first *Studies in Classic American Literature* is that the real people are much less attractive. Lawrence is outraged at Taos by Indians who forbid whites taking pictures and entering the Catholic church there (*MM* 127). He feels the same way about the Apache who tells him he cannot enter the kiva at Stone Lake (118–19), interjecting an 'Ugh!' of disgust at the sounds made by the Apache dancers there (116). Despite this disgust, however, Lawrence also maintains the view that the native peoples of the continent live in closer contact with the divine than whites do: 'the Indians keep burning an eternal fire, the sacred fire of the old dark religion' (110). He compares Taos Pueblo to the monasteries of Europe in the Dark Ages in its 'nodality', its continued existence as a place of spiritual life in the cultural wasteland which surrounds it (125). He even uses a theosophical image for the pueblo, calling it a 'dark ganglion, spinning invisible threads of consciousness' (126). The published version of 'Indians and an Englishman' ends with Lawrence's firm rejection of aboriginal Indian religion: 'There is no going back. Always onward, still further . . . My way is my own, old red father; I can't cluster at the drum any more' (120). On the other hand, at the end of 'Certain Americans and an Englishman', Lawrence expresses precisely the opposite sentiment: 'Let us try to adjust ourselves again to the Indian outlook, to take up the old dark thread from their vision' (110). Despite the 'shock' of his first encounters with Native Americans (116), which forced him to revise his earlier ideas about them, Lawrence never entirely loses his belief in the authenticity of their religious lives.

Lawrence's relationship to the indigenous peoples of America changes when he visits Mexico for the first time. It is in particular the Temple of Quetzalcoatl at Teotihuacan that fires his imagination. Uncovered just four years before Lawrence's visit, the temple is a pyramid from whose tiers project a series of giant serpent heads encircled by feathers, with open mouths full of fangs. These serpent heads alternate with heads of 'an unidentified scaly creature' (Berrin and Pasztory 51), which has 'only an upper jaw' and a 'face divided into rectangular segments that could be read as "scales" or "crocodilian" markings' (Pasztory 110). On the slopes between the panels from which these heads project 'feathered serpents are shown in an undulating position' (Pasztory 110), and serpent heads also project from the balustrade of the stairway. In Lawrence's account, 'Huge, gnashing heads jut out jagged from the wall-face of the low pyramid, and a huge snake stretches along the base, and one grasps at carved fish' (*MM* 132). *Terry's Guide to Mexico*, which Lawrence used in Mexico, calls these sculptures 'singularly barbaric' (426a). Terry also points out that the word Teotihuacan, the name given by the Aztecs to the ancient city, means 'place where the gods reside or come' (425). Witter Bynner recalls Lawrence's reaction to the temple:

> In the great quadrangle of Quetzalcoatl, we saw Lawrence stand looking and brooding. The coloured stone heads of feathered snakes in one of the temples were a match for him. The stone serpents and owls held something that he obviously feared. (24)

Lawrence responds to the experience of seeing the temple of Quetzalcoatl in the essay 'Au Revoir, U.S.A.', written shortly after his visit to Teotihuacan. Mexico is a place of violence, he writes, a violence summed up perfectly in the 'dragons of San Juan Teotihuacán' (*MM* 131). The Mexican spirit of place indicates a deeper and truer religious consciousness, for Lawrence, than that of the United States. It is in the indigenous peoples of the country that Lawrence sees this kind of consciousness: 'the peon still grins his Indian grin behind the Cross . . . He knows his gods'. Underneath the veneer of Spanish Christianity, the Mexican Indian 'knows his gods' (132). In this essay, Lawrence thinks of the pre-Aztec and Aztec worship of Quetzalcoatl as a primitive form of religious consciousness. The Mesoamerican cultures 'never got any higher' than Quetzalcoatl, he writes; 'they hadn't got even as far' as the phallic gods of the ancient Europeans (132–3). Nevertheless, this primitive, violent religion is a real one, for Lawrence. The ancient Mesoamericans were 'dead in earnest' about their cruel gods, with their 'fangs, and cold serpent folds, and bird-snakes with fierce cold blood and claws', and this authentic passion remains, simmering beneath American expansionism and Spanish Catholicism, today. 'The gods bit', as Lawrence puts it, in ancient Mexico, and 'everybody knows' that they are going to bite again 'within the next five minutes' (133). Lawrence finds in Mexico what

he had looked for in the American Southwest, a place in the world
where aboriginal religion is still alive. Mexican religion may be cruel,
for Lawrence, but it is living. It is only once he has encountered it
that he can return to the United States and begin to learn, as he had
hoped to, from the native peoples of the American Southwest.

Essays on Native American religion, 1924

In April 1924, Lawrence attended dances at Taos Pueblo and at Santo
Domingo Pueblo. In the same month, he writes the first two of three
essays on Native American religion that he would later include in
Mornings in Mexico, a collection for which he suggested the title,
'Days and Dances in Mexico' (*L* 5: 581). These are 'Indians and
Entertainment' and 'The Dance of the Sprouting Corn'. In the first
essay, Lawrence begins with a theological reflection on the nature
of the theatre. Following Jane Harrison's thesis in *Ancient Art and*
Ritual (136–49), which he had read in 1913 (*L* 2: 90), Lawrence argues
that ancient Greek drama developed out of a ritual offered to a god or
goddess. As the specifically religious function of the drama declined,
the place of the watching god became assumed by the spectator.
The Western theatre, Lawrence claims, ascribes to the spectator
the role of a god, encouraging him to believe that he is like a god,
his mind governing his life as the mind of God governs the life of
the universe (*MM* 59–60, 67). When one watches an Indian ritual,
however, it is clear that a completely different theology underlies it.
To the Indian, Lawrence writes, there is no God, there is no Creator
and hence he is not the creature of God (66). The Indian distinguishes
neither between Creator and created, nor between Spirit and Matter.
Rather, 'Creation is a great flood, forever flowing, in lovely and terrible
waves. In everything the shimmer of creation, and never the finality
of the created' (66). It is the many different things represented in the
dances that lead Lawrence to this conclusion. On the one hand the
dancers represent beautiful, gentle things like deer or pine trees, and
on the other, terrifying beasts of prey and 'atrocious' enemies like the
Apache. All are part of the dances. Even Christian figures of worship
are integrated into the pre-Christian dances (66–7). Everything,
however good or evil, is raised into the sacred by its inclusion in the

dances, which leads Lawrence to see a theology at work in them: 'things utterly opposite are still pure wonder of creation' (66).

Lawrence's longest and most detailed reflection on the religious beliefs he sees at work in Native American ceremonies is 'The Hopi Snake Dance'. In 'Indians and Entertainment', he had described the animistic beliefs he ascribed to the Pueblo Indians with considerable respect. In 'The Hopi Snake Dance', written four months later in August 1924, Lawrence begins to speak in his own voice. As he tells Murry, the essay 'defines somewhat my position' (L 5: 109). To his agent Nancy Pearn, he writes, 'I value [the] article rather highly', and insists that it must not be cut by a publisher (L 5: 110).

Lawrence wrote and published two essays on the Hopi Snake Dance, the contrast between which is striking. The first essay, 'Just Back from the Snake Dance', is short, angry and insulting, not only to the tourists who come to watch the Snake Dance but even to the Indians themselves. Neil Roberts calls it a 'flippant, debunking piece' (90). This is in part explicable by the context in which Lawrence wrote the essay. Early in August, Lawrence had begun to spit 'bright red blood' (Brett 139). David Ellis writes, 'From August 1924 it is legitimate to regard him as tubercular' (195). He was still unwell ten days later, when Mabel and Tony took him and Frieda for a two-week car trip to Arizona in which they would see the annual Snake Dance at the Hopi reservation, which had for several decades been a tourist attraction because of the live rattlesnakes the priests hold in their mouths during the ceremony. Mabel Luhan chronicles how her relationship with Lawrence had all but fallen apart by the time of the trip. Lawrence was unwell on the trip, she recalls, and she herself was ill and depressed. She paints a vivid picture of the tension between her and Lawrence the night after the Snake Dance:

> I was very cross and Lawrence had an ear-ache. Lawrence wanted the coffee made weak and I wanted it made strong . . . So we made it twice, in a venomous silence, each conducting furiously an inner dialogue with the other. (267)

The following night, Lawrence handed her the essay 'Just Back from the Snake Dance'. 'Disappointed and incensed', she remained in Santa Fe while the rest of the party returned to Taos. Lawrence said to her as they left, she recalls, 'I know you didn't like that article of mine. I'll try and do another one' (268). A week later, he wrote 'The Hopi Snake Dance'.

In 'The Hopi Snake Dance', Lawrence begins his reflection on the meaning of the dance by expanding his earlier thoughts on the 'animistic religion' of the Pueblo Indians. In this religion, he writes, there is no Spirit, no God, no Creator. 'There is strictly no God at all: because all is alive' (81). There is no God in the animistic worldview of the Hopi, he writes, but rather 'the great living source of life: say the Sun of existence' (81). As we will see below, the word 'say' does a lot of work here. It allows Lawrence to develop religious ideas of his own while seeming to be representing those of the Hopi, a process that continues throughout the essay, with a free indirect style so porous as to blur the distinction between his own views and those of the Indians about whom he is writing. In this way, Lawrence develops the following religious ideas. There is no God, but only the Sun of existence. This Sun is not personal and so one cannot pray to it. It is 'nameless' and 'we call [it] Sun because the other name is too fearful'. It is the 'original One' (92). There emerge from it 'the great potencies, the invisible influences which make shine and warmth and rain' (81) and thunder and light (82). These things are not personal, but they are alive (82). From them in turn emerge corn, the seed of life, animals and people. These potencies can also be called dragons. Indeed, 'they are dragons'. The mystic Sun from which they emanate is also 'a dragon most terrible' (83). Neither the potencies nor their Source are gods. Rather, 'the only gods on earth are men'. Gods do not pre-exist the cosmos, but are 'created and evolved gradually, with aeons of effort'. They are 'the highest thing created', and the highest thing created in and by the cosmos thus far is man: 'the cosmos is a great furnace, a dragon's den, where heroes and demi-gods, men, forge themselves into being' (MM 83).

Lawrence describes these beliefs as 'the religion of all aboriginal America'. There may be different expressions of it among different peoples – in Mexico, there is more emphasis on horror, whereas in the pueblos of the United States, 'the most terrible dragon is still somewhat gentle-hearted' (83) – but this religion is shared by the 'settled pueblo Indians and the wandering Navajo, the ancient Maya and the surviving Aztec' (94). Indeed, it is 'perhaps the aboriginal religion of all the world' (83).

The mystic Sun, the Source of life, is 'willing and unwilling that we should have being'. 'Systole and diastole, it pulses its willingness and unwillingness' (92). Hence, human life is 'a battle, a wrestling all the time' with the Sun and its dragons. To forge his divine being, man must both 'submit to the strange beneficence' of the Source and also 'conquer [its] strange malevolence' (93). The modern West attempts to do this with the scientific conquest of nature (84). The Hopi attempt to do it with the Snake Dance. The Snake Dance, Lawrence writes, is an expression of 'the mystic living will that is in man, pitted against the living will of the dragon-cosmos' (84). Snakes are 'nearer' than men to the nameless Sun and to its dragons, like the rain, so the Hopi consider them 'emissaries to the rain-god'. The logic of the Hopi ceremony, in which the snakes are sent to the spirits to ask for rain, leads Lawrence to elaborate a further cosmological principle, that there is a dark sun at the centre of the earth. Its relationship to the dark Sun, the Source of all, is not specified, and seems to exist beyond the difference between literal and metaphorical language. Snakes, however, are closer to both suns than men and women are:

> To the cultured animist, and the pueblo Indian is such, the earth's dark centre holds its dark sun, our source of isolated being, round which our world coils its folds like a great snake. (84)

The 'heavy, rhythmic stamp' of the dancers, their 'low, sombre . . . chant-call' (86) and the paint they wear on their bodies (88) are all means of coming into closer contact with the dark sun at the centre of the earth. The snakes themselves, when set free in the desert after the dance, take the people's prayers down to the same place (91–2), both as 'rays of love' to its beneficent aspect and as 'arrows shot clean by man's sapience and courage' to its malevolent aspect (92).

Lawrence and the Hopi

In his survey of Lawrence's writing on Native Americans, L. D. Clark uses constructions like 'the animistic thought the Indians inspired in Lawrence' ('American Indian' 358), which acknowledge a difference between the views of the Hopi and the views Lawrence ascribes to

them, but which do not specify in what that difference consists. For
Mark Kinkead-Weekes, 'Lawrence is the only major English writer
in his lifetime . . . who tries seriously to imagine under the skin of
a third-world culture and religion' ('Gringo Señora' 254). Margaret
Storch agrees, speaking of Lawrence's 'wish to encounter the true
spirit of the region and its people' ('"But Not the America"' 50).
These critics rightly acknowledge the distinction between Native
American religious beliefs and Lawrence's representations of these
beliefs: Kinkead-Weekes speaks of Lawrence's attempt to imagine
a Third-World culture, and Storch of his wish to encounter such a
culture. The question of the extent to which Lawrence has succeeded
in representing the beliefs of the Native American peoples he
encountered, however, remains unasked.

    The main exception to this rule has been Wayne Templeton, who
criticizes Lawrence for the 'colonialist sensibility' which leads him
to misrepresent Native American cultures and religious beliefs (15).
Templeton argues that, 'without knowing anything of the languages,
religions, histories and traditions' of the Native American peoples he
observed, Lawrence '"read" and "interpreted" them, representing
what he thought they were, and alleging that they were typical'
(18–19). In particular, he argues that Lawrence misunderstands
tribalism, the primacy of land and the historical engagement of Native
American peoples with the United States. Neil Roberts develops
these claims, analysing the historical and political contexts of the
Hopi Snake Dance and arguing that Lawrence's essays 'regard the
ceremonials as, essentially, timeless' (93) although they all, 'and the
Snake Dance perhaps above all, had a political and contemporary as
well as a religious and archaic dimension' (94). Scholars of Lawrence's
American travel writing have emphasized the contemporary cultural
context in which the figure of the Native American is being constructed
in a variety of economic and cultural interests. Judith Ruderman
refers to the work of Edward Sapir, Ruth Benedict and Margaret
Mead, which 'implied that primitive cultures could be models for
American society' ('Lawrence as Ethnographer' 43), as examples of
the context of 'Americans' appropriation of "Indianness" to construct
personal and national identities' (37) in which Lawrence wrote about
Native American religion. Carey Snyder adds that the economy of
Southwestern tourism in the interwar period causes its discourse to

seep into that of ethnography, resulting in a double practice of 'turning native cultures into objects of scientific curiosity and spectacles for touristic consumption' (664), a practice from which Lawrence does not succeed in distancing himself (665–72).

This critical debate allows us to ask the question of the extent to which the beliefs Lawrence expounds in 'The Hopi Snake Dance' and the other essays on Native American religion are those of the peoples to whom he ascribes them and the extent to which they are his own. We will begin with the concept of animism, which Lawrence attributes both to the Hopi and to the other Pueblo peoples whose ceremonies he witnessed. Lawrence learned the view that animism was the original religion of mankind, still practiced as such by primitive peoples in the modern world, from E. B. Tylor's *Primitive Culture*, which he had read in Cornwall in 1916, and which he described as 'a very good sound substantial book' (*L* 2: 593). Tylor defines religion as 'the belief in Spiritual Beings' (i, 424), or more simply 'Animism' (i, 426). From the twin facts of the difference between a live body and a dead one, and of the human forms that appear in dreams and visions, Tylor argues, 'the ancient savage philosophers' formed the concept of the human soul, 'an animating, separable, surviving entity, the vehicle of individual personal existence' (i, 428, 501). They attributed souls of this kind to animals, in whom they also observed the difference between life and death and apparition in dreams, and thence to plants and inanimate objects. Furthermore, the universe itself became peopled, in the animistic logic of the savage mind, with disembodied beings like souls, which Tylor distinguishes from the latter as 'spirits'. 'The conception of a human soul . . . served as a type or model on which [man] framed . . . his ideas of spiritual beings in general, from the tiniest elf that sports in the long grass up to the heavenly Creator and Ruler of the world' (ii, 110). Animism so defined, Tylor argues, is 'the fundamental religious condition of mankind', an 'ancient and world-wide philosophy' that constitutes the 'groundwork of the Philosophy of Religion, from that of savages up to that of civilised men' (i, 426–7).

Lawrence takes from Tylor his view that the Indian peoples of the United States and of Mexico practice the earliest form of religion. He calls the beliefs and practices of the Hopi 'the religion of all aboriginal America' and 'perhaps the aboriginal religion of all the world' (*MM* 81). For Tylor, the name of this aboriginal religion is animism. In New

Mexico, Lawrence had read the anthropologist Adolf Bandelier's novel *The Delight Makers* in which, the author wrote, 'by clothing sober facts in the garb of romance I have hoped to make the "Truth about the Pueblo Indians" more accessible and perhaps more acceptable to the public in general' (v). In this novel, Bandelier describes the world view of the Pueblo Indians as animistic in Tylor's sense:

> Whatever there is in nature which the Indian cannot grasp at once, he attributes to mysterious supernatural agencies. He believes that nature is pervaded by spiritual essence individualized into an infinite number of distinct powers. Everything in nature has a soul according to him, and it is that soul which causes it to move or to act upon its surroundings in general. (43)

Lawrence has read both Tylor's account of animism and Bandelier's assertion that the worldview of the Pueblo Indians is animistic, but in his essays he redefines the concept of animism. He follows his anthropological sources in attributing the oldest form of human religious thought and practice to the Hopi and in calling this religion animism. However, he revises the nature of this aboriginal religion. He writes, 'To the animistic vision, there is no perfect God behind us, who created us from His knowledge' (82). For Tylor, this would be a contradiction in terms, as would Lawrence's claim that 'the animistic religion, as we call it, is not the religion of the Spirit' (81). But for Lawrence, in the aboriginal animism of America, 'behind us lies only the terrific, terrible, crude Source, the mystic Sun, the well-head of all things', from which the potencies or Dragons emanate (82). He says of this mystic Sun, 'You can no more pray to [it] than you can pray to Electricity' (81). It is not personal, not conceived on the model of the human personality or soul. Nor are the Dragons which emanate from it: 'They are alive . . . But they are not personal gods' (82). Lawrence redefines the aboriginal religion of the human race, which he sees to be practiced by the Hopi, as a religion of the living cosmos, which we could perhaps call 'vitalism', rather than as animism in Tylor's sense. This religion knows no personal gods but rather worships the living universe and its unknowable source. Lawrence retains Tylor's term 'animism' to describe this religion in order to make a claim that he believes is anthropologically true, that the oldest religion of the world is still practiced in the Hopi Snake Dance. Although he gives the impression of expounding anthropological facts, however, Lawrence revises his sources, and makes a claim of his own, that the aboriginal religion of America and perhaps of the world is one in which the universe is alive, but not personally so, and derives as such from a greater, unknown and impersonal source of life. L. D. Clark sees echoes of three books on Native Americans in Lawrence's work (*Dark Night* 103, 109–10). Lawrence himself refers only to Bandelier's novel. Whatever his additional sources, print or oral, he has acquired a considerable knowledge of Pueblo beliefs. In 'Just Back from the Snake Dance', it is clear that he understands, according to the anthropological knowledge of his time, the purpose of the Hopi Snake Dance:

> He [the Hopi] says the snakes are emissaries to his rain god, to tell him to send rain to the corn on the Hopi Reservation, so the Hopis will have lots of corn meal. (*MM* 187)

This is true. The purpose of the Snake Dance is that the snakes act as intercessors to the spirits of the dead who appear as clouds. If the dance is performed correctly, the snakes will ask the spirits for rain, in order to make the corn, the staple Hopi crop, grow. Jesse Fewkes, one of the first anthropologists to study the dance, wrote in a paper published in 1900, of which Mabel Luhan may have owned a copy, '[The snakes] are intercessors between man and the rain gods, and if the proper ceremonies with them are performed in prescribed sequence and in traditional ways, the rains must come because they came in the ancient times in the house of the Snake maid' (1008).

The fact that Lawrence's longest accurate statement concerning Hopi religion occurs in 'Just Back from the Snake Dance', the essay in which he is angry and insulting, even towards the Hopi themselves, makes clear that, in 'The Hopi Snake Dance', exposition of Hopi beliefs is not his primary concern. This is at first a surprise, since at one point in the essay Lawrence commits himself to the principle of accurate representation. If you are to understand the Snake Dance, he writes, 'you must have some spark of understanding of the sort of religion implied' (81). He criticizes a fellow spectator's account of the dance as 'very nice, only more Hindoo than Hopi' (81). Keith Cushman argues that 'The Hopi Snake Dance' should not necessarily be privileged over against 'Just Back from the Snake Dance' because it is more complex and considered, especially since

Lawrence published both essays. Rather, he writes, we should 'allow Lawrence the complexity of his responses to the ritual dances of the Southwestern Indians' ('Indians' 121–2). This is true, and the relative emphasis of the accurate descriptions of the Snake Dance in the first and second essays is an example of this complexity. It makes clear that, in 'The Hopi Snake Dance', Lawrence is interested less in representation of Hopi beliefs than in developing his own religious ideas on the basis of the images and concepts suggested to him by the Snake Dance.

In fact, the central religious ideas of the essay are Lawrence's own. First among these is that of the mystic Sun, from which the dragons of the cosmos emerge. The sun plays a central role in Hopi religion, but it is not that of Lawrence's Sun of existence. The Hopi Sun Chief Don Talayesva, who wrote an autobiography in the late 1930s, describes his lifelong devotion to the Sun god. This god is the most important in the Hopi pantheon, he writes: 'The Sun god is chief over all, and gives heat and light, without which there would be no life' (Talayesva 175). Talayesva describes the 'strict custom' according to which new-born Hopi children are named, through which he himself passed (30). He was presented to the sun, in a ritual in which his godmother, 'holding me before the Sun god' at dawn, offered prayers and performed prescribed ritual actions:

> As she concluded, she prayed again for my long life and called out to the Sun god the different names that I had received, in order that he might hear me and recognize me. (32)

Talayesva frequently describes prayers and offerings to the Sun god, whom the Sun Clan refer to as 'our great-uncle', 'asking him to send rain and to keep away the bad winds that destroy our crops' (59). He once saw him in a dream, 'in the form of a middle-aged man and white as snow'. He was 'kind and polite', and 'said with a friendly voice that he was the Sun god himself and that he saw and heard everything that I did' (87). Although chief among the gods, the Hopi Sun god, to whom Talayesva describes prayers and intercessions, and with whom he even describes conversations, is not in any way Lawrence's impersonal Sun of existence, the unknown source of all the living forces of the cosmos.

The sun is involved in creation in Hopi religion, as in Lawrence's thought. Harold Courlander comments that, in the Hopi creation myth, 'The paramount deity . . . is Tawa, the sun':

> What is meant, Hopi informants state, is the sun spirit or the sun force, conceived as male in its attributes. The sun impregnates the earth and the earth gives birth to living things. A distinction is made between the sun spirit, the supreme deity, and the sun that the people [in the Hopi creation myth] put in the sky to provide light and warmth in the Upper World. (205)

The Sun spirit plays the role of Creator in the Hopi emergence myth, which recounts the story of the emergence of the peoples of the earth through three previous worlds into this, the fourth world. The Hopi seem to be more concerned with the emergence of human beings from the Third World, beneath this one, than with an initial act of divine creation. When this part of the myth is told, however, according to Courlander's sources, it begins like this:

> In the beginning, there was only Tokpella, Endless Space . . . Only Tawa, the Sun Spirit, existed, along with some lesser gods. Tawa . . . gathered the elements of Endless Space and put some of his own substance into them, and in this way, he created the First World. (17)

Bandelier too expounds a Pueblo emergence myth. The sun and the moon, in *The Delight Makers*, pre-exist the emergence, and seem to be responsible for it:

> Pāyatyama our Father [the sun] and Sanashtyaya our Mother [the moon] saw that the world existed ere there was light, and so the tribe lived in the dark . . . The earth is round and flat, but it is also thick like a cake. The other three wombs are down below inside, one beneath the other. At Shipapu, the people came out upon this world which is the fourth womb, but it was cold and dark. Then the great sun rose in the heavens above. In it, Pāyatyama dwells, and on it he rides around the world in one day and one night to see everything which happens. (33)

The Sun god plays the closest role to that of creator among all the Hopi deities, but this role is in no way that of Lawrence's mystic Sun of existence, from which the potencies or dragons emerge, from which in turn emerges all else in the universe. In 'The Hopi Snake Dance', Lawrence is drawing on his considerable knowledge of Pueblo religion, which includes but is not limited to Bandelier's novel, and using images, motifs and ideas from that religion in order to express religious views that are in fact his own.

It is the same with the concept of the dragons of the cosmos. There is a Water Serpent in the Hopi pantheon, who is 'male/female and who sends forth water from the below to form clouds' (Loftin 42). Simmons adds, 'Serpent deities live in the springs and control the water supplies' (Talayesva 17). In *The Delight Makers*, Lawrence had read that the Shiuana, the spirits prayed to by the Pueblo Indians in the novel, live in the clouds (90) and can be depicted as serpents (154). Bandelier adds that, among the many gods and spirits of the world of the novel, the most 'prominent' are 'the sun-father and his spouse the moon-mother. It is principally the latter that moves the hearts of men, and with whom mankind is in most constant relations' (209). That is to say, it is the elemental forces of nature, which Lawrence describes as dragons, which play the greatest part in the religious life of the Indians portrayed in the novel. Neither the serpent spirits of Hopi religion, however, nor the deified natural elements of Bandelier's novel, correspond to Lawrence's elemental forces, which emanate from the Sun of existence and which bring forth all created things. With the dragons of the cosmos as with the Sun of existence, as for that matter with the dark sun at the centre of the earth, Lawrence has transformed the raw material of his knowledge of Pueblo religion into ideas that are entirely his own.

A second significant source of Lawrence's concept of the dragon is the work of Frederick Carter. An admirer of Lawrence's work, Carter wrote to him in New Mexico asking for Lawrence's opinion of a manuscript he had written on the astrological symbolism of the book of Revelation (*L* 4: 365). In the introduction he wrote for a revised version of this text, Lawrence describes how his imagination was fired when he first read it. The astrological details meant little to him: they were 'confused' and 'a chaos' (*A* 45). Nevertheless, he felt a 'marvellous release' (46) of the imagination in the astrological space opened up by Carter's work. Carter published a part of his manuscript in 1926 as *The Dragon of the Alchemists*, a meditation on the psychological and astrological symbol of the dragon. He attaches many meanings to this symbol, but focuses at greatest length on the position of the constellation Draco in the skies. The stars that compose it give the impression of guarding the pole star, and earlier in astronomical time it even contained the polestar. The Dragon, therefore, is the centre of the zodiac. It contains 'the one unchanging point' in the sky 'forever amid its coils': 'in the centre of the circle of the great types of life – the Zodiac – the Dragon rides in glory' (38–9). Since the dragon is at the centre of the macrocosm, it is also at the centre of the microcosm, and the constellation symbolizes 'that central life which intertwines and conjoins in the complex of man's psyche the major energies of sensual life' (43).

Lawrence says in his introduction to Carter's work, 'I was very often smothered in words. And then would come a page, or a chapter, that would release my imagination' (*A* 45). This is indeed what happened. Neil Roberts observes that the interpretative section of 'The Hopi Snake Dance' '*precedes* the vivid and detailed account of the ceremony itself' (98), and argues that this is a result of the textual way in which Lawrence interprets an experience of the other in the light of the 'voices of [his] . . . education' to which he refers in his poem 'Snake' (98–9). A reading of Carter makes clear how Lawrence uses these voices. Carter is concerned with the constellation of the Dragon, and with its counterpart in the microcosm of the human person. Lawrence takes this series of ideas and images and turns them into something new, the powers of the natural world described as dragons because they are 'alive and potent, but like the vastest of beasts, inscrutable and incomprehensible' (*MM* 82). The ideas he outlines in 'The Hopi Snake Dance' have a variety of sources, and each of these sources, from his knowledge of Pueblo religion to Carter's occult astrology, constitute the raw material out of which he has developed his own religious beliefs.

Pan in America

In May 1924, Lawrence moved to Kiowa ranch, and began repairing it 'with a couple of Indians and a workman' (*L* 5: 38). He writes:

> We have the camp just above the cabin, under the hanging stars,
> and we sit with the Indians round the fire, and they sing till late
> into the night, and sometimes we all dance the Indian tread-dance.
> (*L* 5: 67)

Just days after the move, he writes 'Pan in America'. In the first
version of this essay, he argues that all modern religions are
forms of pantheism, an 'ideal pantheism' in which 'the flesh and
its functions' are 'redeemed . . . into pure consciousness, into
spirituality'. This is the religion of Wordsworth, Emerson, Thoreau
and Whitman (*MM* 200). Despite its claim that 'everything is God',
Lawrence argues, it quickly resolves into the 'fatal dualism' in which
'Spirit is all good, or God, and Matter is just negative, not-God' (200).
The Pan worship in which Lawrence is interested is not that of the
modern age but that of a prehistoric age, 'back beyond the Greeks
with their passion for intellectualisation', in which 'there is no god
and not-god . . ., no Spirit and no Matter. There is only Pan' (201).
This is the kind of religion he sees still alive in the Indians in whose
dances he takes part after the day's work at the ranch. As he puts it
in the final version of the essay, 'It is what, in a way, the aboriginal
Indians say, and still *mean*, intensely: especially when they dance
the sacred dance, with the tree: or with the spruce twigs tied above
their elbows' (159).

In the first version of the essay, he describes the religion of the
'men of Pan'. In the second, published, version, these men are
specified as the 'Indians' with whom Lawrence sits 'around a big
camp fire' on his 'little ranch under the Rocky Mountains' (157, 159).
As he puts it most succinctly, 'In America, among the Indians, the
oldest Pan is still alive' (164). Lawrence's vision of Pan, which he sees
among the Indians with whom he shares a camp fire, is that of a
relationship between living human beings and the living universe,
a 'vivid relatedness between the man and the living universe that
surrounds him' (160). He imagines the relationship between a man of
Pan and a pine tree, like the huge tree in front of his cabin at Kiowa:

> The tree is asserting itself as much as I am. It gives out life as I give
> out life. Our two lives meet and cross one another, unknowingly:
> the tree's life penetrates my life, and my life, the tree's. (158)

Lawrence imagines a man of Pan conversing with the tree, as his life interacts with that of the tree: 'Oh you, you big tree . . . I am going to cut you down and take your life and make you into beams for my house, and into a fire. Prepare to deliver up your life to me' (159). In the same way he imagines an 'old hunter', 'in the stillness of the eternal Pan', conversing with the deer he is stalking (161). Here Lawrence represents Pueblo thought with considerable accuracy. Talayesva describes hunting a coyote as follows:

> Petting its tail, I gently moved up to its shoulders and said softly, 'Well, coyote, I know you were sent by your Mother to be trapped in answer to my prayers.' (266)

When he kills turtles to use their shells for rattles in a sacred dance, he recalls, 'I made a speech to the turtles before killing them, telling them we had nothing to give them now but that when we got home we would make pahos [prayer feathers] for them' (109). Talayesva's thinking is more animistic than pantheistic – it is to the spirit of the coyote and of the turtles, analogous to the soul that animates the human body, that he speaks, rather than as one part of the living universe to another, as Lawrence's Indian man of Pan does. 'Pan in America' is thus a kind of early version of 'The Hopi Snake Dance', in which Lawrence describes, on the basis of his understanding of Pueblo thought and practice, the religion of the living universe that his experience of Pueblo peoples and individuals has allowed him to develop.

'The Woman Who Rode Away': The question of gender

During his time at Kiowa, from May to October 1924, Lawrence wrote two stories and a novella set in the Southwest, 'The Woman Who Rode Away', St Mawr and 'The Princess', in which he articulates some of the ideas he has been formulating in his essays on Native American religion. The first of these stories was in part inspired by a trip Lawrence took in May to an Indian ceremonial cave, high on the

side of a mountain above the village of Arroyo Seco (Frieda Lawrence
151; Brett 87). Mabel Luhan describes the cave as follows:

> The vast, pelvic-shaped aperture faces the west and yawns upward
> to the sky; and over it descends the mountain water, falling thirty
> feet across the face of the entrance to form an icy pool below . . .
> At the right-hand side of the back wall of the place there are a
> number of rude climbing steps that lead up to a shelving ledge . . .
> One by one we climbed to the high altar. (209)

'At the winter solstice', Mabel writes, 'when the water has turned
to an icy column, as the sun turns to go south, it shines through
the erect, transparent pillar of ice and falls precisely upon the altar'
(210).

In 'The Woman Who Rode Away', a white woman rides alone into
the Sierra Madre mountains of Chihuahua. She is initially inspired
by a 'foolish romanticism' when she hears a young friend of her
husband speaking with a 'vague enthusiasm for unknown Indians'
like those who live in the mountains around them, and she feels that
it is her 'destiny' to wander among them (WRA 42). Her husband
tells her of the Chilchui tribe, 'the sacred tribe of all the Indians'. The
descendants of the Aztec kings live among them, and their priests
continue to practice the 'ancient religion', with its human sacrifices
(42). As the woman rides alone into the mountains, she encounters
three Indians, whom she tells that she wants to visit the Chilchui and
to 'know their Gods' (47). When she is led to the tribe's elder, she
tells him, 'I came away from the white man's God . . . I came to look
for the God of the Chilchui' (51). She is 'weary' of the white man's
God, she tells him, and 'would like to serve the gods of the Chilchui'
(52). She is stripped, ceremonially dressed in ritual garments and
given a sweetened herb liquor to drink, which induces in her a cosmic
consciousness, an 'exquisite sense of bleeding out into the higher
beauty and harmony of things' (62). She is kept alone until midwinter,
when she is led through a series of ceremonies, at the end of which
she is carried up to a cave similar to the one Lawrence had visited
with Mabel Luhan, laid on a stone altar and sacrificed with a flint knife
in order that, as one Indian tells her, 'our gods will begin to make the
world again, and the white man's gods will fall to pieces' (61).

Lawrence had first read Sir James Frazer's *The Golden Bough*, along with *Totemism and Exogamy*, in 1915. Brett recalls that he was re-reading the former, on loan from Mabel, at Kiowa the month before he wrote 'The Woman Who Rode Away' (81). Although she recounts Lawrence criticizing Frazer as one of 'these people who write books from their armchairs' (81), the sacrificial rituals of *The Golden Bough* form the basis for the ritual Lawrence would portray in 'The Woman Who Rode Away'. The story owes most to the chapter, 'Killing the God in Mexico', which would have made a particular impression on Lawrence on this re-reading, with the religion of the native peoples of the American continent uppermost in his mind. Frazer begins the chapter, 'By no people does the custom of sacrificing the human representative of a god appear to have been observed so commonly and with so much solemnity as by the Aztecs of ancient Mexico' (607), possibly suggesting to Lawrence that a story about the religion of the native peoples of the American continent would be a story about a human sacrifice. The way in which the chapter influences the story most, however, is Frazer's emphasis on and examples of the fact that many women, as well as men, were sacrificed to the gods of Mexico:

> The honour of living for a short time in the character of a god and dying a violent death . . . was not restricted to men in Mexico; women were allowed, or rather compelled, to enjoy the glory and to share the doom as representatives of goddesses (612).

Lawrence writes many features of the human sacrifices, both of women and of men, that Frazer describes into 'The Woman Who Rode Away'. Frazer's victims are frequently dressed in ritually significant clothing (608, 614–15), as Lawrence's woman is (55). They are honoured for a period of time, 'for a year in some feasts, in others six months, and in others less' (610), just as Lawrence's woman is guarded for 'days and . . . weeks' (58), perhaps months, until she is sacrificed at the winter solstice. The victims Frazer describes are well fed, well housed and treated with respect and reverence. The young man sacrificed to Tezcatlipoca each year is 'honourably lodged in the temple where the nobles waited on him and paid him homage, bringing him meat and serving him like a prince' (608). In a similar way, Lawrence's woman is treated respectfully by the young Indian who guards her – he 'told her she might have what she wanted', and brings her 'a basket-tray containing food, tortillas and corn-mush with bits of meat . . . and a drink made of honey, and some fresh plums' (56). Several of Frazer's victims are imprisoned and guarded, as Lawrence's woman is, 'lest [they] should fly' (611). The slave sacrificed to Quetzalcoatl is ritually washed before being dressed for the sacrifice: 'before his clothing they did cleanse him, washing him twice in a lake, which they called the lake of the gods' (611), and in Lawrence's story, when the woman is first presented to the old cacique, a similar ceremony of undressing, washing and dressing in new clothes takes place (55). On the day before the sacrifice, the same kind of ritual occurs: the Indian priests 'took off her clothes . . ., washed her all over with water' and 'later, they put a short blue tunic on her' (66–7). The slave sacrificed to Quetzalcoatl that Frazer describes is garlanded (611), just as the young Indian who guards Lawrence's woman 'brought her also a long garland of red and yellow flowers with knots of blue buds at the end' (56). He is also drugged: 'they made a drink mingled with another liquor made of cacao, giving it to him to drink . . . they said that he would offer himself cheerfully to death, being enchanted with this drink' (612). This drink makes the slave forget his coming death, 'returning to his former dancing and mirth', which augurs well for the sacrifice (612). In a similar way, Lawrence's woman is given a 'liquor . . . made with herbs and sweetened with honey', which induces a 'great soothing languor' in her (56), and then the cosmic consciousness which may also contribute to the efficacy of the sacrifice. Some of Frazer's victims are even kept ignorant of their coming fate with ambiguous language, just as in Lawrence's story (Frazer 617; WRA 61).

Frazer writes that 'dances . . . formed a conspicuous feature of the festivities' leading up to the sacrifice to Tezcatlipoca, and refers frequently to dances preceding the sacrifice of victims in other rituals (609, 613–16). At the sacrifice to Toci, the dances 'began in the afternoon and lasted till the sun went down' and lasted for eight days (617), just as in Lawrence's story, several dances precede the sacrifice of the woman, the first of which is described in great detail, lasts 'all day', and is watched by the woman 'for hours and hours' (60). The sacrifice itself in 'The Woman Who Rode Away' has features that derive from Frazer. The several stages of ceremony leading up to the final sacrifice in the story are reminiscent of Frazer's account of the sacrifice to Tezcatlipoca, in which he describes the ceremonies 'twenty days before [the victim] was to die', those which occur 'during the last five days', and finally the events 'on the last day' (609). One Mexican victim is carried to the place of sacrifice on a litter, 'a portable framework or palanquin' (619), as is Lawrence's woman (68). The victims that Frazer describes are always led upwards to the place of sacrifice, as is Lawrence's woman, and most of them are presented to the people for whom the sacrifice is carried out, as is the woman at the end of Lawrence's story (Frazer 607–9; WRA 70). The sacrifice itself, in which 'they laid her on a large flat stone, the four powerful men holding her by the outstretched arms and legs' (70), is also reminiscent of Frazer's accounts of Mexican sacrifices. 'He was seized and held down by the priests on his back upon a block of stone' (609); 'They threw her on her back on the block, and while five men held her down . . . the priest cut open her breast with his knife' (613). Frazer even mentions the 'analogy' of Mexican sacrifices, according to which the Native American Pawnees also sacrificed female victims (Abridged edn 591).

The story is one of Lawrence's most controversial works. The feminist critiques of Carol Dix and Carol Siegel are perhaps most striking since both authors take a generally positive view of Lawrence's portrayals of women. Dix, who writes that 'Lawrence treats women with a respect hardly ever accorded them by male writers' (12), describes 'The Woman Who Rode Away' as 'one of Lawrence's ultimate statements about his fear of women, his hatred of them, and the vengeance he seeks over them' (116). Siegel, who argues that Lawrence belongs to the tradition of women's literature, writes that his novels portray 'a feminized cosmos that most often seems to affirm a female character's point of view' (10). When she discusses 'The Woman Who Rode Away', however, she describes it as a story in which 'female essence [is] meaningful only at the moment of its destruction, as the woman passes into utility within a primitive patriarchal culture' (31). If there can be said to be any kind of consensus among the story's critics, it would perhaps be that it is more complex and equivocal than Kate Millett's critique in Sexual Politics (285–93) had acknowledged. Laurence Steven argues that, if

Lawrence victimizes the woman, he does so unconsciously, since it is the 'white consciousness of the West which strips people of their autonomy and turns them into objects' that the story is really against (216). Peter Balbert agrees that it is the woman's husband and the Indians that the story portrays negatively, and argues that feminist critique of the story 'fails to catch the subtle suggestions of *strength* in the Woman' (260), a point which Barbara Schapiro develops from a psychoanalytic perspective (129). Mark Kinkead-Weekes accepts feminist responses to the story, but adds, 'I do not believe that they . . . do anything like justice either to the experience or to its form' ('Gringo Señora' 254). It is the woman's 'White imperialism and racial superiority' (257) of which the story narrates the destruction, he argues, rather than her will or autonomy as a woman. In a similar way, Sheila Contreras criticizes the ethnocentric assumptions of both Lawrence and his critics in their understanding of the Indians as 'dirty, misogynistic and intent on overthrowing the master-race' (96). 'If the final scene does portray the submission/sacrifice of the female to the "doctrine of male supremacy"', she writes, 'we must recognize this doctrine as Lawrence's creation projected upon his fictitious Chilchui culture' (98). Neil Roberts, by contrast, argues that, while the Southwestern stories 'can be . . . considered as misogynist fantasies' (100), in 'The Woman Who Rode Away', Lawrence succeeds to a considerable extent in portraying the difference of the other culture (107–10).

I refer to this critical debate in order to ask the question of the gender politics of the religion portrayed in the story. As the debate makes clear, 'The Woman Who Rode Away' is a complex story. Despite its complexities, however, the dominant trajectory of the story is one in which the cosmos is to be restored to order, in a way in which the story values – the aboriginal religion of America is to triumph over the dead religion on which modern industrial life is based – at the cost of the death of a woman. This vision of cosmic order is one propounded entirely by men. Critics who have discussed the religious meanings of the story have largely found it to be a positive one. Sheila MacLeod argues that the woman is a kind of female Christ figure. If the woman surrenders her will and her individuality, MacLeod writes, it is 'not because she is a model of female passivity, but because she has embarked on a spiritual or religious quest. Such a quest can no more be called passive than can the practice of yoga' (124). The story articulates a kind of feminist religion, for MacLeod, a 'modern fertility myth' (127), which differs from those of 'Orpheus, Osiris, Thammuz, the Fisher King, and even Jesus Christ', whose 'male blood' is said to possesses fertilizing or redemptive power. Rather, 'The Woman Who Rode Away' 'points . . . towards a true recognition that it is female blood which is shed in menstruation and childbirth and is thus a primary creative agent' (129). Laurie McCollum too finds the religious ideas in the story empowering to women. She argues that the woman's sacrifice is to be understood in René Girard's terms, as the kind of ritual murder upon which all cultural order is founded. In 'The Woman Who Rode Away', 'the female enacts cultural salvation, and the sacrifice of the Woman is ultimately empowering as it places women at the nexus of culture formation' (230). The woman, indeed, may become a goddess to the Chilchui, 'representing female power and influence in the culture' and establishing a model for female political power, since, as Girard argues, ritual sacrifice is linked to the development of royal authority (238).

MacLeod and McCollum are right to an extent, that the story does articulate a redemptive journey for the woman. But in my view, it is impossible to overlook the fact that, within the complex and mutually contradictory trajectories of meaning that make up the story, the dominant trajectory, with respect to the religious beliefs it articulates, is a patriarchal one. If the woman is redeemed from the empty life with which she begins in the story, it is a redemption that comprises her being killed, both bodily and as an autonomous individual, by men. The religion of the story cannot therefore be described as redemptive, despite its apparent intention to the contrary. MacLeod speaks of her own unease with her positive interpretation. Having described the female fertility myth that the story articulates, she writes, 'I confess I am uneasy about the sacrifice . . . Once again [Lawrence] is making an overt connection between the male principle and cruelty and bloodshed, between the act of penetration and the infliction of pain or even death' (129). There is not enough evidence, furthermore, to support MacLeod's claim that the woman restores potency to the women of the Chilchui in particular, far less that her restoration of the men in the tribe is dependent upon her restoration of the women. Twice the Indian who guards the woman tells her, 'the Indian women get the moon back' as a result of her sacrifice (62; cf. 65). But the Chilchui women are mentioned so infrequently with respect to the men, and the rituals involved in the woman's sacrifice are described so entirely as the design and work of the men of the tribe, that it is impossible to say that her sacrifice restores the cosmos to the women of the tribe in particular or, *a fortiori*, that this restoration enables that of the men. While McCollum's Girardian reading is in many respects convincing, the story itself does not bear out her claim that the sacrifice of the woman is ultimately empowering, since this empowerment, if it occurs, will only do so in the future of the society represented. In the story itself, the empowerment that the woman does achieve is surely overwhelmed by the fact that she does so only at the cost of her life.

So, what kind of religion is portrayed in the story? First, it is striking that the ritual dances which culminate in the woman's sacrifice are recognizably those which Lawrence values in his essays on Native American religion. L. D. Clark points out that the ceremonies and ritual dress of the story are similar to those Lawrence witnessed in the corn dance at Santo Domingo (*Dark Night* 39–40). Furthermore, the Indians in 'The Woman Who Rode Away' dance with the 'tread' step, which closely symbolizes the dancer's journey to the dark centre of himself in Lawrence's essays (*MM* 63–4, 74, 116, 179). This tread dance is entirely positive in Lawrence's religious reflections. It is the 'bird-tread' in which 'they are giving themselves again to the pulsing, incalculable fall of the blood, which forever seeks to fall to the centre of the earth' (*MM* 63), that 'brings [the dancer's] life down, down, down, down from the mind . . . and plunges deep from the ball of the foot into the earth, towards the earth's red centre, where these men belong' (*MM* 74). In 'The Woman Who Rode Away', it is this positive religious phenomenon that characterizes the Indians and their rituals in which the woman is sacrificed. The first Indians she encounters guide her to the Chilchui village 'with the slow, soft, heavy tread of the Indian' (50). In the 'big dance' which precedes the day of her sacrifice, the men dance 'bending slightly forward and stamping the earth in their absorbed, monotonous stamp of the dance', and they are each followed by a woman 'rhythmically and subtly beating the earth with her bare feet' (59). At the sacrifice itself, as the woman is carried up to the cave where she will be killed, 'everybody danced the tread of the dance-step, even, subtly the litter-bearers' (68).

If this tread-step is recognizable from 'Indians and Entertainment' and 'The Dance of the Sprouting Corn', the values of 'Pan in America' are also a part of the religion of 'The Woman Who Rode Away'. After the big dance which obliterates the woman's sense of individual independence, the men of the village gather round the fire at night and sing and dance, just as Lawrence describes his Indian companions at Kiowa doing. In 'Pan in America', Lawrence writes that the Pan-consciousness, which he values as genuinely religious, can be witnessed by anyone who '[sits] with the Indians around a big camp-fire . . . in the mountains at night, when a man rises and turns his breast and his . . . bronze face away from the blaze, and stands voluptuously warming his thighs and buttocks and loins . . . faintly smiling the inscrutable Pan-smile' (*MM* 159–60). In 'The Woman Who Rode Away', the woman hears 'the strange uplifted savage sound of men singing round the drum . . . Sometimes there would be a fire, and in the fire-glow, men in their white shirts or naked save for a loin-cloth, would be dancing and stamping like spectres . . . or drooping squatting by the fire to rest' (60–1). The young Indian who guards the woman explains the meaning of the dance to her in precisely the terms Lawrence uses in the early version of 'Pan in America'. In the essay, the man of Pan sits by the fire, watching the sun, and saying to the woman, 'Oh woman, you are dark like the dark places between the stars' (205), just as the young Indian in the story tells the woman, 'Our men are the fire and the daytime, and our women are the spaces between the stars at night' (61). The first time Lawrence portrays in fiction the religion of Pan, the religion of all aboriginal America, whose tenets he has formulated in his Native American essays, he portrays it as a patriarchal one. There is no reason in principle why the religious beliefs he has articulated in these essays should entail patriarchal beliefs and practices but, in 'The Woman Who Rode Away', they do in fact entail such beliefs and practices. Birkin in *Women in Love* and Somers in *Kangaroo* had derived hierarchical gender relations from their religious beliefs, but Ursula and Harriett had maintained a constant criticism of these beliefs. In 'The Woman Who Rode Away', there is no such criticism. Although the religious ideas Lawrence works out in America do not necessarily lead to hierarchical gender relations, in 'The Woman Who Rode Away' they do so in fact.

Apophasis in *St Mawr*

The religion of Pan is also the object of *St Mawr*, which Lawrence began writing at about the same time as 'The Woman Who Rode Away' and then re-wrote between June and September 1924. Pan is first mentioned in conversation between Lou Witt and the artist Cartwright, based on Frederick Carter. Cartwright asks Lou, 'Don't you imagine Pan once *was* a great god, before the anthropomorphic Greeks turned him into half a man?' (65). Before they did so, he says, Pan was 'the god that was hidden in everything'. Indeed, he cannot truly be said to be a god at all:

> Pan was the hidden mystery – the hidden cause. That's how it was a Great God. Pan wasn't *he* at all: not even a great God. He was Pan. All: what you see when you see in full. (65)

You could only see the god hidden in things at night, or more truly in a kind of spiritual night, with the 'third eye', 'which sees only the things that can't be seen' and which is 'darkness' (65). Both Lou and Mrs Witt agree that they see Pan in this way in St Mawr.

In the novella, Pan is associated both with Celtic and with American Indian religion. Bob Smith argues that the Welsh groom Lewis and the Indian groom Phoenix represent the 'mind' and the 'animal' halves respectively of the figure of the centaur, the myth of which Lawrence transposes into the modern age (202–3), but this is not the case. Rather, James Cowan is correct in speaking of the 'syncretism' of the story's chain of associations (92). In *Fantasia*, Lawrence had expressed his belief that in 'the Glacial Period', the sea-level was lower than it is today, much of the earth's water being contained in glaciers, 'so that the Azores rose up mountainous from the plains of Atlantis, where the Atlantic now washes', and 'men wandered back and forth from Atlantis to the Polynesian Continent as we now sail from Europe to America' (*PUFU* 63). In *The Plumed Serpent*, the 'mysticism of the aboriginal Celtic or Iberian people', which 'lay at the bottom of [Kate's] soul' as an Irishwoman, and 'which lives on from the pre-Flood world', is directly related, through the myth of Atlantis, to 'that which is aboriginal in America' (415). It is in this syncretic way that Pan, which Lou and Mrs Witt see in St Mawr, is associated in the novella with the aboriginal religion both of the Celtic and of the American Indian peoples.

As Keith Sagar points out, there is no Christian St Mawr, but there is St Maurus or Maur, disciple and successor of St Benedict, the founder of Western monasticism (*Life into Art* 266), who it was believed brought the Benedictine order to France and founded the Abbey of Saint Maur-sur-Loire in Anjou (Mershman; Gellhaus 375). Lawrence would have learnt of St Maurus during his visit to the Benedictine abbey of Monte Cassino, where the guest master he befriended had taken his monastic name after the saint. Don Mauro is also mentioned in Maurice Magnus' article on Monte Cassino (14), which Lawrence read. Furthermore, as Sagar points out, Lawrence read in the General Prologue to *The Canterbury Tales* Chaucer's account of the worldly monk who found 'old and somdel strait' 'The reule of seint Maure and of seint Beneit' (ll. 173–4). Lawrence turns the name of this Christian saint and monk into a Welsh one, associating thereby the Celtic and the religious in the figure of St Mawr.

St Mawr is closely associated with his Welsh groom Lewis, and Lewis too, as an 'aboriginal' Celt, is associated with Pan. He responds to Mrs Witt's question about God from 'the darkness of the old Pan' (107). He rejects contemporary Christianity (103) and in its place, like a man of Pan, feels a living part of the living cosmos. He feels that oak leaves are more alive than people, and he knows that trees interact with those people who know how to hear them:

> The trees . . . watch and listen with their leaves. And I think they say to me: *Is that you passing there, Morgan Lewis?* . . . And if you cut a tree down without asking pardon, trees will hurt you sometime in your life. (107)

Lewis' Celtic religion is precisely the religion of the men of Pan that Lawrence describes in his essays on Native American religion.

This chain of associations is made explicit in *St Mawr* with the association of the Indian groom Phoenix with the Welsh horse and groom. The religion of Pan is all but effaced in the Westernized Phoenix, however, and it is in the American ranch in which it is most authentically found. Keith Sagar writes, 'The form of *St Mawr* is that of the religious quest, the quest for union with God' (269), and the object of this quest is the spirit of place of Las Chivas ranch. The spirit of the ranch is what Lawrence calls 'the religion of all aboriginal America' (*MM* 83). This is made clear in its effect on the New England woman who, as a Christian with an 'egoistic passion of service', has expected to find in the ranch 'the earthly paradise of the spirit' (*SM* 146), an expression of her belief in a God of Love. The spirit of place of Las Chivas erodes this belief, however. It is a 'grey, rat-like spirit', and it forces upon her the realization that '*there was no merciful God in the heavens . . . There is no Almighty loving God. The God there is shaggy as the pine-trees, and horrible as the lightning*' (147).

Keith Brown observes, 'Criticism of *St Mawr* speaks, perhaps, too readily of "Pan"' (160), and there is a sense in which this is true. Not even Pan, which is the closest the novella has come to naming the relationship of man living in the living cosmos, is exactly the right name for the object of the religious quest of the novella. The truth is, there is no name. In an apophatic manner, *St Mawr* constantly crosses through and re-writes terms and images, resting finally in none of them, for the thing that constitutes the object of Lou's quest, the alternative to her empty life in the modern world. It is because of this refusal to name, and therefore to authorize any person or institution to speak for, the sacred that *St Mawr* constitutes a more successful articulation of this alternative than 'The Woman Who Rode Away'.

There is one sense in the novella in which the spirit of place of the ranch is that of Pan. All the associations in the novel have led up to this climax, in which Pan is not only seen in St Mawr, but in an entire place in which Lou can realistically live. The spirit of the place is described as that of the living universe which men of Pan understand and live within, a 'vast and living landscape', which 'lived, and lived as the world of the gods' (146). So, in one sense the story is a journey from the modern world to the aboriginal world of Pan, in which Lou first glimpses this world in St Mawr, and then is finally able to imagine living in it daily at Las Chivas. But Lawrence also describes the ranch in grimmer terms than those in which he describes the religion of Pan. In 'Pan in America', he emphasizes a man's relationship to a tree, in whose life he lives while he reverently cuts it down and burns it for his fire, and a hunter's relationship to a deer, which he kills for himself and his family to eat. One of the dominant symbols of the spirit of place of Las Chivas, however, is the rat. We hear not only of the landscape's 'intense, bristling life', but also of its 'undertone of savage sordidness' (148) and its 'hatred of man's onward-struggle towards further creation' (150). Lawrence writes in 'Pan in America', 'Among the creatures of Pan, there is an eternal struggle for life, between lives' (*MM* 162). The emphasis in the essay, however, is on men winning this struggle, whereas in the final section of *St Mawr* it is on a woman losing it. The victory and the loss are both part of what Lawrence sees to be aboriginal American religion: 'the great dragons from which we draw our vitality are all the time willing and unwilling that we should have being' (*MM* 92). 'Pan' is the term with which the novella comes closest to naming the sacred living of man in the living cosmos which is its object, and it also shows, in its final section, that this term is inadequate, and that others are constantly needing to be written and re-written across it, such as the symbol of the rat, the concept of the sordid, and even Lou's sexual metaphysics – 'to it, my sex is deep and sacred, deeper than I am, with a deep nature, aware deep down of my sex' (155). The religion of all aboriginal America, which *St Mawr* articulates, is a religion whose God remains absolutely unknown. Lawrence describes it to E. M. Forster, while writing *St Mawr*, as 'the X – I don't know what to call it, but not God or the Universe' (*L* 5: 77). One's relationship to it is 'primary' and 'religious', he writes, but it remains unknown. Behind the religion of Pan, which he works out in America, there remains Lawrence's unknown God. It is for this reason that *St Mawr* is an ethically more successful expression of this religion than 'The Woman Who Rode Away'. Because the sacred in the novella is ultimately unknowable, no person or institution can speak for it, and so the oppressive results of 'The Woman Who Rode Away' do not follow from Lawrence's representation of it. If 'The Woman Who Rode Away' lacks the internal criticism of *Women in Love* or *Kangaroo*, that criticism in *St Mawr* is articulated by the apophatic discourse of the final section. Pan is the best word for the object of the religion of the novella, but it is inadequate, like all its substitutes, because behind Pan, behind living men and women in the living universe, is the X, about which no one can know and for which no one can therefore claim the authority to speak.

3

'The dark God': From *Kangaroo* to *The Plumed Serpent*

trp ḋṿ...ᴨhᴨᴊ Jᴛᴜᴜ ℓiᴛ

Kangaroo

In *Kangaroo*, written in June and July 1922, and revised in October, Lawrence begins to work out, in the form of the novel, how his religious ideas might be put into practice at the level of an entire society. The action of the novel is almost entirely discursive, consisting primarily of the development of Somers' ideas on the kind of beliefs on which post-war Australian society should be based. Birkin's religion of the incomprehensible has developed into a religion of the dark God, and Somers works out the beliefs and practice of this religion in order to articulate a third and better way of life for contemporary Australia than the right wing politics of Kangaroo or the left wing politics of Willie Struthers.

Kangaroo's authoritarian politics are not exactly those of the Fascists whom Lawrence had observed in Italy, and whom he criticizes in the 'Epilogue' to *Movements in European History*. There he describes Fascism as 'only another kind of bullying', which 'has degenerated into a mere worship of Force' (263). Cornelia Nixon argues that 'Lawrence denounced fascism itself; nevertheless his views were similar in many respects to those held by some contemporary European intellectuals sympathetic to fascism' (5), and there are certain similarities between the Diggers of *Kangaroo* and the Fascists Lawrence had seen in Italy. Philip Morgan writes that 'as their name [*fasci di combattimento*] indicated and in a deliberate attempt to stress their connections to the war experience, the *fasci* were also "combat" organisations, which would be prepared to act decisively and use violence to resolve problems' (46), adding that the movement was geared to appeal to ex-servicemen, for whom 'the egalitarian-hierarchical trench community was the model of the anticipated relationship between elites and masses' (47). The difference between Kangaroo's Diggers and the Italian Fascists lies in the philosophy of love on which Kangaroo bases his politics. Fascists did use pseudo-religious language of the Italian nation (Griffin 44, 54–5), but Kangaroo's post-Christian philosophy of love is distinct from anything found in Italian Fascism. The opposing philosophies of Kangaroo and Willie Struthers, between which Somers steers a third course to his dark God are not that of Fascism and Communism as such, therefore, but rather of right and left wing developments of the Christian philosophy of love into contemporary political movements. It is beyond these developments of Christianity that Somers seeks to go with his religion of the dark God.

Somers reflects on the rage that 'everybody, except those that have got hold of the money or the power', feels about the war, in which men had been '*compelled* into the service of a dead ideal, that of 'Love, Self-Sacrifice, and Humanity, united in love, brotherhood, and peace' (264). This ideal is, in Lawrence's view, an ultimately Christian one. Kangaroo, Somers reflects, articulates little more than a development of it: 'Kangaroo insisted on the old idea as hard as ever, though on the *Power* of Love rather than on the Submission and Sacrifice of Love' (265). It is the same with Willie Struthers. His powerfully articulated socialism, Somers reflects, is ultimately no more than a logical development of Christianity: 'If the old ideal still had a logical leaf to put forth, it was this last leaf of communism – before the lily-tree of humanity rooted in love died its final death' (265).

Somers rejects this ultimately Christian love on which both Kangaroo's and Struthers' politics are based. As he tells Kangaroo simply, 'There is something else' (134). In an earlier draft of their discussion, he had spoken of 'that other principle, that other god' in which he believes, who 'does not move out of love for man alone, but according to far more unsearchable purposes in creation' (430). The reason he rejects Kangaroo's idea of love is that, deriving as it does from Christian tradition, it is an idea that emphasizes the spirit and neglects the body, 'working everything from the spirit', with 'the lower self as an instrument of the spirit' (135). The god in which Somers believes, on the other hand, is 'dark'. He believes that God exists but in a way completely unknown to human beings. The word 'God', therefore, is simply the best word that he has to refer to this unknown thing, but its meaning is completely unknown to him, as to others. This is what he means by calling God a 'glyph', or by speaking of 'the great living darkness which we represent by the glyph, God' (266). He predicates the verb to be of God: 'there *is* God'. But nothing about this God, including the way in which he is, is known or knowable. He is, but he is 'forever dark', 'the Unutterable Name, because it can never have a name' (266). All the names that men and women have given to their gods refer ultimately to this nameless God: 'The great dark God outside the gate is all these gods', Thor, Zeus, Bacchus, Venus and 'all the gods' (285). When they come in through the gate of human consciousness, Somers believes, they are 'personified', made analogous to human beings, but 'outside the gate', in itself, 'it is one dark God, the Unknown' (285).

This unknown God calls to men and women, and has always done so. It calls from the dark, unknown parts of the self. In the Victorian age, with its confidence in science, progress and Christian morality, we lived in 'a compound so brilliantly lit with electric light, that really, there *was* no outside' (285), but this was an illusion. It is from the darkness, outside the circle of human knowledge, consciousness and control, that Somers' God calls. He locates God 'on the threshold of my lower self', which he calls 'the dark self, the phallic self' (135). If God is to enter us, it will be 'from below, not from above' (135), from the dark, sensual parts of the psyche, and not from the consciously controlled ego. To these parts of the psyche, God is constantly calling. Indeed, this is the meaning of the Biblical text, 'Behold, I stand at the door and knock' (Rev 3:20), Somers reflects, that 'the Lord thy God is the invisible stranger at the gate in the night, knocking'. It is outside the gate of our consciousness, knocking, 'getting angry' with Lawrence's generation for listening so little, and indeed, as that generation secretly knows and fears, will be 'kicking the door in just now' (285).

Somers is convinced that these beliefs are scientifically true. He describes as a 'fact' a statement that, although 'purely unscientific', 'we must take on trust' if 'any of the so-called humane sciences' are to produce any valid results. This first principle is that, as Lawrence had said in *Psychoanalysis* and *Fantasia*, 'every living creature has an individual soul . . . which connects it individually with the source of all life as man . . . is connected with God' (295). From 'an ant or a louse' to a human being, every individual living being is 'in contact with the great life-urge which we call God'. The nature of this connection has developed, since the essays on the unconscious, into 'a will-to-live in the further sense, a will-to-change, a will-to-evolve, a will towards the further creation of self' (295). Lawrence means that, in a way that the discourse of natural science cannot articulate, because of their relationship to the unknown God, living beings develop, grow and become greater than they were. The theory of evolution knows something of this force, but it is not 'a cause-and-effect sequence' as in such a theory. Rather, it is 'an answer to the strange creative urge, the God-whisper', in which God calls all living beings to grow into something greater and beyond themselves (295).

All men and women can feel, at least if they pay the right kind of attention, this God-urge, but most are 'helpless to interpret' it (296). To understand 'the new prompting of the God-urge' in a new generation or a new time, it takes 'some few exquisitely sensitive and fearless souls who struggle with all their might to make that strange translation of the low, dark throbbing into open act or speech' (296). God presses at the phallic self, prompting one to respond to his call to grow greater than one is, than human beings are, at present, but this call is inarticulate. It is a 'throb-throb, throb-throb-throb', like the 'almost inaudible beating of a wireless machine'. Most people, deafened by the details of their everyday lives in the modern world, hear nothing. Some few hear it, but only interpret it in the old language, in the terms of the old religion and morality (296). President Wilson was such a man. What each age needs is some select man or woman among even the few who can hear the calling of the unknown to interpret this call into the language of his contemporaries, as Somers and as Lawrence are trying to do in *Kangaroo*. 'There is no morse-code', Lawrence writes, 'There never will be', and 'Every new code supersedes the current code' (296). Indeed, 'it needs a new term of speech, invented each time', 'a whole new concept of the universe gradually born, shedding the old concept' (297). What the person who wants to interpret the inarticulate calling of God at the threshold of the lower self needs to do in his time is to create the new language necessary in which to say the new thing to which he hears God calling him and his whole society.

On reading the manuscript of *Kangaroo*, Robert Mountsier, Lawrence's American agent, asked him to cut the 'Nightmare' chapter (*L* 4: 320). Lawrence refused to do so, telling Mountsier when he had revised the typescript, 'I am keeping in the war episode: it must be so. The book is now as I want it' (*L* 4: 323). In terms of the religious ideas articulated in the novel, Lawrence was right: the 'Nightmare' chapter is integral to the meaning of *Kangaroo*. It is the first place in which he develops the theology of the dark God, and the novel shows that this theology is a response to the experience of the war. The dark God, which Somers seeks, is dark because of the war. The war was fought, he reflects, for the 'dead ideal' of 'Love, Self-sacrifice, and Humanity united in love, brotherhood and peace', an ideal based firmly on Western Christianity (264). Men had been 'sold' into the service of this dead ideal, and they felt it. Indeed, they had been 'desecrated' (262), a word Somers uses to describe the violation of the soul, of that part of a person that is in relation to God. The war had been fought in the name of Christianity, with its spiritual ideal of love, self-sacrifice and the brotherhood of man, and in the name of precisely this ideal had violated men's relationship to God. Every Christian ideal, therefore, indeed Christianity itself and all its developments, including Kangaroo's authoritarianism and Struthers' socialism, has not only ceased to function as a way to God, but also positively hinders, indeed violates the sacred relationship of men and women to God. God cannot be found in the light of Christianity, because that so-called light led directly to the mob violence of the war. If God is to be found after the war, Somers passionately reflects, he is to be found in the dark, since the light led only to the war. This is what he means when he says:

> Now, all he wanted was to cut himself clear. To be clear . . . of love, and pity, and hate . . . To cut himself finally clear from the last encircling arm of the octopus humanity. To turn to the old dark gods, who had waited so long in the outer dark. (265)

One of the most striking things about the way in which Lawrence expresses his theology of the dark God in *Kangaroo* is the extent to which he repeats the views that he takes most seriously in the novel in a comic or parodic form. He does this in passages of extended self-parody, in the chapters 'Harriett and Lovatt at Sea in Marriage' and 'Bits', and through the critical voice of Harriett, responding to Somers' ideas. In the first of these two chapters, the narrator, speaking from a point of view very close to that of Harriett, mocks Lawrence's concept of the phoenix. This voice finds Somers ridiculous, pointing out roundly the laughable contradiction between the grandeur of his ideas and the wretchedness of his person. 'He was the most forlorn and isolated creature in the world', 'he was hardly a man at all, among men'. Indeed, the narrator, sounding very like Harriett, says, 'Among men, he was like some unbelievable creature – an emu, for example. Like an emu in the streets or a railway carriage. He might well say phoenix' (175). It is only because he has nothing but his wife in this world, this voice mocks, that he has such grand ideas about men in the first place. 'He *wanted* to be male and unique, like a freak of a phoenix'; indeed, he wants to turn Harriett into a nest that he can sit on, 'like the one and only phoenix in the desert of the world, gurgling hymns of salvation' (175). Although the symbol of the phoenix plays only a relatively minor role in this novel, it stands here as a symbol for all the religious ideas at the heart of Lawrence's concerns in it, and he counterpoints these concerns with a comic strain of parody of that which also matters most to him. 'Bits' is the same. Here Somers begins by undercutting his own religious ideas. 'He could have kicked himself for wanting to help mankind', and 'he kicked himself still harder thinking of his frantic struggles with the "soul" and the "dark god"'. All these struggles, the religious ideas at the heart of the novel, Richard calls 'Blarney – blarney – blarney'. 'He was a preacher and a blatherer and he hated himself for it' (272).

Paul Eggert argues that this 'chameleon attitude' (142), in which Lawrence is able to respond in a comic voice to a principle in which he fervently expresses belief in another voice, is characteristic of his entire work. Such passages of comedy emphasize the 'provisionality' (141) of Lawrence's art, Eggert argues, according to which Lawrence is 'not casuistical in regard to what he espoused, but changeable in his address to it – and thus changeable about the very basis of "espousal"'

(135). Indeed, 'some undercutting might even offer, serendipitously, opportunities for development or variation of the basic terms' (142). These claims are true, and Eggert's argument sheds some light on the nature of Lawrence's theology of the dark God in *Kangaroo*. First, it is an apophatic theology. Lawrence emphasizes formally, what he also asserts directly, that the God in whom Somers believes cannot be known or named, including in the very discourse in which he says that this is true. Lawrence is serious enough in his belief in God's darkness, and therefore in the apophatic discourse necessary to respond to it, clearly to emphasize that his own discourse on God's darkness is no exception to the rule that we can neither know nor say anything truly about it.

Second, Lawrence is repeatedly concerned with the meaninglessness of language throughout *Kangaroo*, and he is clear that his own language, for those things that mean most to him, suffers as much as society's in general from a constant tendency towards meaninglessness. Somers reflects that 'meaning is a dead letter', that 'nothing is so meaningless as meanings', and that, as a result, 'human beings should learn to make weird, wordless cries, like animals, and cast off the clutter of words' (333). Many of Lawrence's own words in the novel approach this state of wordlessness, such as the 'antics and ant-tricks' than which men's actions are nothing more (123), and the 'Beatitudes, beatitudes. Bee-attitudes' of Kangaroo's pseudo-Christian philosophy (283). This is how he finds speech in Australia, done 'merely for the sake of making a sound of some sort' (345). The new country of Australia, indeed, comes to function as a symbol of the meaninglessness of language in Western society in general. 'Australia – Authority – Anarchy: a multiplication of the alpha' (22): it is a place where the emptiness which the sound of language covers is too vast to disguise. This is true also of Somers' theological language. It is 'blarney', the words of a 'blatherer', like a dog 'barking, barking' and 'yap-yap-yapping' (351). His language, even at the point at which he is trying to express a solution to the meaninglessness of society after the war, suffers from and tends towards precisely the emptiness that he sees to be the problem.

This is not to say that Lawrence doubts or disbelieves the theological views that constitute the heart of the novel. At the end of the parodic chapter 'Harriett and Lovatt at Sea in Marriage', for example,

Somers still affirms, in a way that the comic tone of the chapter does not finally undercut, that he 'must open the doors of his soul and let in a dark Lord and Master for himself, the dark god he had sensed outside the door' (176). There is nothing comic or parodic about this conclusion to the comic and parodic chapter. Lawrence means it. What Lawrence doubts and disbelieves is the possibility, which is the concern of the entire novel, of putting his theological views into practice in society. Here I would add to Eggert's account of the provisionality of Lawrence's art the claim that this is the most significant source of the comic parodies in *Kangaroo*. 'Chapter follows chapter, and nothing doing', Lawrence writes, correctly, three-quarters of the way into the novel (284). *Kangaroo* has almost no plot, in the sense of a meaningful progression of actions. It is primarily a series of dialogues, with respect to how society is to be governed after the war. Michael Wilding calls it a 'thought-drama' (183). Nothing happens. Unable to commit either to Kangaroo's or to Struthers' causes, even only as a writer, Somers simply leaves the country of whose future the entire novel has been a discussion. Wilding argues that this represents a radical criticism of the spectrum of available political action (183) but, in my view, it is more like a failure to imagine an alternative to that spectrum that will work in society, as Kangaroo and Struthers believe that their programs will. These two features of the plot, that nothing happens and that Somers simply leaves at the end, indicate the same thing as the comic parodies of Somers' theological views, that Lawrence cannot see how these views are to be put into concrete social practice. He has no doubts about the theology of the dark God, but he does not know how that theology is to work in practice to do what he believes it can and should, re-build Western society after the disaster of the war. *Kangaroo* is the record of this question without an answer, the question of how to put into practice the religious beliefs that Lawrence believes can and must regenerate society.

Mexican religion

In April 1923, shortly after his arrival in Mexico City, Lawrence visited the distinguished American anthropologist Zelia Nuttall. When he returned in October 1924, he renewed their acquaintance (*L* 5: 155,

156). Frieda recalls that Lawrence read Nuttall's large comparative study, *Fundamental Principles of Old and New World Religion* (Tindall 115). Virginia Hyde has argued that Lawrence found in this book an account of Aztec history in which the Aztecs were originally governed jointly by a male and a female ruler, but that 'the equality of the sexes had eroded during the fiercely misogynistic dominance of Huitzilopochtli' ('Kate and the Goddess' 256), a history Hyde sees Lawrence working to reverse in *The Plumed Serpent*. Hyde is certainly right to see a dialogism in the novel, which may indeed derive from Lawrence's wish to write back to the history he reads in Nuttall. There are several more direct ways, I would add, in which Nuttall's work influences the religious ideas Lawrence articulates in *The Plumed Serpent*. First, and this is the first thing that would have struck him about the book, since it is its first claim, is Nuttall's argument that the outward complexities of Aztec religion are in fact all forms of worship of one, unknown God. On the very first page of the book, she writes that the apparently 'numberless' Aztec deities had, over the course of her study of their 'respective symbols, attributes and names', 'dwindled in a remarkable way', such that she had come to conclude that 'the Mexicans painted one and the same god under a different aspect "with different colours" according to the various names they gave him in each instance' (7–8). Mexican prayers, she argues, were addressed to 'a supreme Creator and ruler, whom they termed "invisible, incomprehensible and impalpable"' (8). She quotes from early Spanish sources, which describe Mexican worship of this unknown God:

> In many parts of the [American] continent, the natives had a particular knowledge of the true God; they believed that He created the Universe and was its Lord and governed it. And it was to him they addressed their sacrifices, their cult and homage. (32)

She even uses the phrase Lawrence had used in *Kangaroo*, 'the Unknown God', to describe the object of Mexican worship (33). Lawrence had already expressed in *Kangaroo* the belief that all the gods of human history represent the one unknown God (*K* 314). In Nuttall's study, he found that a belief very similar to this one underlay the complex pantheon of Mexican religion, suggesting to him that a novel portraying a modern revival of such religion would be a particularly appropriate form in which to express his belief in the one dark God worshipped as many gods.

Lawrence learnt in detail about the cult and mythology of Quetzalcoatl from Nuttall's book and this is the second way in which *The Plumed Serpent* is influenced by her work. In particular, she identifies Quetzalcoatl with the representation of the unknown God:

> 'The invisible and imageless god of the Chichimecs was named Yoalli-ehecatl . . . which means the invisible and impalpable god . . . by whose virtue all live, who directs by merely exerting his will.' In the Codex Fuenleal . . . the remarkable title of 'wheel of the winds = Yahualliehecatl,' is recorded as another name for Quetzalcoatl. (33)

The serpent is the dominant image in Mexican religion of the unknown God: 'The Mexicans and Mayas employed the serpent as an expressive symbol merely, signifying the generative force of the Creator to whom alone they rendered homage' (32). As Nuttall puts it most simply, 'The feathered serpent was an image of the divinity' (70).

In *The Plumed Serpent*, Lawrence's central image for the unknown God is that of the dark sun. Takeo Iida has given a broad account of the European cultural traditions by which Lawrence was 'strongly, even if unconsciously, influenced' (279–80) in developing this image throughout his work. Peter Balbert argues that 'it is a composite statement of Lawrencean belief, for the crux of his credo always turns on the paradoxical interrelation of dark and light' (258). In the light of these claims, the following passage from Lawrence's account of the instinctive life of the colliers he had known as a child, in 'Nottingham and the Mining Countryside', is illuminating:

> The miners worked underground as a sort of intimate community . . . They brought with them above-ground the curious dark intimacy of the mine, the naked sort of contact, and if I think of my childhood, it is always as if there were a lustrous sort of inner darkness, like the gloss of coal, in which we moved and had our real being. (*LEA* 289–90)

Lawrence speaks of his childhood sense of something both dark and bright at the heart of the earth, like coal, which is dark with a bright 'gloss'. It is also an 'inner' darkness, and it is a place where men are truly themselves and truly associate with one another – 'they knew each other practically naked, and with curious close intimacy' (289). Lawrence's Biblical language even suggests that it is a place where they meet in God, since like God in Acts 17:28, 'we moved and had our . . . being' in it. It is possible that the image of the dark sun, whether at the centre of earth as in 'The Hopi Snake Dance', or behind the sun as in *The Plumed Serpent*, owes something to the formation of Lawrence's sensibility in the coal-mining country of his youth.

Such an assertion must remain at the level of speculation, however. We can say with greater certainty that Lawrence found the image of the dark sun, the central theological image of *The Plumed Serpent*, in Zelia Nuttall's work. This is the third way in which her book influences the religious ideas he expresses in the novel. She writes that 'the Mexicans had conceived the idea of two suns, a young day sun and an ancient night or black sun' (13). The 'fundamental principles' that Nuttall sees at work in all ancient religions are a sevenfold division of the cosmos into Centre, Above, Below and the four quarters. She argues that the 'cult of the Above' was directed towards the sun and its associated stars, and that the 'cult of the Below' was directed towards the moon, the pole star and 'possibly in the same way towards the enigmatical "Black Sun" figured in [one ancient manuscript]' (54). She quotes from a study of the Zuni Indians which speaks of the Zuni belief in both a 'light and dark sun' (100). Nuttall also provides a dramatic account of Mexican religious thinking which may have suggested to Lawrence the concept of the sun behind the sun of which he makes use in *The Plumed Serpent* as an image of the imageless divinity. In a passage in which she describes the displacement of the worship of the sun by the worship of the pole star, Nuttall describes a 'native American ruler and reformer' who 'actually employed the following reasoning':

> It is not possible that the sun should be the God who created all things, for if so he would sometimes rest and light up the world from one spot. Thus it cannot be otherwise that there is someone who directs him and this truly is the true Creator. (22)

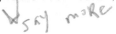

This passage is one of the sources of the concept of the sun behind the sun, which is Lawrence's central figure for the divinity in *The Plumed Serpent*. Nuttall means that the more powerful divinity behind the sun, which had initially appeared divine, is the fixed pole star, a concept of which Lawrence makes no use. From her work, however, he learnt that ancient Mexican religion posited not only a dark sun but also a divine power behind the sun, which was more profoundly associated with the unknown God than the sun itself.

Theresa Mae Thompson describes the 'apparently effortless assumption' in *The Plumed Serpent*, 'as in Pueblo spirituality, that gods interact with human beings as part of the material world, not as separate forces' (224). She mentions Hopi religion as an example of this kind of spirituality, but Lawrence encountered it more explicitly in his reading in Mexican religion. In Terry's *Guide*, Lawrence read that Quetzalcoatl was 'the most important of the Aztec divinities', but also about 'his residence on earth', about his birth from a virgin, about his physical appearance – 'he was said to have been tall in stature, with a white skin, long, dark hair and a flowing beard' – and that he was the 'high priest' of Anahuac (304). He learnt the same thing from Nuttall's book, and this is the final way in which her work influenced *The Plumed Serpent*, that the distinction between gods and men, especially in the cult of Quetzalcoatl, is not rigorously drawn in Mexican religion. Nuttall makes clear that the high priests of the Mexican gods, and particularly the high priest of Quetzalcoatl, were considered human embodiments of those gods. In *The Plumed Serpent*, Don Ramón and Cipriano become 'the living Quetzalcoatl' and 'the living Huitzilopochtli' (289). From Nuttall, Lawrence learnt that 'the high priest of the temple was [the representative of] the god Quetzalcoatl' and 'assumed the name Quetzalcoatl' (71). She writes, 'The Mexican Quetzalcoatl was regarded as the visible representative of the celestial ruler of the universe' (74). She even uses the phrase, in discussing the Aztec ruler Montezuma, that he was 'the living personification of Huitzilopochtli' (71).

A second major influence on the religious ideas of *The Plumed Serpent* is Lewis Spence's book *The Gods of Mexico*, which Brett records that Lawrence and she read shortly after Christmas 1924 (203). In *Quetzalcoatl*, the embodiment of the Mexican gods by Ramón and Cipriano is a simpler and clearer process than in *The Plumed Serpent*.

The first time that the phrase 'the living Quetzalcoatl' is used, it is in a way clearly indebted to Peter's recognition of Christ in Matthew 16:16, 'Thou art the Christ, the Son of the living God'. Cipriano says to Ramón that in him, 'I recognise something beyond me. You are the living Quetzalcoatl' (*Q* 183). Cipriano also explains the meaning of the phrase more clearly than in the second novel:

> Ramón is . . . only a man, and he knows it . . . But the deepest root of his soul goes down to God, and he rises from God, and he is the living Quetzalcoatl. (*Q* 218)

Lawrence read in Lewis Spence's book more about the embodiment of the Mexican gods by their high priests, and by the time he finishes *The Plumed Serpent*, he portrays it as a more seamless, almost more reified, process. In Spence's accounts, as in the second novel, no rigorous distinction is drawn between Quetzalcoatl as a man, usually a high priest, and Quetzalcoatl as a god. In one Spanish account, for example:

> Quetzalcoatl was high-priest of Tollan, whence he migrated to Cholula . . . He then passed on to Cholula, where he was adored as a god. When he had resided there for twenty years, he was expelled by [the god] Tezcatlipocâ. (Spence 125–6)

Indeed, Spence cites the statement of Bernardino de Sahagún, that Quetzalcoatl was 'a man who became a god' (140). He adds that the high priest of Quetzalcoatl, just as Ramón would attempt to become in *The Plumed Serpent*, was 'the most venerated ecclesiastic in Mexico' (137).

Lawrence found in Spence the association of Quetzalcoatl with the morning star, of which he makes considerable use in *The Plumed Serpent*. He had learnt from Nuttall that the name Quetzalcoatl meant both 'plumed serpent' and 'divine twin', and she emphasizes the duality of the god, calling him 'the dual . . . Force', 'The Divine Twin' (42) and expounding invocations to him as 'our celestial father and mother, great lord and great lady, whose title is Ome-Tecuhtli (literally, two-lord = twin lord) and Ome-Cihuatl (literally, two-lady = twin lady)' (32). In *Quetzalcoatl*, Lawrence makes full use of the duality of the symbol of the plumed serpent, the serpent symbolizing the earth and the eagle the heavens – 'the serpent sleeps in my bowels, the knower of the under-earth. And the eagle sleeps in my heart, the strength of the skies' (153; cf. 98–100, 112, 237). However, it is only in *The Plumed Serpent* that he makes use of the symbol of the morning star to explore the many complex dualities for which Quetzalcoatl stands, and it was from Spence that he learnt the details of the ways in which this planet was identified in Mexican religion with the god. Spence reproduces a wall painting that represents Quetzalcoatl 'in his variant of the planet Venus' (122), and he quotes a colonial account of the god in this variant:

They name him One Cane, which is the star Venus . . . Tlavizcalpantecutli is the star Venus, the first created light . . . This star (Venus) is Quecalcoatle . . . Tlavizcalpantecutli is God of the Morning when it begins to dawn: he is also the Lord of Twilight on the approach of the night. (129)

He cites another colonial account, which says, 'They adored [Quetzalcoatle] as a god . . . for they believed it certain that he had ascended into heaven and was that star which was visible at the north of the sun at the break of day, which is the planet Venus' (131). Indeed, Lawrence also found some of the language he would use to express the significance of Quetzalcoatl as the morning star in *The Plumed Serpent* in Spence's appendix on the Aztec *tonalmatl*, or book of days. In this book, each day and night has a series of gods assigned to it, which Spence describes as 'Lords of the Night' and 'Lords of the Day-Hours' (364–5), just as Don Ramón describes himself as 'lord of the day and night . . . lord of the two ways' (*PS* 159).

As several critics have pointed out, the many hymns and songs of the Quetzalcoatl religion that Lawrence puts into *The Plumed Serpent* are influenced by the songs Spence transcribes from colonial sources in *The Gods of Mexico*. There are some songs and hymns in *Quetzalcoatl*, but the character of Spence's hymns has influenced Lawrence's development and multiplication of these songs and hymns in the revised novel. In *Quetzalcoatl*, the songs are much more like liturgies than the kind of lyrics Lawrence would find in Spence. The song described as 'the coming of Quetzalcoatl', for example, is sung responsively, in two parts, Jesús taking the part of Quetzalcoatl and Francisco and Rafael the parts of Jesus and Mary, a device Lawrence abandons in *The Plumed*

Serpent. The parts are in long, prose lines (*Q* 147–8), resembling a liturgy much more than the lyric poems with formal titles that predominate in the revised novel. The 'Fourth Hymn' of *Quetzalcoatl* is written largely in prose in the first novel (170–2), but becomes a poem entitled 'What Quetzalcoatl Saw in Mexico' in the second (256–60). In the same way, the long lines of the song in which Jesus bids farewell to Mexico in the first novel (178–9) become the more formally versified lyric with the title 'Jesus' Farewell' in the second (279–80).

Lawrence was already moving in the direction of formalized hymnody in *Quetzalcoatl.* The last songs of Quetzalcoatl (227–8) and of Huitzilopochtli (248, 252–3) are the kind of lyric poems that he would develop in full in the re-writing of the novel. Nevertheless, he was clearly influenced in the final move in this direction when he wrote *The Plumed Serpent* by the hymns he had read in Spence. Many of these have titles, such as 'The Song of Uitzilopochtli', 'Song of the Shield', 'Song of the God of Music and Games' (Spence 80, 81, 200), a device Lawrence uses in *The Plumed Serpent,* with 'Jesus' Farewell', 'Welcome to Quetzalcoatl', Huitzilopochtli's Watch', *et cetera.* (*PS* 279, 349, 383). Indeed, the novel contains a '*First Song of Huitzilopochtli*' (373), clearly indebted to Spence's 'Song of Uitzilopochtli'. Sandra Gilbert has analysed the relationship of Spence's hymns to Lawrence's (*Acts* 233–40), and I will add one or two points here with respect to their contribution to the kind of religion Lawrence portrays in his novel. First, Spence's hymns frequently list a series of qualities of the god, proclaiming who the god is and what he or she has done in the mythological past, and Lawrence's hymns also often use this kerygmatic device. So, in Spence, he read:

O, she has become a goddess of the melon cactus
Our mother Itzpapalotl, the obsidian butterfly.
Her food is on the Nine Plains,
She was nurtured on the hearts of deer. (30)

This kind of list of qualities of the god, following from the first mention of his or her name, appears also in Lawrence's hymns:

I am the inward star invisible
And the star is the lamp in the hand of the Unknown Mover (308)

The Lord of the Morning Star
Stood between the day and the night . . .
With the bright wing on the right
And the wing of the dark on the left (158)

Second, Lawrence picks up the archaisms of Spence's hymns. Archaic forms like 'For, our mother, thou leavest us. /Thou returnest to Tlalocan' (171) can be seen in Lawrence's 'Ye that perceive me' (158), 'Lo! / I am coming' (104) or 'Yea, I am always here' (158). He found numerous archaic inversions in Spence's hymns – 'Thirteen eagles is our mother' (180), 'Ripe has the *octli* become' (200) – and uses the device with equal frequency himself – 'In the stillness where waters are born / Slept I, Quetzalcoatl' (103); 'The multitudes see me not' (158). Third, Spence's hymns often use imperatives addressed to an implied fellow worshipper, such as:

Our enemies, the people from Amantlan, assemble; meet me there.
So will in their own house the enemy be. Meet me there. (80)

Lawrence's frequently use the same device:

Put sleep as black as beauty in the secret of my belly.
Put star-oil over me.
Call me a man. (314)

Lawrence read in Spence that the Toltec myths of Quetzalcoatl were 'the earliest religious influences in Mexico' (10), and that the hymns 'probably date from a more archaic period than the myths' (11). I would suggest that he modelled his own hymns in *The Plumed Serpent* on those that Spence had transcribed in *The Gods of Mexico* because the latter suggested an authentic form of expression of what Lawrence believes to be 'the religion of all aboriginal America' (*MM* 88), to which he wished to portray a meaningful modern return in his novel.

Gilbert points out that the 'motif of the periodic migration of the gods', dominant in the mythology of *The Plumed Serpent*, can be found in one of Spence's hymns (*Acts* 236), but more striking sources for the theology and rites of the departure of Jesus and the return of Quetzalcoatl in the novel are the historical accounts of the Spanish Conquest Lawrence read before writing *Quetzalcoatl*. Most influential among these is Bernal Díaz del Castillo's *True History of the Conquest of New Spain*. It is primarily from Bernal Díaz that Lawrence learns the motif of the physical replacement of the images of an established religion in Mexico with those of a new, better and true one. Over and over again, in Díaz's *True History*, native idols are dramatically destroyed, to be replaced by an altar, a cross and an image of the Virgin Mary. At Cempoala, for example, the first town the conquistadors reach after their landing at Vera Cruz, the chiefs offer Cortés and his men their daughters in a gesture of friendship. Before he will consent to this friendship, however, Cortés insists that the town's idols must come down, and that the women become Christians. The chiefs and priests refuse to give up their gods, but Cortés argues, 'How can we ever accomplish anything worth doing if for the honour of God we do not first abolish these sacrifices made to idols?' (80). This eventually occurs:

> More than fifty of us soldiers had clambered up [to the temple] and had thrown down their idols which came rolling down the steps shattered to pieces . . . When they saw their idols broken to pieces the caciques and priests who were with them wept and covered their eyes . . . Cortés ordered all the idols which we had overthrown and broken to pieces to be taken out of sight and burned. Then eight priests who had charge of the idols came out of a chamber and carried them back to the house whence they had come, and burned them. (81)

As in each of Díaz's accounts of this kind of event, Cortés sets up an altar and an image of the Virgin Mary in the place of the native idols (82). One of Díaz's polemical concerns in his narrative is to rebut the attack, 'in the name of Christian evangelization and justice', by Fray Bartolomé de las Casas, in his *Brief Account of the Destruction of the Indies*, on the brutality and injustice of colonial practices (Adorno, 'Bernal Díaz' 392). A dominant theme, as a result, of his *True History*, is the replacement, for the good of the native peoples, of their 'cursed' idolatry with 'our holy religion' (78, 65). Both the dramatic events and the ritual details of the physical replacement of the images of native Mexican religion with those of Spanish Catholicism in his narrative influence Lawrence's portrayal of the reversal of this process in his Mexican novel. In a passage particularly close to the hymnody of *The Plumed Serpent*, Díaz describes the Aztec gods telling their priests that they want to leave Mexico:

> As soon as we had placed the image of Our Lady and the Cross on the Altar which we had made on the Great Cue [temple pyramid] . . ., it seems it seems that Huichilobos and Tezcatepuca spoke to the priests, and told them that they wished to leave their country as they were so badly treated by the Teules [the Spaniards], and they did not wish to stay where those figures and the Cross had been placed. (205–6)

It is from a passage like this that Lawrence derives the image, of which he makes much use in the hymns of the novel, of both Quetzalcoatl and Jesus leaving Mexico, as if physically, once their worship ceases to be the way to God there, and of Quetzalcoatl returning in the same way once he becomes again the way to the unknown God (124–5, 225–8, 279–80, 281).

Quetzalcoatl

The religious ideas portrayed in *Quetzalcoatl*, written in Chapala in May and June 1923, are a development of those of *Kangaroo* in the light of Lawrence's experiences and reading in Native American and Mexican religion. In the first version of the novel, Don Ramón's Indian ethnicity is emphasized. He tells Kate that 'the white man doesn't belong to this continent' (*Q* 91), with their 'white blood and white minds' (92), and although Kate can ask him, 'Don't you think of yourself as a white man?', he replies emphatically, 'No, my skin allows me no place among the elect . . . My heart is no whiter than my hair' (92). In accordance with his more Indian blood in this version of the novel, Ramón's theology is more racially inflected, particularly in the first three-quarters of the novel, than in the final version. He believes in one unknown God, 'the inscrutable God', who makes man in such a way that he 'makes these mysterious differences between the great races of mankind', so that, as Ramón says directly, 'each race needs its own religion' (113). Whereas in *The Plumed Serpent*, Christianity had once led men and women to God in Mexico, but can function in this way no longer, in *Quetzalcoatl* it has never done so, because it is a European religion, which cannot as such lead the Indian race to the unknown God. 'Jesus with all his beautiful and liberating words could not quicken the Indian blood to the last bright flame' (113). The native peoples of Mexico are therefore 'men as yet unmade' in Ramón's first theology (112). Christ has completed the manhood of European men by having 'cleaved a way' to God for them, just as Mohammed has done for Arab men (112). But 'no man had broken the invisible walls that shut the Indians of America from their own' (112). Ramón, therefore, looks for a native Mexican to lead the Indian race in the Indian way necessary to God. 'A race must produce its own heroes, its own God-men. Men, some men, some man, must take the heroic step into his own Godhead, in the sight of all his people: or there *is* no godhead for this people' (114). He himself and Don Cipriano will be these Indian god-men.

Kangaroo had wanted to establish the state of Australia as a 'kind of Church', with himself as 'a patriarch, or a pope' (*K* 112). The concept of the Catholic Church has its most detailed development in Lawrence's work in *Quetzalcoatl*, as Ramón and Cipriano 'talk theology' with the bishop of Guadalajara (167). Ramón agrees with the bishop, who is also a Mexican Indian in the first version of the novel (166, 169), that 'the Church is universal' (167). He believes in 'the One Great God with an Unutterable Name', but not in one Mediator. 'The Mediator is not one and exclusive. He is many' (167). 'There must be mediation', he says – he is 'not a protestant' who believes that 'men can come in one leap to Almighty God' – and that mediation is the work of the Sons and Daughters of God of each race who are its great religious leaders, of whom Jesus was one (168). These beliefs all remain in *The Plumed Serpent*, but in *Quetzalcoatl* the institutional structure of Ramón's revisionary Catholic Church is specified in some detail. He intends to make all the land around Lake Sayula belong to 'the commune', which will be run on a system 'something like the old Indian village system', with a 'war chief, a cacique, and a peace chief', although Ramón's system will also include the innovations of 'a chieftainess and a woman cacique who will suffer with the women' (208). The men will farm and the women weave and spin. The peace chief of the men will 'divide the land and be chief judge and the living Quetzalcoatl' in the pueblo of Sayula, just as the peace chief of each pueblo in Mexico will be the living Quetzalcoatl there. Ramón will be 'the living Quetzalcoatl of Mexico' (208). Later in the novel, when Ramón speaks to the chief clergy of Mexico about the spreading Quetzalcoatl movement, he tells them that he is a 'Catholic of Catholics' and that he wants there to be 'one Catholic Church in the world' (235). In his vision, however, this church will be governed by 'one esoteric priesthood'. The One God will be worshipped in many religions throughout the world, each with its own gods and its own 'honest, passionate priests' (235). But these priests will be initiated by 'degrees into the central mystery of the One Everlasting God, and united in concentric circles in the one Church of the Earth' (235). Ramón even allows that the centre of this esoteric Catholic Church should continue be 'Old Rome'.

While Lawrence was writing Quetzalcoatl, he received Frederick Carter's manuscript of The Dragon of the Alchemists (L 4: 456, 459). In the penultimate chapter of Quetzalcoatl, as a result, Ramón begins to speak in theosophical terms, a language Lawrence did not entirely abandon until his revision of the typescript of The Plumed Serpent (PS 547–8). Once again in the context of the relationship of the Quetzalcoatl religion to the Catholic Church in Mexico, Ramón reflects that his religion is that of 'the redeemed Adam' (281). He explains to Kate that in the 'Old Mysteries', the body of Adam was buried at the foot of the cross, from which the blood of Christ fell upon him, so that he 'rose again, as before the Fall'. So, in Rosicrucian language, 'the cross is again enclosed in the circle of Unity' (281), 'the rose is exalted around the cross' (282), which means that the soul is no longer fallen, as in Christianity, with its 'naked cross', but 'whole again over and above her divisions'. Ramón stresses that this theosophical language should not be taken too literally. He tells Kate that it is 'only the language of the old symbols', 'only the semi-barbaric method of thinking in images' (282). This was 'once supposed to be the finest and purest form of thinking', and in Quetzalcoatl Ramón still consciously values it, since 'the mysteries become so real' in it (282).

Ramón concludes his explanation of his religion of the risen Adam with a revisionary creation myth. He tells Kate that the human soul climbs down through the 'seven heavens' into matter, seeking it as a bride seeks her bridegroom, 'accomplishing herself in the flesh' (283). She climbs down through the spheres of the stars, of the sun and of the moon, each time becoming more fleshly, until on earth she becomes fully incarnate. In this state, Ramón says, 'the souls of man and woman danced on earth, in the perfect rapture of their consummation, the glory of their incarnation' (284). Into this paradise comes the serpent, who had also climbed down from the state of pure spirit in which he was created into incarnation, but he 'failed in one of the stages', which meant that he failed to forget, as the soul did, his more spiritual state in each of the previous spheres. He was not content to be incarnate, therefore, but 'desired again the state of pure spirit' (285). In his envy of Adam and Eve, he tempts them to eat from the 'Tree of Memory', and so instils his 'poison of discontent' with the incarnate state in them (286). Thus begins what Ramón calls 'the Æon of the Little Creation of the Logos' (283), the age of Western culture, with its Platonic and Christian privileging of the spirit over against the body. This Æon is now over, Ramón proclaims, and the followers of the living Quetzalcoatl 'stand at the gates of the sun', watching those who reject the marriage of soul and body flying back to become pure spirit. They themselves step forward through the sun to earth as 'lords of the earth', 'the Dark Pearl of the new flesh', and 'the axle of the turning of the Æon' (288). This is of course a revisionary use of theosophical ideas and images. In theosophy, as we have seen, the soul progresses through seven stages of increasingly pure spirituality, a journey which Pryse calls the 'process of transcendental self-conquest, the giving birth to oneself as a spiritual being' (9). Lawrence retains the concept of progression, but in Ramón's creation myth, the direction of this progression is downwards, towards an increasingly holistic state of union between the soul and the body, which he calls 'incarnation' and 'marriage'. Lawrence had responded in this way to Carter:

> For my part, I should like to see the end of this Return [to the upper centres of the psyche]. The end of the Little Creation of the Logos. A fresh start, in the first great direction, with the polarity downwards, as it was in the great pre-Greek Æons, all Egypt and Chaldea . . . The great *down* direction, away from mind, to power. (*L* 4: 461)

It is precisely this fresh start, this account of the perfection of the soul in its union with the body, that Ramón seeks to make in the revisionary theosophical language of *Quetzalcoatl*.

The *Adelphi* articles

Lawrence expresses many of Don Ramón's views directly as his own in the series of essays he writes for John Middleton Murry's *Adelphi* magazine between September 1923 and early 1924. In the fragment, 'There is no real battle . . .', written in the notebook from which he tore the completed essays, Lawrence sounds very like Don Ramón speaking with the bishop. He writes that 'there is no real battle between me and Christianity', because 'at the depth, my nature is catholic' (*RDP* 385). By this he means, as Ramón does, that there is one 'all-overshadowing' God, that Jesus is one of the Sons of God, but not the only one. Everyone who believes in God 'naturally' forms a Church, in which, and in the 'authority' of which, Lawrence believes. Although he cannot align himself with nonconformity, 'on the religious fundamentals, there is no breach between me and the Catholic Church'. He cannot believe in the Church of Christ – indeed, 'one hates Christianity', because it claims that it is the only way to God. The true Church in which Lawrence believes, by contrast, knows that there are 'a few great roads to God, and many, many small tracks' (385).

In 'On Being Religious', Lawrence affirms his central belief in God, who is unknowable. Reflecting on the word 'God', he argues that it 'isn't really quite a word' at all, but rather 'an ejaculation and a glyph', 'just a noise and a shape, like pop! or Ra or Om' (*RDP* 187). The word 'God' is just a sound, that is – it has no definition, nor known meaning, although Lawrence does feel that it means 'something we can none of us ever quite get away from' (187). In this essay, he uses astrological imagery, of the kind he found in Carter, to express his belief that there are many ways to the one God, that Christianity has been one such way, and that it is no longer. He speaks of 'an everlasting . . . pair of truths', that 'there is always the Great God' and that 'as regards man, He shifts his position in the Cosmos' (189). Just as the stars move through the heavens, just as even the apparently fixed pole star moves, so God 'slowly and silently and invisibly shifts His throne, inch by inch, across the Cosmos' (190). Jesus was once the way to God, but the foot of his Cross too, has shifted over the horizon of the heavens, and he is the way no longer. As Lawrence says in 'Books', 'I know the greatness of Christianity: it is a past greatness' (*RDP* 200). He adds in 'On Being Religious' that even the way of Christianity has been shifting in itself, with the changes of the Reformation and of the Enlightenment, which he describes as 'curves' in the Christian way to God. As he stresses over and over again in the *Adelphi* essays, modern men and women are now without any of the old ways to God, and they must find a new way. What that way will be, Lawrence does not know in these essays. 'For the moment we are lost . . . None of us knows the way to God'. What he knows, in 'On Being Religious', is that 'the Holy Ghost' remains, 'forever Ghostly' and 'unrealisable'. It is the Holy Ghost within us, he argues, that, like Francis Thompson's Hound of Heaven, can 'scent the new tracks of the Great God across the Cosmos of Creation' (191). Lawrence's Holy Ghost is of course not the third person of the Christian Trinity. He is, as Lawrence puts it apophatically, 'nothing, if you like' (192). He is not, not a being nor of any substance. He is simply 'the strange calling' which, Lawrence says, it is 'God's own good fun' to follow in the modern world (192, 193). In each one of the works discussed in this book, Lawrence himself is doing precisely this, expressing his sense, which he believes comes to him from the unknown God, of the new way to that God by which alone modern men and women will be able to live genuinely human lives.

In 'Books', Lawrence changes his theological image of the Holy Ghost to the psychological claim that 'man is a thought-adventurer', a position he had worked towards in the first of the *Adelphi* essays, 'The Proper Study', that human life is 'an endless venture into consciousness' (*RDP* 197, 169). Lawrence finds that only another Biblical image will express his meaning here, adding that we are led in that venture, when it is authentic, by 'the pillar of cloud by day, the pillar of fire by night' (197). In 'Books', he argues that the great value of Christianity in human history was that, during the Dark Ages, after the fall of Rome, man's adventure into consciousness was kept alive by Christianity, in particular in the monasteries. 'The monks and bishops of the early Church carried the soul and spirit of man unbroken, unabated, undiminished over the howling flood of the Dark Ages', like Noah in the Ark (200). It was these early Christians who kept the human spirit alive through the Dark Ages, Lawrence claims, and he writes, 'If I had lived in the year four hundred, pray God I should have been a true and passionate Christian' (200). In 'On Human Destiny', he calls them 'a scattered, tiny minority of men, who had found a new way to God', and their religious lives 'tiny but perfect flames of purest God-knowledge' (*RDP* 207). In 1924, however, 'the Christian venture is done', and 'we must start on a new venture towards God' (200). It is this, Lawrence argues, in which human destiny consists, following the calling of the Holy Ghost in the new adventure towards consciousness, 'which is, essentially, the light of human God-knowledge' (207), towards God today.

In 'The Proper Study', Lawrence argues that Jesus was such a thought-adventurer. That is why his symbol became the fish, he jokes, because Jesus was one of those Sons of God who dared to fall into the great Ocean of non-knowledge by which human consciousness is surrounded. 'He had the other consciousness of the Ocean which is the divine End of us all' (*RDP* 171). In 'The Proper Study', Lawrence concludes his religious reflections with an aesthetic point, of the kind he had developed earlier in 'The Future of the Novel'. The literature of the future, he argues in 'The Proper Study', will come from man's thought-adventure towards God. 'Any new book must needs be a new stride', in which the novelist steps out of what he knows about himself and about other men and women into the Ocean of the unknown, 'where the first and greatest relation of every man and every woman is the Ocean itself, the great God of the End' (173). In 'The Future of the Novel' Lawrence had described the Gospels as novels of this kind (*STH* 154), and in 'The Proper Study' he adds that the same can be said of St Paul's letters (173). This is precisely the goal of Lawrence's own work, from *Kangaroo* to *The Plumed Serpent* and beyond, to articulate, whether in the form of the novel or otherwise, the new way towards God, which he sees to be the most pressing need of modern men and women.   _hmm_ ..

The Plumed Serpent: The morning star

Lawrence had repeatedly described *Quetzalcoatl* as the 'first rough draft' of a novel (*L* 4: 454, 457). In November 1924, he began the final version by revising the typescript of *Quetzalcoatl*, but at a certain point, as L. D. Clark points out, decided that it was inadequate for his new purposes and began a new draft altogether (*PS* xxxi–ii). Clark speaks of Lawrence's 'realization that he must transform the work by delving much deeper into the Mexican national and mythical consciousness' (quoted in *QM* 328–9). It is true that, in the religious beliefs and practices it portrays, *The Plumed Serpent* is a substantially different novel than the first draft. It is primarily with the concept of the morning star that Ramón's beliefs have developed. The religion of *Quetzalcoatl* is fundamentally one of the blood. In his expositions of the symbol of the plumed serpent, Ramón frequently privileges the serpent of the body, the bowels or the blood over against the eagle of the spirit. He tells Kate, 'I will bring back the Mexican gods, and deliver the snake from the claws of the eagle' (*Q* 98). He even contrasts Doña Carlota's empty Catholicism with his own authentic religion in these terms: 'You . . . are the Mexican eagle of the sky, and I am the Mexican serpent of the lower earth' (*Q* 108). The religion of *The Plumed Serpent*, by contrast, is fundamentally one of the morning star, of that third place that emerges between the spirit and the blood, the eagle and the serpent, a man and a woman, a man and a man, or a person and God. Kate first experiences the morning star in the dance in the plaza. In the dance, her individual femininity becomes her 'greater' femininity, as her partner's individual masculinity becomes his 'greater' masculinity. The relationship Kate experiences between her deeper self and her partner's Lawrence calls the morning star, 'the spark of contact lingering like a morning star between her and the man, her woman's greater self and the greater self of man' (131). The man of Quetzalcoatl she had encountered in the lake had told her that the men of Quetzalcoatl 'wait till the Morning Star rises' (91), and she had meditated on the symbol, 'the watcher between the night and the day, the gleaming clue to the two opposites' (94). In the dance in the plaza, she begins to experience it for herself.

In the sermon that precedes the dance in the plaza, the man of Quetzalcoatl identifies Quetzalcoatl with the Morning Star. He tells the story which dominates the hymnody of the novel, that Quetzalcoatl left Mexico at the time of the Conquest to return to God, who sent Jesus and Mary down in his place. They have now returned to God, since they no longer constitute the way to him in Mexico, and Quetzalcoatl is returning to the country to constitute the new way to him. In this sermon, the unknown God is spoken of in a variety of apophatic images, 'the Master Sun', 'the dark one of the unuttered name', 'the greatest of the great suns . . . back of the sun', and 'the Great One, whose name has never been spoken' (124, 125). He sees the Morning Star, and asks him, 'Who art thou, bright watchman?', to which the answer is, 'It is I, the Morning Star, who in Mexico was Quetzalcoatl' (125). The Morning Star here is a kind of intermediate deity between the unknown God – like the latter, he '[looks] at the yellow sun from behind' (125) – and Quetzalcoatl, one of the Sons of God or Saviours who constitute a way to him. Indeed, the phrase, 'the Morning Star, who in Mexico was Quetzalcoatl' suggests something that neither Ramón nor Lawrence say directly elsewhere, that the Sons of God and Saviours are all manifestations of the one Morning Star, itself a creation of the unknown God.

In a passage in which Ramón reflects with disgust on love, particularly on the kind that his Catholic wife has for him, he develops his fundamental exposition of the morning star. Two souls cannot meet in what the world calls love, but, in order for the soul to love, 'the quick of a man must turn to God alone' (252). Here is where one finds one's true self, before God and before all other true selves. As Ramón reflects, 'That which we get from the beyond, we get it alone. The final me I am, comes from the farthest off, from the Morning Star' (252). The Morning Star is Ramón's name for the true self one finds when one gives up one's everyday, worldly self: he calls it 'the quick of himself, . . . the Quick of all being and existence' (253). It is the place where one meets God. He reflects, 'There is only one thing that a man really wants to do, all his life; and that is, to find his way to his God, his Morning Star, and be alone there' (253). Finally it is the place, where, meeting God as one's true self, one can also truly meet another self: 'Then afterwards, in the Morning Star, salute his fellow man, and enjoy the woman who has come the long way with him' (253).

The Plumed Serpent: Religion in society

In both *Quetzalcoatl* and *The Plumed Serpent*, Lawrence envisages and portrays the spread and practices of the religious beliefs he expresses in the novels at work throughout an entire society. In *Quetzalcoatl*, Lawrence portrays the Quetzalcoatl religion spreading throughout Mexico, and the responses of the government and the President to it. 'The government in Mexico City' is anti-Catholic, so 'not at all hostile . . . to this rise of a new, national religious impulse, seeing it as a wonderful instrument against the Catholic Church' (166). We even hear the President's views on its political valences (166). Ramón and Cipriano both negotiate in great detail with numerous political bodies and institutions within the republic. We hear Ramón's attempts to persuade the Catholic clergy and the liberal intellectuals, and Cipriano's to persuade the Knights of Columbus, the unions and the army of the value to them, in their own terms, of the Quetzalcoatl religion (234–9). Lawrence is serious in imagining and portraying the spread of this religion throughout modern Mexico. He means to portray it as a religion by which men and women in 1923 genuinely can and should live in the modern world.

Louis L. Martz argues that, in *The Plumed Serpent*, Lawrence writes in a more mythical mode, exemplified by the fictional place names of the novel, than in the first draft of the novel, in which the growth of the Quetzalcoatl religion from the spirit of place of Lake Chapala was emphasized. He calls Sayula a 'mythic realm' (*QM* 331). Lawrence remains fully concerned in *The Plumed Serpent*, however, with portraying the spread and the practice of his religious beliefs throughout Mexican society. Cipriano discusses Ramón and the spread of the Quetzalcoatl religion with the President of Mexico, who wants to begin a political relationship with Ramón, 'perhaps that you could give him your moral support', as Cipriano says, 'perhaps that you might be Secretary, and President when Montes' term is up' (190). Although Ramón rejects political office and influence, he constantly envisages his religion as an alternative to the concrete historical politics of recent Mexican leaders – 'I know you want me to be another Porfírio Diaz, or something like that. But for me that would be failure' (191); 'Men like Benito Juarez, with their Reform and their Liberty . . . they are the Anti-Christ' (209). In the latter part of the novel, to an even greater extent than in *Quetzalcoatl*, Lawrence portrays the spread of the Quetzalcoatl religion throughout contemporary Mexican society, and the responses of the political institutions in that society. The president of the Republic's reform policies begins a rebellion, in which conditions the Catholic Church and the Knights of Cortés are 'preparing against' Ramón. The priests 'began to denounce him from the pulpits', but with Cipriano 'and with Cipriano the army of the west' beside him, he is safe. The President's response to the religion continues to be important (247). Cipriano is for getting the President to declare, 'The Religion of Quetzalcoatl is the religion of Mexico', and then 'backing up the declaration with the army' (359), and although Ramón is against this, it happens towards the end of the novel, where we hear that 'the Quetzalcoatl movement had spread in the country . . . . The Archbishop had declared against it, Ramón and Cipriano and their adherents were excommunicated' and 'an attempt had been made to assassinate Montes' (419). In Mexico City, the Church of San Juan Bautisto is taken over by the Quetzalcoatl religion and becomes the 'Metropolitan House of Quetzalcoatl', which precipitates what 'looked like the beginning of a religious war', a 'wild moment' in which General Narciso Beltran 'declared against Montes and for the Church', but Cipriano and his 'Huitzilopochtli soldiers' defeat the General's army and shoot him (420). 'Then Montes declared the old Church illegal in Mexico, and caused a law to be passed, making the religion of Quetzalcoatl the national religion of the Republic' (420).

Ramón is always against political force in the spread of his religion. He tells Cipriano, 'Politics and all this *social* religion that Montes has got is like washing the outside of the egg, to make it look clean. But I myself, I want to get inside the egg . . . to start it growing into a new bird' (191). Despite this, Lawrence himself remains fully committed to imagining and portraying the spread of Ramón's religious beliefs throughout Mexican society, in a real, material, even institutional way. His constant refusal, in the character of Ramón, to accept the value of political force, suggests a doubt, a lack of confidence in his own vision, splitting the political vision of the novel. The lack of clear division between Cipriano as a political operator and Ramón as a detached religious leader operates in the same way. Barbara Mensch writes that Cipriano is 'a foil to Don Ramón, assures a Lawrencian balance of opposites in the novel' (223), but this opposition is not at all rigorously maintained. Rather, in both versions of the novel, it is posited on the one hand and undercut on the other. In *The Plumed Serpent*, Ramón rejects political solutions, as we have seen, in favour of his religious teachings, but he also willingly allows these teachings to spread through political force and institutions. He is determined to 'keep free from the taint of politics', Lawrence writes, but when political bodies like the Church and the Knights of Cortés begin to organize against him, he knows that 'with Cipriano beside him . . . and with Cipriano the army of the west, he had not much to fear' (247). It is ultimately for a political reason, negotiation with the Church, that Ramón goes to see the Bishop of Guadalajara. He tells Cipriano, 'I will see [Bishop] Jimenez . . . Yes, I intend to use every means in my power'. He even adds, '[President] Montes will stand for us, because he hates the Church and hates any hint of dictation from outside. He sees the possibility of a "national" church' (247). Although he adds, 'Though myself, I don't care about national churches', his involvement in the political aspect of the spread of the Quetzalcoatl has already begun in these considerations and decisions. In a similar way, Cipriano is presented primarily as the political arm of the Quetzalcoatl religion – 'Why should you not be Secretary . . .? And follow to the Presidency?' (191); 'Cipriano was . . . for getting Montes to declare: The Religion of Quetzalcoatl is the religion of Mexico . . . Then backing up the declaration with the army' (359) – but he also bleeds into precisely the kind of religious leader that Don Ramón is, in contrast to these views. It could be Don Ramón speaking and acting as Cipriano teaches his soldiers to 'dance naked, with the breech-cloth, to rub themselves with red earth-powder, over the oil', and tells them, 'If you know how to tread the dance, you can tread deeper and deeper, till you touch the middle of the earth with your foot . . . Get the second strength. Get it, get it out of the earth, get it from behind the sun' (366). *The Plumed Serpent* represents Lawrence's most ambitious attempt to envision the spread of his religious beliefs throughout a contemporary society, in the material, historical context of that society. The fact that his religious leader in the novel refuses to accept the value of what the author nevertheless remains committed to portraying is indicative of a split in Lawrence's religious thinking at this point in his work. He both wants to but cannot fully believe in his vision of an entire society practicing the religion that he believes will save it.

If Lawrence fails to convince himself aesthetically of the spread of Don Ramón's religious beliefs throughout the political institutions of a contemporary society in *The Plumed Serpent*, he is far more successful in portraying the practice of these beliefs at a local level. First at Don Ramón's hacienda and second in the town of Sayula, the greatest success of Lawrence's religious thought in *The Plumed Serpent* is his portrayal of the transformation of daily, communal life into religious life, in such a way that the division between secular and sacred no longer remains, as in the cultures of the Pueblo Indians he had witnessed earlier in the year.

Ramón's hacienda is a community whose life is becoming entirely religious. The men who live and work on the hacienda are engaged in making the symbols, vestments and other paraphernalia of the Quetzalcoatl religion. In the smithy, a man and a boy are smelting one of the symbols of Quetzalcoatl in iron, and Ramón carefully directs the production of the symbol, a bird in inside the sun, 'for a symbol to the people' (171). His servants also make his ceremonial clothes, the sarapes, the sashes and the sandals, on the hacienda. We see an artist making a wooden head of Ramón in his newly invented posture of prayer, for which Ramón sits for a while, before he moves on to the house where 'Manuel and his wife and children, and two assistants, were spinning and weaving' (173). Lawrence describes in careful detail and at length both the means of production of the sarape and the ceremonial design of the product itself, 'the same as the iron symbol the smith was making: a snake with his tail in his mouth, the black triangles on his back being the outside of the circle: and in the middle a blue eagle standing erect with slim wings' (174). In this long episode, as we watch Ramón touring the courtyard of the hacienda, where the work is done, and supervising the various kinds of production of the ceremonial objects of his religion, we see the hacienda turn into a religious community, something like the monasteries Lawrence praises in the *Adelphi* essays, which keep the human search for God alive in the spiritual darkness of the contemporary world. On the model of these monasteries, Jamiltepec becomes a self-sufficient community, producing all it needs for its communal religious life.

The dominant impression made upon the reader of *The Plumed Serpent* is the immense detail and proliferation of the rites, sacraments, vestments and other ceremonial forms of the Quetzalcoatl religion that Lawrence describes. Many critics see this as an aesthetic failure, but it is nevertheless an impressive feat of the imagination, in which Lawrence attempts to portray the daily practice of an entire religion and furthermore the transformation of the entire life of a community, the town of Sayula, into a religious one. He describes in great detail, to name only the most extended ceremonies, a rain ceremony (193–200), the 'marriage by Quetzalcoatl' of Kate and

Cipriano (328–31), the worship of Quetzalcoatl in the former Sayula church (336–45), Cipriano's assumption of the living Huitzilopochtli (367–9), 'the Huitzilopochtli ceremony' in which Cipriano executes those who betrayed Don Ramón (372–86), and Kate's marriage as Malintzi to Cipriano as Huitzilopochtli (391–3). The liturgies, gestures, vestments, sacraments, hymns, sermons, art and architecture of the ceremonies are described in close, multi-sensual detail. In the worship of Quetzalcoatl in the former church, for example, Ramón enacts a sacrament in which four men put four garments of different colours on four different parts of his body – a blue crown on the brow, a red belt around the breast, a yellow belt around his middle and a white belt around his loins. These four men then touch four glass bowls, each with a different colour liquid in it – white, red, yellow and dark, respectively – to these four parts of Ramón's body, hold them to the light and pour them into a silver mixing-bowl. Ramón mixes this liquid, saying a series of liturgical prayers over it, offers it to the image of Quetzalcoatl and throws it into the altar fire before the image, which causes an explosion of successively different coloured fires. Ramón's liturgical prayers expound the significance of this elaborate sacrament as he performs it: 'Save the Unknown God pours His Spirit over my head and fire into my heart, and send his power like a fountain of oil into my belly, and His lightning like a hot spring into my loins, I am not'; 'Fourfold is man but the star is one star' (341).

In the latter part of the novel, once Ramón brings the public practice of the Quetzalcoatl religion to the church in Sayula, Lawrence portrays the transformation of the everyday life of the people of Sayula into religious life. The kind of ceremonies he describes in such detail permeate from the sacred context of the newly organized religion into the fabric of the daily life of the people of Sayula, such that the distinction between secular and sacred ceases to be rigorously clear. By the last quarter of the novel, the Indian drums, which have replaced the church bells, sound from the church at mid-day each day, 'when every man should glance at the sun, and stand silent with a little prayer', which Lawrence transcribes (356). There is also a 'Dawn-Verse', chanted each day at dawn from the church tower, in response to which all the men in the town 'stood silent, with arm uplifted' and all the women 'covered their faces and bent their heads' so that 'all was changeless still for the moment of change' (358). Lawrence transcribes the Dawn-Verse, as he does the complementary verse which is chanted from the tower at sunset each day, at the sound of which the men and women of the town perform the same ritual gestures. There is even a light drum and a shorter verse at nine and three o'clock, and a heavy drum at noon (358). The very passage of time in Sayula has become sacred, transformed into such by these rituals. It is this process, the transformation of everyday life into the sacred, which Lawrence repeatedly describes as the 'new world' that is emerging in the novel at this point. 'The world was somehow different, all different', he writes, as he begins to describe the rituals of the hours of the day (357). 'It was as if', he concludes, 'from Ramón and Cipriano, from Jamiltepec and the lake region, a new world was unfolding' (359). The world has become sacred in this section of the novel, and this is the climax of Lawrence's religious vision in *The Plumed Serpent*, that living itself has become an act of worship of the unknown God and the living cosmos.

The question of authority

Since reading Heraclitus during the war, Lawrence's religious beliefs had been closely associated with authoritarian politics, and this association comes to its climax in *The Plumed Serpent*. From his letters to Russell onwards, Lawrence has been developing the concept of natural aristocracy, of what Richard Somers calls 'the mystic recognition of difference and innate priority, the joy of obedience and the sacred responsibility of authority' (*K* 107). As First Man of Quetzalcoatl, Don Ramón envisages himself in communion with the First Men and Women of all the gods of all the peoples of the world, who will constitute a 'Natural Aristocracy of the World' (*PS* 248). It is in *The Plumed Serpent* that Lawrence derives this concept most closely from his religious beliefs. Towards the end of the novel, Kate comes to realize that Don Ramón has a 'supremacy, even a godliness' that makes him fit to lead (417). He gets this neither from the blood nor spirit, but from 'a star within him' which shines between both (417). Lawrence derives an authoritarian politics from the theology of the Morning Star. 'Some men', he writes, 'are not divine at all. They have only faculties. They are slaves, or they should be slaves' (418). Some men have their 'spark of divinity' ground out of them by their mechanized life in modern society. What is needed in this situation? 'Only the man of a great star, a great divinity, can bring the opposites together again', the spirit and the blood, in a 'new unison' and bring men back to life again (418). This is what it is to be a natural aristocrat, and this is what it is that justifies Don Ramón's role as leader, that his star is greater than that of others, and so therefore is his divine power to unite the spirit and the blood both in himself and in those who follow him.

The practice of natural aristocracy in the Quetzalcoatl religion is disturbing to readers in the post-Holocaust age. Its violence is clearest in the episode of Huitzilopochtli's Night, in which Cipriano claims the right to execute without trial the peons who attempted to kill Don Ramón. Even critics who emphasize most strongly the dialogism of the novel, or who identify feminist or anti-colonialist narratives within it, find this episode unacceptable. Virginia Hyde writes, 'Even though the plot seems to grope for some newly innocuous form of sacrifice . . . it fails to naturalize this scene into the novel's larger fabric and only raises troubling issues that are never resolved' ('Mexican Cypresses' 203). Neil Roberts calls the episode 'perhaps the most repellent in the novel' (142). Cipriano derives explicitly from the relative greatness of his star or divinity the right to execute those whose star or divinity he judges to be less than his own: 'Men that are more than men have the judgement of men that are less than men' (379).

The practice of the Quetzalcoatl religion is also patriarchal, enforcing in its liturgy and sacraments the submission of women to men. In the first public worship of Quetzalcoatl, the men are instructed to 'stand erect' in the former church, because 'to the new God no man shall kneel'. The women, however, must 'cover their faces' and 'sit upon the floor' (337). Although it is not stated directly, the liturgical symbolism implies a hierarchical relationship between the sexes, in which agency and the dignity that follows from it belong primarily to men. In the marriage by Quetzalcoatl of Kate and Cipriano, which Ramón conducts in a liturgy heavy with the theology of the morning star, Kate as the bride is required to kiss the groom's feet (329). Cipriano, on the other hand, has only to kiss Kate's brow and breast, in a posture that implies less submission before her. She kisses his feet and ascribes strength to him; he does not so abase himself physically and ascribes peace and childbearing to her. Later, when the two are also married legally, Cipriano denies Kate the 'satisfaction' of orgasm in their sexual relationship. He 'recoiled' from this desire of hers, because it was 'repulsive' to him. She comes to learn, in this sexual relationship, the 'worthlessness' of the 'white ecstasy of frictional satisfaction', and to learn from her husband a 'new, soft, heavy, hot flow, when she was like a fountain gushing noiseless and with urgent softness from the volcanic deeps', in which 'there was no such thing as conscious "satisfaction"' (422). Carol Siegel has argued that 'Lawrence's later female characters reject such interpretations of their ritualistic sexual posturing' as I am articulating here, namely that they are patriarchal, and see them rather as 'a means to escape the traditional confines of intimacy with a man and to discover their own selfhood' (17). It seems to me, however, that earlier feminist critics were correct in condemning these passages as oppressive. The higher level of relationship between the sexes than equality posited in the sexual politics of the Quetzalcoatl religion is a patriarchal fantasy, which has no reference in the real world.

We need, therefore, to address two related questions. First, does the kind of violence that we have come to condemn in the authoritarian politics Lawrence derives in *Kangaroo* and *The Plumed Serpent* from the religious beliefs expressed in those novels render those beliefs unethical? Second, do the patriarchal gender relations that are, in my view, as well as that of critics such as Judith Ruderman (*Devouring Mother* 142–53) and Margaret Storch (*Sons and Adversaries* 157–78), an integral part of these politics render these beliefs unethical from a feminist point of view? In my view, the answer to both questions is no, for two reasons. First, the theology of the dark God that Somers and Don Ramón develop does not logically necessitate the politics of natural aristocracy. It is true that Lawrence in fact derives the latter from the former, but, in principle, the theology of the dark God is independent from the politics of any religious or state institution. Second, the novel articulates a conspicuous failure to resolve its own doubts and questions about the politics of the Quetzalcoatl religion. This occurs primarily in Kate's ideological struggles over whether or not to marry Cipriano and stay in Mexico as the living Malintzi, and in Lawrence's continued process of re-writing the end of these struggles, at the very end of the novel, which itself ends in the ambiguous last line of the published text, '"You won't let me go!" she said to him' (444).

As Harriett had done with Somers' ideas in *Kangaroo* and Ursula with Birkin's in *Women in Love*, Kate voices a continual criticism of the Quetzalcoatl religion in *The Plumed Serpent*, particularly of its sexual politics. When Cipriano urges her to be the bride of Huitzilopochtli, 'giving her a name', Malintzi, she refuses, reflecting, 'They want to put it over me, with their high-flown bunk, and their Malintzi. Malintzi! I am Kate Forrester, really. I am neither Kate Leslie nor Kate Tylor. I am sick of these men putting names over me' (371). Virginia Hyde has emphasized the 'dialogism' of *The Plumed Serpent*, and nowhere is this more present, nor more unresolved, than in Kate's responses to the sexual politics of the Quetzalcoatl religion. She is fascinated by the power of the will at work in Ramón and Cipriano, but, 'as is so often the case with any spell, it did not bind her completely. She was spell-bound, but not utterly acquiescent. In one corner of her soul was revulsion and a touch of nausea' (387). Indeed, Kate broaches some feminist theology of her own, arguing that she has 'a tiny Morning Star inside her, which was herself', as opposed to the 'two potent and reciprocal currents between which the Morning Star flashed like a spark out of nowhere' of Don Ramón's teaching (388). Cipriano, she knows, does not value her for herself, for her own morning star – 'the tiny star of her very self he would never see. To him she was but the answer to his call' (388).

The greatest aesthetic failure of the novel is what seems to be the narrator's attempt to coerce Kate into accepting the hierarchical terms of the Quetzalcoatl religion, as Don Ramón and Cipriano expound it, and to accept a hierarchical marriage, in which she will submit as goddess wife to her god husband, despite her struggle against precisely such a submission. This aesthetic failure, however, is precisely the ethical strength of the novel. Lawrence as an artist simply will not let himself, although he seems also to be trying, resolve the questions of sexual politics raised by Kate in the hierarchical vision of Don Ramón's natural aristocracy. The novel tries intensely, but ultimately fails, to envision and persuasively portray the hierarchical politics Ramón and Cipriano derive from their religious beliefs. Many studies of Lawrence's writing on women argue that his fiction belies his theoretical statements on gender relations (Simpson 109; McLeod 228–30; Nixon 16–17; Siegel 9–12; Hyde, 'To "Undiscovered Land"' 174). As Hilary Simpson puts it, 'In contrast to the dogmatism of the essays . . . the novels [*Aaron's Rod*, *Kangaroo* and *The Plumed Serpent*] remain explorations, and rather tentative ones at that. Lawrence's failure to be convinced by his own new theories is honestly set down in these novels' (109). Lawrence maxim in 'Morality and the Novel' is true of his own fiction: 'If you try to nail anything down, in the novel, either it kills the novel or the novel gets up and walks away with the nail' (*STH* 172). *The Plumed Serpent* gets up and walks away with the nail. Neil Roberts speaks of the 'discursive manipulation' by which Kate is made repeatedly, in the final sections of the novel, to accept the postulates of the Quetzalcoatl religion although her earlier resistance to them is honest and persuasive (161). One reason for speaking of the relative ethical success of the novel, however, is the extent to which this coercion ultimately fails, the extent to which the novel gets up and walks away with the nail of the authoritarian politics of the Quetzalcoatl religion.

Lawrence cannot make himself believe what he tries to persuade his readers of, that the politics, authoritarian and patriarchal, he portrays following from the religion of the dark God, are just. *The Plumed Serpent* portrays the spread of a religion throughout a contemporary society, but in the form of a question that it cannot answer. Lawrence's great achievement in *The Plumed Serpent* is his detailed imagination of what it would look like if his religious beliefs were put into practice at the level of an entire society. His greater achievement, however, is to have effectively admitted, in the flaws, gaps and contradictions of that portrayal, that he ultimately cannot imagine it. In practice, the novel shows, the political forms in particular of the Quetzalcoatl religion, despite being the best that Lawrence can conceive of at the time and place of writing, simply will not suffice, simply are not what they claim to be, just.

As L. D. Clark shows, Lawrence 'rewrote nearly eighty per cent of the last chapter' of *The Plumed Serpent* (*PS* xxxix), in two major stages, revising the typescript in June and July 1925, and then revising the galley proofs based on that revision in October 1925. He did not give the chapter a title until November 1925, and seems to have done so only in response to his publisher's insistence (*L* 5: 336), just two months before the novel's final publication. Frieda recalls, 'Later on he told me he wished he had finished it differently' (Frieda Lawrence

149), and an examination of the revisions Lawrence makes to the final chapter shows that he was constantly changing and re-changing his mind, and that he was unable to bring the novel to a decisive resolution with any of the endings he wrote for it, including the final, published one. It is in particular with respect to the question of the sexual politics of the Quetzalcoatl religion that he changes and re-changes the ending, suggesting that he remains, throughout the manuscript, revised typescript and galley proof stages of writing and re-writing unable to find an ending for Kate in her struggle between personal independence and religious submission in marriage to Cipriano that constituted, even to himself, a convincing resolution of this struggle.

In the manuscript version of the text, which Lawrence completed in February 1925, Kate is going to leave Mexico to spread the theological core, expressed primarily in theosophical language, of the Quetzalcoatl religion, to her own people in Europe. Don Ramón encourages her to do so, knowing that in her freedom to leave, she will also return:

'You don't think I am wrong to go?' she said
'No no! You are like Persephone. You must go between two worlds.'
'I know the greater world is here,' she said, wavering.
'Therefore you will never abandon it.' (*PPS* 458)

The ending of the manuscript version seems to bear the evidence of Lawrence's dissatisfaction, however, in an odd change of tone at the very end of Ramón's long sermon to Kate on the theosophical truths she is to carry to Europe. In the last three short paragraphs, his tone becomes suddenly flippant, in contrast to the gravity of the message he has been conveying thus far:

Tell them anything, or tell them nothing, what does it matter! Tell them it is all a joke, and their symbols are pretty play-things, and they are all great-god Peter-Pans.
Tell them what they want to hear, that they are the cutest ever. (*PPS* 460)

Although the manuscript seems to have the least conflicted ending, with Kate about to preach the Quetzalcoatl religion in Europe, and then return to Mexico, it clearly dissatisfies Lawrence, and this ending is inadequate to the grandeur of the religious vision of the final sections of the novel.

In the revised typescript, Lawrence takes out Ramón's theosophical teaching and replaces it with a relatively ordinary conversation between Kate and Ramón, but in the middle of which Kate articulates a sustained feminist critique of his religion (*PPS* 460–2). At the galley proofs stage, however, Lawrence decided to cut this passage of feminist criticism, and replace it in turn with the passage in the published version, in which Kate is 'aware of a duality in herself, and she suffered from it' (429). In the first revision, of June 1925, Kate criticizes Don Ramón's religion in the name both of her individual independence, which she sees to be violated by the terms of that religion, and of religious ideas of her own, which seem no less impressive or persuasive than those of Don Ramón. Not only does Ramón fail to recognize that, as Kate Forrester, Kate is 'ten times as real and important as any Malintzi, or any living Quetzalcoatl either' (*PPS* 460), but in doing so he even fails to recognize 'the real Lord that is behind me' (461). She says, 'There is no God behind you', and that 'the Lord that is behind me is much greater' (461). We have seen that, in the final text, Kate begins to develop a feminist theology of the morning star, the central concept of Don Ramón's religion. Here in the penultimate version of the final chapter, she goes even further, and starts to develop a feminist theology of her own that she altogether opposes to that of Don Ramón. While he has much to say in response, she remains defiant. Her last words in their dialogue are, 'I am not afraid' (462).

So in June 1925, Lawrence gave Kate a feminist theology, undiminished for the reader by Ramón's critique in response. By October, though, when he came to revise the galley proofs, he struck out this passage, and replaced it with the altogether different final text, in which all Kate's certainty of her self, as well as her theological reflections based on this certainty, has vanished. Indeed, in the passage which he wrote in its place, 'It was as if she had two selves' (*PS* 429), one of which belonged to Ramón, Cipriano and the Quetzalcoatl religion, the other to her European life. In her 'old, accomplished self', no doubt the one which had articulated the feminist critique of Ramón in the earlier draft of the passage, she was 'an individual and her own mistress'; in the 'other self', she was 'vulnerable, and organically connected with Cipriano . . . and so was not "free" at all' (429). She is aware of the 'duality' in herself, and she 'suffers' from it. Above all, 'she could not definitely commit herself, either to the old way of life, or to the new' (429). These extremely different versions of Lawrence's attempt to resolve what Graham Hough called the two plots of the novel, to portray Kate both fully becoming herself and also submitting as a goddess wife to her god husband, suggest very strongly that he repeatedly found himself unable to do so, unable to imagine what both becoming oneself and submitting to one's husband and god could in practice mean for a modern woman like Kate.

At the end of the revised typescript in June, the novel's final sentence was, '"Le gueux m'a plantée là [The rogue has abandoned me]!" she said to herself, in the words of an old song' (*PPS* 462). In October, Lawrence changed this to the final version, '"You won't let me go!' she said to him' (*PS* 444). Virginia Hyde rightly points out that it is possible to read this last line as 'a statement of trust and hope' ('Picking Up "Life-Threads"' 180). Kate has repeatedly asked herself, Ramón and Cipriano whether or not she should 'go', and she tells Ramón, 'I don't really want to go away from you'. Her last question to Cipriano is one in which she 'pleaded', 'You don't want me to go, do you?' In this context, the line can indeed be read to mean that Kate is glad to see that Cipriano is not so indifferent to her as to be willing to live without her. On the other hand, the most obvious sense of the phrase, that Kate is expressing a sense of constraint, that Cipriano will not allow her the freedom to be herself and to make her own choices, comes most immediately to the reader's mind. Furthermore, it too makes sense in the context of the passage: in their previous conversation, Cipriano had reflected that 'he could use the law and have her prevented from leaving the country – or even from leaving Sayula – since she was legally married to him' (437). Hyde, who sees *The Plumed Serpent* as a novel in which Lawrence is 'working toward mutuality rather than dominance', more than previous critics have acknowledged ('Kate and the Goddess' 251), argues that Lawrence's refusal, in all three stages of revision, to give the final chapter a title, indicates that he was 'perhaps reluctant to resolve the novel's dialogic play' ('Picking Up "Life-Threads"' 178). She is right to point out the dialogism of the novel, but I see in the constant play of writing and re-writing of the final chapter, and in the constitutive ambiguity of the final line, not a reluctance but a series of attempts to resolve its two plots. It seems to me that Lawrence tried, with all the seriousness of purpose that accompanied his portrayal of the practice of his religious beliefs in a contemporary society, to portray them as realistically as he could. The re-writings, and their ultimately ambiguous result, is, in my view, an indication that, extremely hard as he tried, he simply could not convince himself that his religious beliefs would work in practice, or at least in the kind of hierarchical practice he envisaged in *The Plumed Serpent*. Lawrence makes a great effort to imagine the Quetzalcoatl religion truly consummating Kate, as he believes it should, but simply could not do so.

4

'Being in touch': Last works

Lady Chatterley's Lover

The problem faced by Connie Chatterley, solved in her sexual relationship with Mellors, is an increasing sense of meaninglessness, an increasing sense that her life, like that of the nation, is turning gradually into nothing. 'To accept the great nothingness of life', she reflects, 'seems to be the one end of living. All the many busy and important little things that make up the grand sum-total of nothingness!' (*LCL* 55). She has a vision of English society as a place full of activity because there is simply nothing to do, a series of institutions built with increasing fragility over nothing (58). Connie finds herself, like the miners who toy with socialism, full of energy, an energy that derives from a real life force within her, but with no outlet for it, such that her life is simply rotting inside her. As she reflects on Clifford's misguided energies, she cannot blame him, at least early in the novel, since his injury has not been his fault – it is rather what she calls 'part of the general catastrophe' (72). The inner emptiness she feels, and that Clifford symbolizes, whose 'bits seemed to grow together again' while 'something inside him had perished' (5, 6), is universal. It affects her, as it affects her entire society.

In the early versions of the novel, Lawrence emphasized Clifford's passion for the idea of the immortality of the soul. In the first version, he speaks to Connie of the soul as 'your essential *you*', and acknowledges that one of his chief concerns is whether the soul 'will reach a state where it is – well, *perfect*' (*FSLC* 49). Connie responds with her contrary belief in 'the immortality of the flesh', but Clifford insists, 'When I am out of the body, perhaps I shall be a real thing. Till then I'm not' (51). In both the first two versions of the novel, Clifford is an avid reader of Plato:

> His view was the old-fashioned Platonist view: the soul of the earnest seeker after truth, after that which is essence, pure and enduring, would reach the upper levels where absolute truth, absolute justice shines in the great eternal gleam. (23)

Clifford even has mystical experiences of this kind of transcendent realm, 'sort of exaltations and experience of identification with the One' (297). Connie, however, expresses Lawrence's view of the matter clearly – it is 'conceited, egoistic, anti-life', as if Clifford were insisting that 'he *was* the One, the great I Am' (297). Clifford's Platonic beliefs in the greater value of the spiritual over against the physical are simply a sign of his failure to live fully, a morally corrupt failure to understand the kind of holistic and ultimately divine life that Connie will find in her sexual relationship with Mellors. Neither the Christian nor the Platonic belief in the immortality of the soul is of any use to Connie in her search for an authentic form of life. She thinks of trying to be 'religious and charitable' in the second version of the novel, but instantly rejects Christianity as unable to satisfy her longing for such life: 'I can't open [my heart] to Jesus! he's too dead! he's too much of death! he's too like Clifford!' (254). Indeed, the religion seems to be of use to no one: Parkin's mother, in this version of the novel, converted to Christianity at a revivalist meeting, but quickly 'dropped off' and now 'has her pint regular' and has become 'as hard as nails' (405). Christianity, like the Platonism on which it is historically based, in its failure to understand the importance of the life of the body, is, in all three versions of *Lady Chatterley's Lover*, part of Connie's problem as she tries to live rather than any kind of solution to that problem.

The kind of sexual relationship that Connie has with Mellors is portrayed as something like a sacrament of the religion that Lawrence articulates in the novel. When Connie sees Mellors washing himself in the wood, 'naked to the hips', it is a 'visionary experience' (*LCL* 66). After they make love, Connie does not bathe, because 'the sense of his flesh touching her, the very stickiness upon her' is 'in a sense, holy' (137). Their sexual intercourse is described as a sacrament of divine power: Mellors' penis enters Connie with 'a ponderous, primordial tenderness, such as made the world in the beginning' (174), and the touch of his hand 'over her tail', 'over her secret places', is like a 'benediction' (265). As Connie drives through Europe with her sister towards the end of the novel, she reflects that her love for Mellors is like that of a monk for God, fulfilling her beyond worldly pleasures like the beauty of the Alpine landscape: 'I'm like Saint Bernard, who could sail down the lake of Lucerne without ever noticing that there were even mountains and green water' (255).

In the final version of the novel, Lawrence returns to the idiom he had forged in *The Rainbow*, in which Biblical texts are used in such a way that the sense in which they are true, for Lawrence, in which they refer to the holiness of the relationships he portrays in the novel, emerges. T. R. Wright has analysed Lawrence's 're-marking' of the Bible in *The Rainbow*, a phrase Wright borrows from Derrida to indicate repetition with difference (*Bible* 84, 17–18). Lawrence returns to something similar in *Lady Chatterley's Lover*, re-investing Biblical texts with heterodox senses in such a way as to constitute not only a redefinition of the nature of the sacred, but also an account of the conditions that have necessitated such a redefinition. When Connie is looking for a relationship which will fulfil her, it is a Biblical text that articulates her desire, a version of Jer. 5:1: 'Go ye into the streets and by-ways of Jerusalem, and see if ye can find a man' (64). As she walks through the wood in the Spring, remembering her vision of Mellors' body, it is primarily Biblical and ecclesiastical phrases that run through her mind: 'Ye must be born again! – I believe in the resurrection of the body! – Except a grain of wheat fall into the earth and die, it shall by no means bring forth.' These Biblical texts (John 3:7 and a version of John 12:24) and the text from the Apostles' Creed function in two ways, as do the plethora of such texts throughout the final version of the novel. They suggest that it is the kind of life that Connie finds in her relationship with Mellors that is the true meaning of the Biblical texts, the true site of the sacred in human life. At the same time, they suggest that the relationship described in the terms of the sacred text of Christianity is, precisely, sacred. As Wright has argued with respect to *The Rainbow*, Lawrence is attempting to do no less than re-write the Bible in *Lady Chatterley's Lover*, to show where in fact the sacred, relationship with God, can be found in contemporary English society.

In *Lady Chatterley's Lover*, Lawrence insists that it is to be found in the physical details of an authentic sexual relationship. Michael Bell argues that the accounts of sexual intercourse in the novel 'do not have the metaphysical ambition of the earlier great novels' (219), which is true, but a theological ambition nevertheless remains in these accounts. When Mellors enters Connie in one of their acts of sexual intercourse, Lawrence writes that 'he had to come into her at once, to enter the peace on earth of her soft, quiescent body' (116), using the language of Luke 2:14, which describes the salvific effect of the birth of Christ. This use of Biblical language functions as a commentary on the nature of the sexual relationship between Connie and Mellors. It says that this relationship is the genuine referent in contemporary society of the language for divine salvation in Luke 2:14, that it constitutes, as the Gospel says that the birth of Christ does, a salvific relationship with God. This portrayed most graphically in Mellors' address to his penis before he and Connie have sex: 'Dost want my lady Jane? . . . Ax 'er then! Ax lady Jane! Say: Lift up your heads O ye gates, that the king of glory may come in' (210). Daniel Sheerin has noted an analogue, what he calls a 'thoroughly devout antecedent', of this address in a sermon of St Quodvultdeus, bishop of Carthage in the mid-fifth century, who discusses the perpetual virginity of the Virgin Mary as follows:

> 'Lift up your gates, O ye princes' (Ps. 24:7) . . . Do not imagine that this gate through which was the passage of the Son of God was such, as was your going in and coming out. For your mother's womb cannot remain intact, for in it, daily, carnal embrace holds sway . . . This gate is eternal, is lofty, for the eternal entered it and came forth from it . . . But neither going in nor going out did he break the seal of the Virgin. (quoted in Sheerin 298)

There is no question of Lawrence's having read this text, but Sheerin is right to point it out as an antecedent of Mellors' use of the Psalm in *Lady Chatterley's Lover*, since in both cases the intention behind the exposition of the text to describe sexual intercourse is devout. Of course, Mellors' use of the text is intended to be shocking. Terry Wright has written of a similar passage (*LCL* 137) that Lawrence is 'trying to shock [his] audience out of their secular complacency by using the word "holy" of acts and substances not normally regarded in that light' ('Holiness' 175). This is certainly true of Mellors' use of the Biblical text to describe his penis entering Connie's vagina. But, as Wright points out, the intention behind the shocking effect is that what is genuinely rather than apparently sacred in human life should emerge. Lawrence is as serious as the bishop of Carthage in expounding the text with reference to the presence of God in human life. Of course, for the bishop, that was achieved in the Incarnation, effected in the Virgin Birth. For Lawrence, it is achieved in the kind of authentic sexual relationship he portrays in his novel. Mellors' use of the Biblical text to describe the physical details of the sexual act makes those details themselves sacred acts, acts in which, as in Psalm 24, God enters into human life.

In the same way, while Connie and Mellors decorate each other's pubic hair with flowers, Mellors says of a campion bud he entwines in 'the fine brown fleece of the mount of Venus', 'That's Moses in the bull-rushes' (223, 224). The text claims by this use of Biblical language that the physical acts of love, whatever form they may take, between Connie and Mellors constitute a sacred, indeed salvific, relationship, a relationship in which God enters human life and in which his will is done, as in the story of Moses. For Connie and Mellors, being together is like 'being in a little ark in the Flood' (216), especially when they are physically or sexually close: 'she laid her cheek on his belly, and pushed her arm around his warm, silent loins. They were alone in the Flood' (218–19). Their relationship is a holy place, Lawrence says in the Biblical imagery he uses throughout the novel, in an unholy world, a relationship that constitutes God's will for human beings, and an authentic relationship to him. Mellors ends the novel very explicitly on this note, describing his and Connie's 'fucking' as his 'Pentecost'. He writes to her: 'It's my Pentecost, the forked flame between me and you' (300–1). He explicitly intends to say that their sexual relationship is the basis of true religion in their lives, since Christianity no longer serves as that basis. 'The old Pentecost isn't quite right', Mellors writes, 'Me and God is a bit uppish somehow'

(301). The Christian account of God and relationship to him no longer works; it is in the new Pentecost, the 'forked flame between me and you', as Mellors tells Connie, that God is now made present in the world. God remains unknown, at the end of Lawrence's last novel. Mellors speaks of his faith in 'the unnamed god' that shields their Pentecost flame. What the novel does know is that it is in the kind of sexual relationship it has portrayed that he is revealed and encountered.

In the early versions of the novel, Lawrence makes explicit that Connie and Mellors, as they make love in the wood, enter a state like that of Adam and Eve in Paradise. In the first version, as the couple stand naked together in the moonlight, Connie says, 'We are Adam and Eve, naked in the garden' (*FSLC* 148). It is in this context that she weaves flowers into Parkin's body hair and around herself. This language remains in the typescript of the final novel: '"Tha'art Eve, an' I'm Adam," he said . . ."We'n got a grand property ca'd Paradise, on'y it isna on' th' map"' (*LCL* 432). In the final version of the novel, Lawrence prefers to understate the scene, and to allow the striking visual images of Connie and Mellors decorating each other's naked bodies with flowers to represent visually, as the paintings he had done on the same theme the previous year had done, of the return to Paradise, the return to the life with God and with one another of Adam and Eve. He prepares the reader for the meaning of the scene just a few pages earlier as Mellors laments that modern society, whether capitalist or bolshevist, is 'making mincemeat of the old Adam and the old Eve' (217).

Lawrence makes clear that he has been revising Christian tradition in the novel in 'A Propos of "Lady Chatterley's Lover"'. There he praises the Catholic view of marriage and identifies his own concerns in the novel with that view. In teaching that sex is the consummation of the sacrament of marriage, Lawrence writes, the Catholic Church, especially in southern Europe, recognizes that sex is 'charged with all the sensual mystery and importance of the old past' (*LCL* 317). It understands that sex is at the heart of physical life and that physical life is at the heart of human relationship to God. 'To the priest', Lawrence writes, 'sex is the clue to marriage and marriage is the clue to the daily life of the people and the church is the clue to the greater life' (318). Later in the essay, he praises the Catholic vision of 'marriage, sacred and inviolable, the great way of earthly fulfilment

for man and woman, in unison, under the spiritual rule of the Church'
(321–2). Lawrence is deeply impressed by the Catholic concept of
the sacrament of marriage, especially as he sees it to be incorporated
into the lives of rural southern Europe, where life is lived according to
the natural rhythms of the earth of which the sexual consummation
of marriage is one. Lawrence is not interested in an 'after-life', in 'A
Propos', especially not the spiritual one posited by Christian tradition.
Hence he emphasizes that marriage is 'eternal', that is, eternal as far
as this, bodily, life goes. 'The Catholic Church does not spend its time
reminding the people that in heaven there is no marrying or giving
in marriage. It insists: if you marry, you marry for ever!' (318). This
revisionary understanding of Catholic teaching with respect to eternity
follows from Lawrence's approval of its teaching with respect to bodily
life, that it is sacramental, the place where one, indeed where people
in relationship, meet God. This is what he means when he writes, 'The
Church established marriage for life, for the fulfilment of the soul during
life, not postponing it for after-death' (322). Indeed, its establishment
of the sacrament of marriage is the point of Christianity, for Lawrence,
the essence of its value for human beings, and not at all its teaching
on the after-life or its doctrine of salvation, which the Protestant and
especially the nonconformist churches emphasize (322): 'the great
saints only live, even Jesus only lives to add a new fulfilment and a
new beauty to the permanent sacrament of marriage' (324). Jesus'
contribution to the religious life of human beings, Lawrence now
writes, is that he and the church founded in his name have taught
that marriage, and its consummation in sexual intercourse, is holy,
and the place above all in human life where human beings encounter
God. Lawrence speaks of marriage as the unity of the two 'rivers of
blood' that husband and wife constitute, unified by the bridge of the
phallus. Marriage so understood is the will of God for human beings,
he writes. Indeed, 'all we know of the will of God is that he wishes
this, this oneness, to take place, fulfilled over a life-time, this oneness
within the great dual bloodstream of humanity' (325).

This is the view that Lawrence expresses in the novel. In the first
version, Parkin calls Connie his 'wife in the wood', by contrast with
her marriage to Clifford 'in a' the rest o' th' world' (*FSLC* 89). Indeed,
Connie learns about the essential nature of marriage as she and Parkin
lie together, his left arm cupping her right breast so that he encircles

her: 'So this was what it was to be a wife! . . . The curious united circle of the man and the woman' (100). Although both of them have been married before, they come close to agreeing that it is only their sexual relationship in the woods that truly constitutes a marriage:

> 'Do you feel I'm your wife in the wood?' she asked, pleased.
> 'My wife onywheer!' he said. 'I've niver 'ad no wife. I niver knowed what a woman wor like, afore. Did thee?'
> 'No, I never really had a man, either.' (102)

In a scene Lawrence removes in the second and final versions, they enact a sacrament of their own, each hammering a nail into a tree to signify their lasting relationship. In a faint echo of Don Ramón, Parkin guides her through the liturgy he devises for the occasion:

> 'Shall yer drive yer nail inter th' oak tree, wi' mine, for good and a'?' he asked her.
> 'Yes!' she said uneasily. (79)

Parkin drives in his nail, and hands another to her, instructing her, 'Nail it in aside of mine'. The ritual performed, he concludes, 'Tha's done it' (79). I would suggest that Lawrence removed this scene from the second and final versions of the novel because he wanted to emphasize that the sexual relationship of Connie and Mellors is itself sacramental, and that no other ritual is needed to show that this is the case. In the second version of the novel, Connie reflects explicitly on the truth of the Anglican marriage service with respect to their relationship: '"With my body I thee worship," says the man to the woman in the marriage service. And she felt it had been so with him: an act of bodily worship' (332). In the final version of the text, Lawrence makes it clear that he is redefining the sacrament of marriage, as he has redefined the Biblical texts he uses to describe the relationship of Connie and Mellors. The couple entwine each other's sexual organs with flowers, like Adam and Eve having regained Paradise. As he decorates her navel and pubic hair, Mellors says, 'That's you in all your glory! . . . Lady Jane at her wedding with John Thomas'. As he decorates his navel and penis, he says, 'This is John Thomas marryin' Lady Jane' (228). Their genuine sexual relationship, these texts say, genuinely constitutes the sacrament of marriage. As 'A Propos' makes clear, the relationship between Connie and Mellors is the essence of the relationship that, for Lawrence, the Catholic Church intends in its teaching on marriage. They commit adultery only according to the letter rather than to the spirit of such teaching. As Martin Jarrett-Kerr puts it, 'Lawrence re-defines [sexual] morality in his own way. And that way is essentially religious' (108). The relationship Lawrence portrays constitutes his understanding of the meaning of the sacrament of marriage.

A view similar to this was taken by John Robinson, the Bishop of Woolwich, at the trial of Penguin Books in 1960 for their publication of the unexpurgated text of *Lady Chatterley's Lover*. Robinson testified that, in his opinion, Lawrence was trying to 'portray the sex relationship as something essentially sacred', and as 'in a real sense an act of holy communion' (Rolph 70, 71). In *D. H. Lawrence and Human Existence*, published in a second edition after the Lady Chatterley trial, Jarrett-Kerr writes: 'Lawrence can teach Christians lessons that they should have known but have forgotten' (12). This is true, he argues, especially of Lawrence's view of the body: 'Christians, it seems to me, owe a debt to Lawrence for insisting again and again that man is not without a body, and expresses himself as man not without his body. And what Lawrence says about sex is true even more widely' (22). Jarrett-Kerr sketches a theological account of sex that involves three 'surrenders', that of the self to the other, that of the mind to the body, and that of both these surrenders to God (22). Put simply, he speaks of 'the full, glad appreciation of divine-human creativity, of gratitude for the body, which should be the mark of a truly Christian theological view' (18). In *Lady Chatterley's Lover*, he argues, Lawrence expresses precisely such a view. In the scene in which Connie initially reflects on the ridiculous nature of sexual intercourse, the act 'remains inoperative until she can accept it humbly, thankfully, at bottom "religiously"' (103). Indeed, Jarrett-Kerr writes, the portrayal of sex in *Lady Chatterley's Lover* functions as a corrective to that element in Christian tradition, in which he includes an article from the *Summa Theologiae*, which fails to understand the integration of mind and body from which a genuinely Christian theology must derive: 'It remains true that Lawrence rightly suspected . . . that something was wrong in the balance of Christian teaching, especially as so often expounded in his day. And we have to thank him for re-emphasizing an element in the doctrine of Creation which has too often been neglected' (104).

In a review of Jarrett-Kerr's book, F. R. Leavis wrote that he viewed 'with the gravest distrust the prospect of Lawrence's being adopted for expository appreciation as almost a Christian by writers whose religious complexion is congenial to Mr [T. S.] Eliot', who had written the introduction to the book (72). Nor were all of Bishop Robinson's Anglican colleagues in agreement with his testimony to this effect at the Lady Chatterley trial. Geoffrey Fisher, the Archbishop of Canterbury, responded, 'The Christian fact is that adultery . . . is always a sin', and that therefore 'the Bishop was mistaken to think he could take part in this trial without becoming a stumbling block and a cause of offence to many ordinary Christians' (quoted in Eric James 97–8). As Mark Roodhouse and Eric James (93–109) have shown, views from church leaders on the extent to which the novel does or does not express Christian values were extremely varied. In terms of Lawrence's own beliefs, however, his novel represents a revisionary reading of Christianity, in which the authentic sexual relationship portrayed in the novel is defined as the place in which human beings meet and are fulfilled by, although they in no way know, God. It is this kind of relationship to which the Bible refers, according to the novel, and it is this kind of relationship that is at the heart of Catholic teaching on the sacrament of marriage. Lawrence is doing no less than writing a new Bible and a new liturgy for the society he portrays in the novel. At the trial, Vivian de Sola Pinto explained that the book has a 'double theme', 'the condemnation of the mechanization of humanity in an industrial society' and 'the necessity for human happiness to find adequate sexual relationship based on tenderness and . . . mutual affection' (Rolph 74). This double theme constitutes a question and answer structure. To the question of the emptiness of life felt across English society, from coal miners to landed gentry, the novel answers in terms of the contemporary sacrament of marriage that constitutes its centre.

The Escaped Cock

Lawrence had been thinking about the meaning of the concept of the resurrection of the flesh since *The Rainbow*. Virginia Hyde writes that Lawrence had 'seemingly been preparing throughout his career to write [the] story' *The Escaped Cock* (*Risen Adam* 214), which he calls a 'story of the Resurrection', on 'what sort of a man "rose up"' after all that other pretty little experience' (*L* 6: 40). Earl Brewster recalls that, during their Etruscan tour, he and Lawrence saw in a shop window on Easter morning 'a toy white rooster escaping from an egg'. Brewster 'suggested a title – "The Escaped Cock – a story of the Resurrection"', and Lawrence replied that he had been 'thinking about writing a story of the Resurrection' (Brewster 123–4). In fact, it was Palm Sunday on which they saw the toy, but Lawrence recalls two years later that the story was 'suggested' by this toy, and that it was written at 'Easter' (*VG* xxvi). He had completed the first draft by the end of April (*L* 6: 44) and the second, published in *Forum* in February 1928, in early May (*L* 6: 51). As he puts it a year later, defending the story against the 'vituperative condemnation' it had received, it was 'an attempt to show the resurrection *in the flesh*, instead of in vacuo and in abstraction' (*L* 6: 378).

The new life of the man who had died begins with 'nausea' and 'revulsion', both physical and emotional. Evelyn Hinz and John Teunissen explain this well, writing that it 'symbolizes the ultimate and logical conclusion to the Christian and Platonic ideal of renunciation' (284). To a preacher and would-be saviour, who has exalted the life of the spirit over against the life of the body, as the man who had died has been, the experience of rising into the physical world is initially a negative and unpleasant one. He feels, physically and emotionally, the *contemptus mundi* he had spent his life preaching.

The man who had died also experiences 'disillusion' in rising, primarily with his former mission, his preaching of the gospel of salvation. In the view of resurrection articulated in the story, after his resurrection Jesus repents of the excessively spiritual nature of the salvation he preached, and indeed of the concept of salvation itself. He calls his preaching 'the day of my interference', and says, 'Death has saved me from my own salvation' (132). In the first manuscript version, even God the Father feels this way: the man who had died says, 'I, now, belong to my father, who owns my greater self, and undertakes neither mission nor the making of gospel' (194). The *Forum* version of Part I ends with the man who had died asking himself 'a last question: From what, and to what, could this infinite whirl be saved?' (215). As Lawrence would write two years later in 'A Propos of "Lady Chatterley's Lover"', 'Salvation seems incomprehensible to me . . . I see the soul as something which must be developed and fulfilled throughout a life-time' (*LCL* 322). The man who had died learns Lawrence's own view in rising from the death of the kind of life he had led, that of a teacher of spiritual salvation, that the concept of salvation itself, the essence of the Christian idea of the good life, is simply a category mistake, 'just jargon' as Lawrence puts it in 'A Propos' (322), and not at all the kind of thing in which the good life consists.

Madeleine remains orthodox, according to the Christian understanding of Jesus' preaching. Since he no longer preaches his message of salvation of the soul, she sees that he is 'not the Messiah', that 'the Messiah had not risen' (134). Indeed, it is precisely insofar as 'her mind discarded the bitterness of reality' that she invents the Christian account of Jesus' resurrection: 'He was risen, but not as man; as pure God, who should not be touched by the flesh, and who should be rapt away into heaven' (134).

The new life into which the man who had died is raised in the story is embodied above all in the natural world. As he looks around him, he sees an urge to live driving through the natural world that he had never had, seen or understood when he was preaching his gospel of salvation of the soul in his previous life. It is this urge to live that the cock symbolizes in the story. Hinz and Teunissen rightly point out that the story 'seems to play down the conventional pun on "cock"' (280). The cock symbolizes not the phallus, as the pun would lead the reader of the title to expect, but what the phallus symbolizes, namely the full life lived in touch with another, with the natural world and with the unknown God from whom they come. As the man looks at the phenomena of the natural world, 'the cool silkiness of the young wheat' and 'the silvery-haired buds of the scarlet anemone', he sees that they are in 'a world that had never died' (127). The man who had died rises up to understand and live the kind of life, a life that is purely itself, which the natural world had been living all along, and which his religion of spiritual salvation had made him unable to see. The cock's crow is a 'challenge from life to death', and it causes the man, for the first time, to '[look] nakedly on life', where he sees 'a vast resoluteness everywhere flinging itself up in stormy or subtle wavecrests' (129) and hears each living thing's 'ringing, ringing defiant challenge to all other things existing' (130). It is this life, life itself, rather than preaching about eternal life, to which the man is raised in Lawrence's story, and it is learning to live in this way that constitutes the resurrection of his Christ figure. As the man who had died says, 'The teacher and the saviour are dead in me; now I can go about my own business, into my own single life' (132).

Part II of the story represents a completion of this process, the consummation of the resurrection into a fully lived life, with the man's sexual relationship with the priestess of Isis. Lawrence wrote in defence of the story:

> Church doctrine teaches the resurrection of the body: and if that doesn't mean the whole man, what does it mean? and if man is whole without a woman – even Jesus – then I'm damned. (L 7: 122)

In 'The Risen Lord', he writes the same thing, asserting directly in prose the idea expressed in fictional form in the story:

> If Jesus rose as a full man, in full flesh and soul, then he rose to take a woman to himself, to live with her, and to know the tenderness and blossoming of the two-ness with her . . . and to have children by her. (LEA 271)

The consummation of the resurrection of the man who died into a fully lived life is his sexual relationship with the priestess. It is essential to Lawrence's vision of a fully lived life that the woman with whom the man has a sexual relationship is a priestess, and that their intercourse takes place in a temple, before the image of a goddess. As in Lady Chatterley's Lover, the consummation of the man and of the woman's lives is the sacrament of marriage, that is, a sexual relationship that puts both partners into relationship with each other and, through each other, with God. As he thinks of her desire for him, and of his own awakening desire for her, the man who had died reflects, 'I have never before stretched my limbs in such sunshine . . . The greatest of all gods granted me this' (155). Their sexual relationship is from the beginning something that takes place in relationship to God.

Lawrence emphasizes this with the technique he used in Lady Chatterley's Lover of using Biblical and theological language for the *[handwritten marginal notes: "plenty of [...] more, let [...] seems to me."]*

details of their sexual relationship. As the woman's anointing of the man before the image of Isis leads to sexual intercourse, the man looks at her crouching before the image and thinks, '"On this rock I build my life" – The deep-folded, penetrable rock of the living woman!' (159). As he 'felt the blaze of his manhood and his power rise up in his loins', he thinks, '"I am risen"'. His 'last thought' before he 'knew her and was at one with her' is 'My hour is upon me' (160). In these uses and echoes of Biblical language, Lawrence reaffirms the twin beliefs he had expressed in *Lady Chatterley's Lover*, first, that the sexual relationship depicted in the story is a sacred one, one that, like the traditional sacrament of marriage, puts the couple into relationship with God through their sexual relationship with each other. Second, that the Biblical texts, which the church holds to express the self-revelation of God, refer as such most truly to the kind of sacramental sexual relationship depicted in the story, such that it is in this kind of relationship that God is most truly known. This kind of relationship is simply the new Bible, the self-revelation of God for Lawrence's contemporaries. As the priestess rubs the man's wounded body with oil, the act that will lead to sexual intercourse before the image of Isis, he begins truly to experience resurrection: 'a new sun was coming up in him, in the perfect inner darkness of himself . . . "I am something new –"' (159). The consummation of the new life that began when he awoke in the tomb, the consummation of life lived fully, is the sexual relationship that begins before the image of the divinity, what the Catholic Church, as Lawrence writes in 'A Propos', calls the sacrament of marriage.

Lawrence's primary source for the myth of Isis and Osiris in the story is *The Golden Bough*. Frazer describes Osiris as 'the god whose death and resurrection were annually celebrated' (366). He compares the cult of Osiris as a dying and rising god to that of Christ, writing that 'as Osiris died and rose again from the dead, so all men hoped to arise like him from death to life eternal' (372). To some extent, Lawrence draws on the pattern of fertility rites he knew from Frazer in having his Christ play the role of Osiris to the priestess of Isis. In Part I of the story, the resurrection of the man who had died is in part his vision of the life of the natural world, 'thronging with greenness' (*VG* 126), associating his resurrection with Frazer's account of the rites of dying and rising gods. Isis, too, in Frazer, is a fertility goddess, the 'corn-goddess' (387). He points out that she was known by epithets such as 'Creatress of green things', 'Green goddess, whose green colour is like unto the greenness of the earth', and that she was 'not only the creatress of the fresh verdure of vegetation which covers the earth, but is actually the green corn-field itself, which is personified as a goddess' (388). Furthermore, her cult too can be compared to Christianity:

> Her stately ritual, with its shaven and tonsured priests, its matins and vespers, its tinkling music, its baptisms and aspersion of holy water, its solemn processions, its jewelled images of the Mother of God, presented many points of similarity to the pomps and ceremonies of Catholicism. (389)

Lawrence knew from his reading of *The Golden Bough* that the cult of Isis and Osiris was, according to Frazer's anthropology, a religion structurally similar to Christianity.

Nevertheless, it is not quite true to say, as Phillip Marcus does, that in Part II of the story it is 'as if Christ had stepped from the New Testament into the world of *The Golden Bough*' (229). Nor do I agree with Larry LeDoux that Lawrence is attempting to 'return Christianity to its vital archetypal sources' in the story, of the kind uncovered by Frazer (138). Lawrence's use of Frazer's accounts of the cults of Osiris and Isis is highly revisionary. It is the phallic element of these cults that he uses in his story, an element that is not in the story reducible to the more fundamental archetype of fertility religion, but which is itself the essence of the religion articulated by the story. In addition to the story of Isis in search, Lawrence read in Frazer about the phallic aspects of the cult of Osiris, considered as a 'god of fertility':

> At his festival women used to go about the villages singing songs in his praise and carrying obscene images of him which they set in motion by means of strings . . . A similar image of him, decked with all the fruits of the earth, is said to have stood in a temple before a figure of Isis, and in the chambers dedicated to him at Philae the dead god is portrayed lying on his bier in an attitude that indicates in the plainest way that even in death his generative virtue was not extinct. (Abridged edn 381)

In these passages, Frazer is arguing that Osiris is a god of fertility. In the sentence which I have elided from the quote above, he wrote, 'The custom was probably a charm to ensure the growth of the crops'. That is not the part that interested Lawrence, however. In *The Escaped Cock*, it is the phallic aspect alone of the story that he uses. The point is not to show that Christianity, like all religions, is a kind of fertility rite, but that true religion, as the cult of Osiris and Isis shows, is phallic. Resurrection, whether that of Osiris or of Christ, is phallic, it is to a new life in which sexual relationship functions as a sacrament, in which the couple experience the mystery of God in the mystery of their encounter with one another.

This is why the priestess serves Isis in search rather than Isis the mother of Horus. Isis does not represent the Great Mother in Lawrence's story, although Frazer tells us that 'in her character as a goddess of fecundity Isis answered to the great mother goddesses of Asia' (387). It is Isis in search who is the presiding deity of *The Escaped Cock*. Merely virile men like Caesar or Anthony, whom the priestess had known when she was young, do not arouse or awake her inner self (144). It is after a philosopher tells her that 'rare women wait for the re-born man' (144) that she finds the cult of Isis 'in whom she spelled her mystery' (145). Isis represents a woman who, like herself, is searching for the re-born man, and whose re-birth will be phallic. This is why the man who had died can be Osiris to her, since her awakening of his dead sexuality constitutes the culmination of his resurrection. Their sacramental sexual intercourse is the fulfilment both of her religion of Isis in search and, in Lawrence's view, of the Christian account of the resurrection. For the man who died and the priestess of Isis, for both Christianity and pagan fertility cults, life becomes most fully itself in the sexual intercourse of the couple before the image of the goddess, or, to put it in the Catholic terms Lawrence will use in 'A Propos', in the sacrament of marriage.

Sketches of Etruscan Places

Lawrence read widely about the Etruscans, both before and after his tour of Etruscan places in April 1927. He re-read George Dennis' *Cities and Cemeteries of Etruria* (*L* 5: 413; 6: 45), which Billy Tracy argues that he had at his side while writing the *Sketches* (441). In May 1926, he had 'read one or two books' on the Etruscans, which he found 'very dreary' in their 'repetition and surmise' (*L* 5: 465). The following month, he reads R. A. L. Fell's *Etruria and Rome*, finding the same thing, that Fell is 'very thorough in washing out once more the few rags of information we have concerning the Etruscans: but not a thing he has to say' (*L* 5: 473). As a result, Lawrence writes:

> I shall just have to start in and go ahead, and be damned to all authorities! There really is next to nothing to be said, *scientifically*, about the Etruscans. Must take the imaginative line. (*L* 5: 473)

As we saw in his essays on Native Americans, Lawrence's account of Etruscan religion is just this, a work of his imagination, in which the Etruscan remains function as a catalyst for the development of his own religious thought.

For Lawrence, Etruscan religion is essentially a religion of life, especially of the life of the body. He found little support for this view in Dennis, who writes:

> The religion of Etruria in her earliest ages bore some resemblance to that of Egypt, but more to the other theological systems of the East. It had the same gloomy, unbending, imperious character, the same impenetrable shroud of mysticism and symbolism; widely unlike the lively, plastic phantasy-full creed of the Greeks, whose joyous sprit found utterance in song. (i, 28)

Fell, too, writes that it is its 'gloomy and repulsive features which are regarded as [the] particular characteristic' of Etruscan religion (142). He argues for a degeneration from an 'earlier confidence in a happy immortality' into a religion of 'fear and despair' (142). For Dennis, the power of Etruscan religion was 'but negative', 'a system of spiritual tyranny that rendered Etruria inferior to Greece' since the minds of most Etruscans were not allowed 'liberty to expand . . . in that field wherein lies man's highest delight and glory', his relationship to God (i, 29–30). Furthermore, Dennis emphasizes, Etruscan religion includes a mythology of 'the dread powers of the lower world' (i, 35). One of these gods, Mania, was 'a fearful deity, who was propitiated by human sacrifices'. Another was Charun, 'the infernal Mercury of the Etruscans', whose 'dread image' is 'hideous as the imagination could conceive'. Indeed, Dennis writes that Charun, 'with his numerous attendant demons and Furies', 'well illustrates the dark and gloomy character of the Etruscan superstition' (i, 36). He adds an appendix to his chapter on the Volterra Museum on 'the Charun of the Etruscans', who, he writes, is 'generally represented as a squalid and hideous old man, with flaming eyes, and savage aspect' and 'the ears, and often the tusks, of a brute' (ii, 183). In depictions of violent death, as on a vase from Vulci, he 'stands by, grinning with savage delight', and 'in the Etruscan mythology, [he] is also the tormentor of guilty souls' (ii, 184). When Lawrence quotes directly from Dennis on the Volterra urns (*SEP* 163–4; cf. Dennis ii, 176), it is from a passage that concludes several pages on Charun's depiction as 'grisly, savage and of brutish aspect' (ii, 173) on those urns. Fell, too, writes of the hideous appearance of Charun, with a 'vulture's beak, animal ears and snaky locks . . ., dragging away guilty souls or threatening them with his hammer' (143). He also discusses the 'still more repulsive . . . demon Tuchulcha' (143).

Lawrence does not emphasize in any way the 'grisly' or 'dread' aspect of Charun and his 'infernal demons', however. Rather, he reads out of the Etruscan remains a religion of life, of touch with the natural world and the body, in which death is nothing to fear, but rather a continuation of the natural life of the body lived in this world:

> Death, to the Etruscan, was a pleasant continuance of life, with jewels and wine and flutes playing for the dance. It was neither an ecstasy of bliss, a heaven, nor a purgatory of torment. It was just a natural continuance of the fullness of life. (19)

These views are in direct contrast to those he finds in Dennis. The latter is impressed by the gaiety of the tomb paintings of Tarquinia, but he denigrates the scenes of sensual enjoyment depicted there in the terms of precisely the kind of spiritualizing Christianity which, for Lawrence, modern men and women must learn from the Etruscans to move beyond:

> Every one, on entering these tombs, must be struck with the inappropriateness of such scenes to a sepulchre; but happily for

us we regard them from the high vantage ground of Christianity, and our view is not bounded by a paradise of mere sensual gratification. (i, 330)

For Lawrence, by contrast, the gorgeous banquets depicted in the tombs of Tarquinia are evidence that, against much of what he read in his sources, Etruscan religion was one in which death represented a natural step in a vision of life lived in touch with the physical world: 'the life on earth was so good, the life below could but be a continuance of it' (46).

For Lawrence, this view of the after-life derives from a 'profound belief in life, acceptance of life', which he sees to be 'characteristic of the Etruscans' (46). The naked slaves who 'joyfully stoop to the wine-jars' are painted in such a way that 'the curves of their limbs show pure pleasure in life' (56). In the dancers, this is a 'pleasure that goes deeper still', in the 'big, long hands thrown out and dancing to the very ends of the fingers'. The 'religion of life' (56) Lawrence sees represented in the Etruscan remains is similar in many respects to the religion he saw in Native American rites, songs and dances. The reason for this is that both sets of religious beliefs and practices stem from the single aboriginal religion of the pre-historic, antediluvian world. Lawrence writes, 'The [Etruscan] religion is in all probability basically aboriginal, belonging to some vast old religion of the prehistoric world' (27). The most fundamental belief of this ancient religion is that the universe is alive:

The old idea of the vitality of the universe was evolved long before history begins, and elaborated into a vast religion before we get a glimpse of it. When history does begin, in China or India, Egypt, Babylonia, even in the pacific and in aboriginal America, we see evidence of one underlying religious idea: the conception of the vitality of the cosmos . . . and man . . . striving . . . to get himself more and more of the gleaming vitality of the cosmos. (57)

Lawrence sees primarily in the Etruscan remains this ancient dual religious idea, that the universe is alive and that the goal of human life is to draw into oneself, 'by vivid attention and subtlety and exerting all his strength' (58), that cosmic life. As he found in Native American religion, the more a person can do this, live with the life of the living universe, the more divine he becomes. This is the meaning of the red colour of the men in the Tarquinian paintings, for Lawrence: 'when [a man] was all himself he painted himself vermilion, like the throat of the dawn, and was god's body' (58). Etruscan religion, Lawrence believes, like that of the Pueblo Indians he encountered, was one in which the goal of human life was to open oneself to the life of the living universe and thereby, since this life is divine, to become a god.

Dennis' strongest criticism of Etruscan religion is of the tyrannical nature of its institutions. It is the 'religion of a caste, imposed for its exclusive benefit on the masses':

> Before the gate of that paradise where the intellect revels unfettered among speculations on its own nature, origin, existence and final destiny, on its relation to the First Cause, to other minds, and to society in general – stood the sacerdotal Lucumo, brandishing in one hand the double-edged sword of secular and ecclesiastical authority; and holding forth in the other the books of Tages, exclaiming, to his awe-struck subjects, 'Believe and obey!' (i, 30)

Fell regards the theocratic nature of Etruscan society as one of the causes of the decline of Etruria into dependence on Rome:

> This theocratical basis, so different from Roman practice, made impossible any gradual equalization of privilege, so that the lowest classes, permanently excluded from power, had less interest in the welfare of their city than Roman citizens in theirs. (136)

As a result, he writes, 'the strength of the city was gravely impaired' (137). For Lawrence, however, the hierarchical nature of Etruscan religion is precisely its strength. As in the Quetzalcoatl religion of *The Plumed Serpent*, it is only the great soul which can contemplate and draw into itself enough of the divine living cosmos to become a god, and which thereby shows its natural fitness to rule, to guide lesser souls to the kind of fulfilment of which they are capable. This is 'the ancient idea of kings, kings who are gods by vividness, because they have gathered into themselves core after core of vital potency from the universe' (*SEP* 58). This institution was the strength of Etruscan religion, for Lawrence, because:

> The people are not initiated into the cosmic ideas, nor into the awakened throb of more vivid consciousness. Try as you may, you can never make the mass of men throb with full awakedness. They *cannot* be more than a little aware. So you must give them symbols, ritual and gesture, which will fill their bodies with life up to their own full measure. (59)

The Lucumo, the 'religious prince' is therefore the heart of Etruscan religion, 'the clue to etruscan life', keeping the people in touch with the mystery of the living universe which is too great for them to grasp. 'The "touch" went down from the Lucumo to the merest slave' (59). Lawrence would write the following year that 'the leader of men is a back number' and that 'the leader-cum-follower relationship is a bore' (*L* 6: 321), but while he is completing *Sketches of Etruscan Places*, in his religious thought at least, his commitment to natural aristocracy remains.

Apocalypse

In August 1929, Lawrence resumed his correspondence with Frederick Carter, and by October had decided to write a commentary on the book of Revelation to complement what remained of Carter's manuscript, *The Dragon of the Apocalypse* (*L* 7: 507). By January 1930, this had become a separate piece of work, which Lawrence intended to 'publish . . . later on, as a small book' (*L* 7: 613). In this text, *Apocalypse*, Lawrence argues that there are 'two kinds of Christianity' – the 'Christianity of tenderness', which focuses on the person and teaching of Jesus, and the 'Christianity of self-glorification', which focuses on the Apocalypse (*A* 65). The strong have taught, with Jesus, Paul and John the evangelist, renunciation and love. The weak, with John of Patmos, have taught '*down with the strong and the powerful, and let the poor be glorified*' (65). Since there are always more weak than strong people in the world, Lawrence argues, it is this second sort of Christianity that 'has triumphed and will triumph'

Nietz

(65). It is this kind of Christianity which is expressed in the book of Revelation, and which has caused that book to appeal to weak minds throughout the history of the church and to continue to do so today.

Lawrence had read in R. H. Charles' commentary that John of Patmos had incorporated earlier sources into his text (I, lxxxix–xci), and that his work had been edited by a 'shallow-brained fanatic and celibate, whose dogmatism varies directly with the narrowness of his understanding' (I, lv), whose ideas are ascetic to the point of heresy. John Oman, whose commentary Lawrence had reviewed in 1924, also took a dim view of the 'incompetent editing' of the book (9). In Alfred Loisy's commentary, Lawrence read of the numerous hypotheses of different authors, sources and editors of the text posited by Biblical critics (10–21) and that, in Loisy's view, the author of the book of Revelation had used a complex, Christianized mix of pagan and Jewish sources (21–37). Lawrence elaborates his own redaction history of the text:

> Down at the bottom is a pagan substratum, probably one of the ancient books of the Aegean civilisation: some sort of a book of a pagan Mystery. This has been written over by Jewish apocalyptists, then extended, and then finally written over by the Jewish-Christian apocalyptist John: and then, after his day, expurgated and corrected and pruned down and added to by Christian editors who wanted to make of it a Christian work. (81)

Lawrence identifies four stages, that is, of writing and editing in the book – a pagan book that is re-written as a Jewish apocalypse, then re-written as a Christian apocalypse by John of Patmos and finally is made more orthodox by Christian editors after his death. Carter recalls that Lawrence went through 'scheme upon scheme to eliminate the Johnisms' in the book of Revelation, convinced as he was that the Christian author had re-written an early pagan text of ancient and universal religion (*Body Mystical* 52–3), eventually settling upon this one:

> Of all the writers dealing with the origins of this Apocalypse he preferred Dupuis' version in the *Religion Universelle*. Not that Lawrence had read Dupuis, but I had, and gave him a synopsis of the argument. This was to the effect that in it existed the only

document that had come down to us of all the secret cults, the sole survivor giving a full description of the Mithraic initiation with its symbols and figures. (53)

Lawrence writes of the base text he hypothesizes of the book of Revelation, 'The oldest part . . . was a pagan work, probably the description of the "secret" ritual of initiation into one of the pagan Mysteries, Artemis, Cybele, even Orphic' (A 85).

The substance of this ancient document, Lawrence argues, is that the universe is alive, and that men and women are living creatures in the living universe: 'We and the cosmos are one. The cosmos is a vast living body, of which we are still parts' (77). This belief implies an ethics, at least for modern readers who understand it, that 'we have to get back to the cosmos', back in touch with the living universe of which we are living, consubstantial parts (78). In *Apocalypse*, Lawrence specifies that it is by worship that this return to touch with the cosmos is to be achieved: 'We can only get the sun by a sort of worship: and the same the moon. By *going forth* to worship the sun, worship that is felt in the blood' (78). There are hints of this view, traces of the original pagan document, Lawrence argues, in the book of Revelation (79).

In 1929, Lawrence re-read John Burnet's *Early Greek Philosophy*, this time in the third edition of 1920. In *Apocalypse*, as a result, he expresses his account of the universal pagan religion in the language of the pre-Socratic philosophers he has been re-reading in Burnet. Lawrence writes, 'To the ancient consciousness, Matter, Materia, or Substantial things are God', a view that he also affirms in his own right (95). He adds, again agreeing with this view himself, that 'those things which move are doubly God'. This ancient and universal view, he argues, can be found in the earliest scientists, the pre-Socratics. 'Today it is almost impossible for us to realise what the old Greeks meant by god, or *theos*. Everything was *theos*; but even so, not at the same moment. At the moment, whatever *struck* you was god' (95). The four elements, being 'things in themselves', were also 'realities, gods, *theoi*' (96). Later in the text, as he comments on the dragon of Rev. 12, he argues that 'the dragon is the symbol of the fluid, rapid, startling movement of life within us' (123). He continues to use the theosophical concept of *kundalini* in explaining this inner force, and he also explains it in pre-Socratic terms: 'The hunger which made Esau sell his birthright would have been called his dragon: later, the Greeks would even have called it a "god" in him', because 'it is something beyond him yet within him' (123).

The ancient world, to put it another way, was 'entirely religious and godless'. The pagans, like the pre-Socratics, whose 'early science is a source of the purest and oldest religion' (131), did not have an anthropomorphic concept of God. When people lived 'breast to breast, as it were, with the cosmos', 'the whole cosmos was alive' and 'there was no room for the intrusion of the god idea' (130–1). There is a kind of fall in the history of religion, Lawrence argues in *Apocalypse*, which occurs with the thought of Socrates, in which individuals become aware of themselves as such, apart from the cosmos, and so the concept of God as a higher mode of individual arises, 'to intervene between man and the cosmos' (131): 'With the coming of Socrates and "the spirit", the cosmos died. For two thousand years, man has been living in a dead or dying cosmos, hoping for a heaven hereafter' (96). In an early version of the text, Lawrence adds in a third stage to this history of religions, which occurs before Plato, the rise of the 'cults of the dying god'. Lawrence acknowledges with Frazer that 'the dying god may have symbolised the death and re-birth of vegetation', but adds that it also 'meant much more than this' (168). Frazer's dying and rising gods, for Lawrence, are primarily an expression of 'the need man felt of death, the death-wish, so that a man might experience mystically, or ritually, the death in the body, the death of the known desires, and a resurrection in a new self' (168). This is why the Orphic mysteries begin at the same time as the dying god cults, Lawrence argues. Eventually, he works out three stages in the history of religion, re-writing Frazer's three stages in the history of thought, those of magic, religion and science. For Lawrence, there are 'three states of man: cosmic-religious, god-religious, and philosophic-scientific' (182).

The book of Revelation contains traces of the first two of these stages in the history of religion. Lawrence finds evidence of the early pagan manuscript primarily in the first seven chapters of the book, up to Rev. 8:1 (107, 108), and again in Rev. 12:1-9 (119). The text in between these passages Lawrence sees primarily to be the work of Jewish apocalyptic thinking, 'the curious distortion of paganism through the Jewish moral and cataclysmic vision' (108). The second part of the book, after the episode of the woman and the dragon, is 'all moral', 'all sin and salvation', the work of John of Patmos' weak Christian apocalyptic thinking and of later Christian editors concerned with church orthodoxy (141), who represent the fall into individual thinking and the concept of God as a higher individual, the fall away from a living relationship with the cosmos. This is 'the Christianity of the middling masses', which Lawrence, who begins *Apocalypse* with an account of his own childhood experience of such Christianity, describes as 'hideous' (144). Taken as the whole text that remains to us, Lawrence concludes, the book of Revelation shows us 'what we are resisting', 'our connection with the cosmos, with mankind, with the nation, with the family'. These things are anathema in the final text and they are anathema to us today, who still live in a culture dominated by precisely the same second-rate, weak Christianity as that of John of Patmos. Nevertheless, 'by its very resistance', Revelation shows us 'the things that the human heart secretly yearns after', 'for the sun and the stars and the earth and the waters of the earth, for nobility and lordship and might, and scarlet and gold, splendour, for passionate love and a proper unison with men' (149). By 'the very frenzy' with which the extant text condemns these things, Lawrence argues, we see how much even the apocalyptic thinkers who re-wrote the pagan text celebrating them wanted them themselves.

In an early version of *Apocalypse*, Lawrence meditates on the concept of power raised by his reading of the book of Revelation. He argues that men and woman are dual creatures: 'man is a being of power, and then a being of love' (*A* 163). Power, however, is not necessarily mere force, but rather can be 'divine, like love', when it is 'in harmony with love' (165). This, Lawrence argues, is 'what Nietzsche meant' by power, a point Lawrence develops into a profession of belief of his own:

A Kosmokrator [ruler of the universe] there is, in spite of all our efforts at denial. There is a great and terrible Ruler of the cosmos, who gives forth life, and takes back life. The Kosmokrator gives us fresh life every day. But if we refuse the Almighty, the Ruler, we refuse the life. (166)

Lawrence identifies the Kosmokrator with the Unknown God, writing, 'My very soul tells me that if the Kosmokrator, the Unknown, at last gives me the kiss of acceptance, that is my happiness' (174). He restates the belief in natural religion he had articulated in *Psychoanalysis* and *Fantasia*, arguing that the soul by nature acknowledges the existence of God: 'From the far corner of the soul comes the confession: There is Almighty God' (175). It is self-evident, Lawrence believes, that the cosmos brought forth everything in itself, including me. There must therefore, he claims, be 'that in the cosmos which can bring forth all things, including mind and will and feeling', 'that in the universe which contains the potentiality of all things, known and unknown', and 'this terrific and frightening and delighted potency I call Almighty God' (175).

This belief in a ruler of the universe translates into a politics of natural or spiritual aristocracy. Long disillusioned in practice by dictatorships like those of Mussolini, Lawrence believes to the end of his life in the value of a spiritual aristocracy. Against all his sources, he praised such an institution among the Etruscans. As he puts it in this early version of *Apocalypse*, 'The most free, the most upstanding, the most dauntless men are happy, splendidly happy to accept the rule of a real man of power, who draws vitality from the cosmos' (167). The unknown God is a ruler of the cosmos, and those who draw most life from him are themselves by nature rulers. Those who draw life from him, but less so than the natural rulers of mankind, have enough such life to recognize and delight in the rule of those cosmic aristocrats. Furthermore, 'the common man wants to be consummated in the splendour and might of the rulers above him', and this is a 'primary, paramount need' in him (167). Secular dictators like Lenin and Napoleon, and socialists like Shelley, for Lawrence, take away this natural love of power, this natural sense of universal hierarchy, from the people they propose but ultimately fail to rule. As Lawrence puts it, 'one man cannot be truly glorious unless all men, according to their degree, are glorified' (167). There is no end, in his religious thinking, to Lawrence's leadership phase, but only a development of it from a vision of concrete political institutions into a vision of a purely natural hierarchy freely acknowledged by all.

'The Last Poems Notebook'

Critics often describe Lawrence's 'Last Poems Notebook' as his most religious work. Sandra Gilbert calls poems like 'The Ship of Death' and 'Shadows' the work of 'a religious poet', whose tone is 'absolutely authentic': 'Like Herbert, [Lawrence] speaks in his best religious verses . . . with a quiet assurance, faith that does not need to rely on the doctrinaire and even morbid melodrama that sometimes seems to characterise the writings of Eliot and even those of Donne' (*Acts* 315). Del Ivan Janik calls 'The Last Poems Notebook' 'a mature statement of religious belief' (309). Holly Laird writes that in the 'Notebook', as in *Sketches* and *Apocalypse*, Lawrence is 'preoccupied with his own religious preparation for death' (222). George Panichas calls the poems 'Lawrence's most fervent religious expression' (180). Earl Brewster recalls that in Lawrence's last months, 'he said to me, "I intend to find God: I wish to realize my relation with Him. I do not any longer object to the word God. My attitude regarding this has changed. I must establish a conscious relation with God"' (224). It is certainly the case that Lawrence uses the word 'God' much more widely in 'The Last Poems Notebook' than in any other of his works. It is also the case that his religious views have developed in these poems, as they have been developing throughout his life. Nevertheless, 'The Last Poems Notebook' is only more explicitly religious than Lawrence's earlier works. The 'Notebook' makes explicit with its use of the words 'God', 'god' and 'gods' what has in fact been the case throughout Lawrence's work, from the 'Foreword to *Sons and Lovers*' on, that the ultimate concern of that work has been religious. If there is any change of the kind that Brewster recalls Lawrence speaking of in his thinking and writing in 'The Last Poems Notebook', it is in his new willingness to use the word 'God', with its previously inadmissible connotations of Christian tradition. With respect to the content of his work, Lawrence's religious quest remains where it had always been, at the heart of his writing.

   In the autumn of 1929, Lawrence was reading Dean Inge's essays on Plotinus and Gilbert Murray's *Five Stages of Greek Religion* (Brewster 305). Achsah Brewster recalls, 'He was annoyed with Murray for teaching that civilization keeps evolving into something better. The old gods were as important to Lawrence as the new, different but not inferior' (305). Despite Lawrence's rejection of Murray's evolutionary view of religious history, he nevertheless incorporates much that he learnt from his book into 'The Last Poems Notebook'. The first group of poems look back nostalgically to the time of the Greek gods and heroes. Lawrence represents it as a kind of golden age, as a time in which men and women lived with, indeed as, gods. The Mediterranean of the present is inhabited only by 'coffee', 'pain grillé' and 'the smoking / ships of the P. & O. and the Orient Line' (*P* 601–2). But the speakers of Lawrence's poems can still see 'Odysseus' ships' and the 'slim black ship of Dionysos come sailing in / with grape-vines up the mast' (601–2):

And the Minoan gods, and the gods of Tiryns
are heard softly laughing and chatting, as ever;
and Dionysos, young and a stranger
leans glistening on the gate, in all respect. (602)

Lawrence read in Murray of the piety of Julian the Apostate and of Sallustius, whose Neoplatonic account of Greek theology Murray translates at the end of his book. The Greek myths 'are all expressions of God and of the goodness of God', for such thinkers, stating in the form of mystery and allegory 'the one tremendous fact that the Gods *are*' (222). Lawrence has no interest in Neoplatonic allegory, but the many references to pious forms of worship of the Greek pantheon in Murray's book constitute the background of his vision in the first group of poems in the 'Notebook', of the value of a time in which the gods dwelt with men. For Lawrence, this is a vision of the good life, a life lived with Dionysos, Hermes and the other Olympians, and it remains a possibility, for those, like the poet, who know how to see the gods today.

The fourth poem in 'The Last Poems Notebook', 'For the heroes are dipped in Scarlet', compares the vibrant living, the rejoicing in their physical life, of the poet's idea of the early Greeks to divinity. 'The thing that is done without the glowing as of god, vermilion, / were best not done at all' (603). Lawrence picks up in the form of a simile what he had directly stated in the previous poem, that the gods can be seen, today as in Greek antiquity, in men. Lawrence learnt from Burnet and from

Murray that, in early Greek thinking, the word *theos* had a much wider range of meanings than those it took on in Christianity. Murray writes:

> τὸ εὐτυχεῖν, 'the fact of success', is 'a god and more than a god'; τὸ γιγνώσκειν φίλους, 'the thrill of recognising a friend after long absence is a 'god'; wine is a 'god' whose body is poured out in libation to the gods; and in the unwritten law of the human conscience 'a great god liveth and groweth not old' (27).

In 'The Last Poems Notebook', Lawrence uses poetry as a form of language that revives a pre-Socratic simplicity, a language that reaches back beyond the oppositions of Platonic metaphysics. So in his poems on the presence of the gods among men, he is able, as Homer and as the early Greeks both of Burnet and Murray were able to do, to speak in a language that does not need dualistic concepts like incarnation or manifestation with which to understand this presence. In poems like 'Middle of the World', the god Dionysos is not incarnate, not manifest in the young stranger leaning on the gate (602); the young stranger simply is Dionysos.

Having said this, it may be that Dionysos himself represents, in 'The Last Poems Notebook', as for Sallustius or Plutarch, about whom Lawrence is reading in Murray, the one unknowable God, as all gods do. Murray writes that 'Plutarch explains in his beautiful way that all religions are really attempts towards the same goal' (171). Even in the second stage of Greek religion, before the Olympian gods are allegorized by Neoplatonic philosophers, Murray writes, the Greek gods are 'artists' dreams, ideals, allegories; they are symbols of something beyond themselves' (99). He concludes his account of Olympian religion in this passage, which deeply informs the theology of 'The Last Poems Notebook':

> In Religion, however precious you may consider the truth you draw from it, you know that it is a truth seen dimly, and possibly seen by others better than by you. You know that all your creeds and definitions are merely metaphors, attempts to use human language for a purpose for which it was never made. Your concepts are, by the nature of things, inadequate . . . Something like this, I take it, was the character of the Olympian Religion in the higher minds of

later Greece. Its gods could awaken man's worship and strengthen his higher aspirations; but at heart they knew themselves to be only metaphors. As the most beautiful image carved by man was not the god, but only a symbol to help towards conceiving the god; so the god himself, when conceived, was not the reality but only a symbol to help towards conceiving the reality. (100–1)

In the 'Notebook' poems in which the Greek gods appear among men and women, especially when those poems are understood in the context of the 'Notebook' as a whole, it is in the sense described by Murray. The poems depict an ideal life in which the gods genuinely appear to men and women, and in which even those gods, our best way of understanding the incomprehensible God, represent that supreme unknown reality itself. In a footnote to the passage quoted above, Murray cites from 'the beautiful defence of idols' by Maximus of Tyre, whose name appears in the titles of two of the 'Notebook' poems in which the Greek gods appear. Maximus wrote:

God himself, the father and fashioner of all that is, older than the Sun or the Sky, greater than time and eternity and all the flow of being, is unnameable by any lawgiver, unutterable by any voice, not to be seen by any eye. But we, being unable to apprehend his essence, use the help of sounds and names and pictures, of beaten gold and ivory and silver, of plants and rivers, mountain-peaks and torrents, yearning for the knowledge of him. (Murray 100)

Shortly after having read this, Lawrence wrote 'Maximus'. The poem begins:

God is older than the sun and moon
and the eye cannot behold him
nor voice describe him. (P 606)

Just as Maximus himself had written, God is, for the speaker of Lawrence's poem, unknowable and unnameable. On the other hand, in the second stanza of the poem, 'a naked man, a stranger' leans on the speaker's gate, is invited in, and sits down by his hearth. He does not at first say his name, but 'such a loveliness / entered me, I smiled to myself, saying: He is God! / So he said: *Hermes!*'. The final stanza of the poem repeats the first three lines on God's incomprehensibility, quoted above, and adds, 'and still, this is the god Hermes, sitting by my hearth' (606). Precisely the same contradiction is experienced in the following poem, 'The Man of Tyre', in which the man of Tyre, walking down to the sea, was 'pondering, for he was Greek, that God is one and all alone and ever more shall be so' (606). But when he sees a naked woman washing herself in the twilight, her 'dim blotch of black maidenhair' is 'like an indicator / giving a message to' him (607). He concludes, 'Lo! God is one god! But here in the twilight / godly and lovely comes Aphrodite out of the sea' (607). In both cases, the speakers of the poems live in a dialectic very like that which Maximus of Tyre himself describes. God is unknowable in himself, but we know him by analogy with created things. For Lawrence, in these two poems, it is above all in human beings, particularly in naked human beings, that we see him. In human beings in their naked beauty, one sees the gods, in these poems on the Greek gods; in the gods, the other 'Notebook' poems on God suggest, one sees God. Lawrence's religion in these poems is what Murray calls Olympian, or at least that of 'the higher minds' Murray posits among the society that worshipped the Olympians. The good life is a life lived with the gods, who appear, above all as human beings, particularly as lovely human beings, in the world, and who themselves are only our best way of representing to ourselves the unrepresentable, unknown God.

The next theme in 'The Last Poems Notebook' is introduced by 'Demiurge'. In *The Philosophy of Plotinus*, which Lawrence is reading while writing the poems, Inge gives an account of the concept of the Demiurge at work in Plotinus' predecessors:

Numenius . . . separated the 'second God' – the Demiurge or Creator, from the Supreme Being, thereby gathering together the crowd of inferior gods, to whom Platonism entrusted the part of administering the universe, into one divine Being . . . The second God, though all his divine qualities are derived from the First Principle, is the active power for good in the world. The 'First God' is concerned only with the spiritual world (τὰ νοητά); the Second with the spiritual and phenomenal both. (94)

In the sequence of five poems from 'Demiurge' to 'The Body of God', originally one long poem entitled 'Demiurge', Lawrence makes use of the pun on the word 'urge' within (and etymologically unrelated to) the word 'Demiurge', which he only makes explicit in the fifth poem. These poems meditate on God and the physical, for which Numenius' Demiurge was responsible, and they conceive of God as a divine 'urge'.

In the first poem, the speaker rejects the Platonic ideas that 'reality exists only in the spirit' and that 'the idea of the form precedes the form substantial' (603). 'What nonsense it is!' he cries, 'as if any Mind could have imagined a lobster / dozing in the under-deeps, then reaching out a savage and iron claw!' Lawrence overturns the Neoplatonic ideas he is reading about in Inge's book:

Even the mind of God can only imagine
those things that have become themselves:
bodies and presences (603)

like the lobster. The 'God' spoken of in this poem is very much a 'second' God, of the kind Lawrence had been reading about in Inge, although in a revisionary sense. Whereas Numenius' Demiurge was subordinate to a 'First God', the Supreme Being, Lawrence's 'God' is subordinate to physical being, to 'creatures with a foothold in creation'. Lawrence turns his reading about the Demiurge as a Second God concerned 'with the spiritual and the phenomenal both' into a metaphysic in which the only God there is is subordinate to the prior and more fundamental reality of physical being. This is true religion, Lawrence had written in the first draft of the poem:

Religion knows better than philosophy
Religion knows that Jesus was never Jesus
till he was born from a womb, and ate soup and bread
and grew up, and became, in the wonder of creation, Jesus,
with a body and with needs, and a lovely spirit. (1270)

'Philosophy' here includes, of course, Platonism and Neoplatonism, but also Christianity, at least as the speaker sees it to be expounded and practised. It is one of those Platonic discourses that privileges spiritual over physical being. The object of true 'religion', on the contrary, is both physical and spiritual in nature. The poem leaves space for the Lawrentian Unknown. But what can be known, it says, is that, whatever Gods we know, including the God of Christianity, are not only spiritual, but also physical. With Christian tradition in our cultural background, we are used to describing such Gods with a small 'g': 'gods'. But Lawrence insists in 'Demiurge', as Madame Blavatsky had done, that the 'God' worshipped by Christians is just one more such god. In Inge Lawrence read about the Neopythagoreans, who spoke of 'a plurality of gods beneath the Godhead' (i, 84). For Lawrence, the God of the Bible is precisely one such god.

In the next poem of the series, 'The work of Creation', Lawrence develops the concept of 'urge' that he finds and likes in the word 'Demiurge'. Etymologically, the word means a public or skilled worker, from the Greek *dēmios*, of the people, and *-ergos*, -working or worker. In this poem, Lawrence again rejects any Platonic concept of God, in whose mind the ideas of things would exist before he (or a demiurge) brings them into being. 'The mystery of creation is the divine urge of creation, / but it is a great, strange urge, it is not a Mind' (603). Lawrence revises the traditional comparison of divine creation to that of an artist, writing that, just as with a human artist, God does not think out his creations in advance, but rather is possessed by a 'strange ache', and 'out of the struggle with his material, in the spell of the urge / his work took place' (604). Once again, the poem leaves space for a greater unknown thing than that which Christians have called 'God', but this is the way the god they have called God in fact creates, according to this poem. It is not with pure spirit or pure will or a pure word, but rather with desire, inarticulate like that of the desire of bodily creatures like human beings. Lawrence's demiurge does not create the world mentally, but with the urge, the desire, by which he is above all characterized. As Lawrence puts it in 'Red Geranium and Godly Mignonette', God created by 'sighing and yearning with tremendous creative yearning . . . / oh for some other beauty' (604).

In 'The Body of God', Lawrence develops this account of his demiurge still further, writing, 'God is the great urge that has not yet found a body / but urges towards incarnation' (605). The god he calls God, the demiurge, does not have a body until his creative urge is fulfilled in the creation of bodies, in which he is incarnate or 'made manifest' (605).

When this divine urge to create physical beings is fulfilled, then that physical creature 'is god', according to this poem. Hence:

> There is no god
> apart from poppies and the flying fish,
> men singing songs, and women brushing their hair in the sun. (605)

God exists, as far as we can know, entirely in the things he has created, or, to put it another way, the things he has fulfilled his creative urge towards incarnation by becoming. Nevertheless, Lawrence adds, at the end of the poem, 'The rest, the undiscoverable, is the demi-urge' (605). This line seems to mean that there remains something else that is unknown and unknowable in addition to the God who is known only in the things he has come into being by creating. Lawrence is continuing to reserve, after the manner of the Neoplatonists he is reading about, an Unknown, a First God, about whom nothing can be said or known once one has known all one can about the second God. This, I take it, is what Lawrence means with his punning phrase the 'demi-urge', that which exists less than all than one can know of God, since it is the cause of existence and cannot therefore 'exist' itself, at least in the sense that the things of the created world exist.

As the sequence of 'The Last Poems Notebook' continues, an increasingly existential note arises. The poems become less theological and more religious, in the sense that the speakers' relationship to God, rather than the nature of God, becomes what matters in them. The first series in which this is the case is that of the four poems beginning with 'The Hands of God'. Lawrence begins the poem with the Biblical text, 'It is a fearful thing to fall into the hands of the living God' (Heb. 10:31), and adds, in the second line, 'But it is a much more fearful thing to fall out of them' (613). In a newly direct manner, Lawrence uses the traditional Christian word 'God', without looking to move beyond its connotations, in order to express what he has been articulating since *The Rainbow*, that the good life is one lived in relationship to, for want of a better word, God. In this series of poems, Lawrence ceases to look for a better word, and speaks directly of relationship to God as his primary concern. 'Let me never know myself apart from the living God' (614). The poems set up an account of the fall that is somewhat revised but that in this case remains close to the traditional Christian doctrine. 'Falling' in 'The Hands of God', consists in 'falling into the ungodly knowledge / of myself as I am without God'. It is knowing oneself without God, rather than being 'at one with the living God' (614), that constitutes evil in these poems. This is described in language very close to traditional Christian language: to live without God is to live in 'the abyss', in 'endless undoing', to which 'there is no bottom' (614, 616). The language Lawrence uses for living with God is equally traditional. 'Pax' begins, 'All that matters is to be at one with the living God / to be a creature in the house of the God of Life', echoing Psalm 84:10 as well as Hebrews 10:31. The calm deriving from the sense of submission to God, expressed in the poem's final stanza, is also traditional, both with respect to its Biblical imagery and its spiritual topography:

> feeling the presence of the living God . . .
> a deep calm in the heart
> a presence
> as of the master sitting at the board
> in his own and greater being,
> in the house of life. (614)

In an unusually direct way, Lawrence articulates a belief in the supreme value of relationship to God in life, using in a way that is only just revisionary the traditional language of the Bible and of Christian spirituality.

In the last series of poems, the poet is preparing himself for death. The series begins with 'The Ship of Death', in which the poet recognizes that it is time 'to bid farewell / to one's own self, and find an exit / from the fallen self' (630). The series begins, that is, with a continuing commitment to the ethics of the earlier series, in which living in oneself alone, without God, is to have fallen from what life could and should be with God. The kind of peace Lawrence had spoken of in 'Pax' now comes from having built one's ship of death. This is true of everyone, the poet affirms, not only of those facing imminent death. 'We are all of us dying / . . . so all we can do / is now to be willing to die, and to build the ship / of death' (631). Building the ship of death, although it is not translated out of the imagery of the poem, means preparing rightly for death, the details of which are made no clearer than the description of the ship as a 'fragile ship of courage' and an 'ark of faith'. Courage and faith, in the face of human fragility, are the ways in which the poet recommends both to himself and to others to face death.

Keith Sagar poses the question, 'Did Lawrence literally believe that after death he would in some sense retain his humanity, manhood and identity?' and answers, 'He could only discover what he truly believed by giving his whole attention to whatever images of death life brought him' (*Poet* 134). Lawrence's vision, that is, of what occurs after death is essentially a work of his imagination. Sandra Gilbert too writes that Lawrence 'attempts imaginatively to penetrate beyond that dark barrier' of death (*Acts* 295), that he is imagining, where he is unable to know or even believe, what may be after death. The nature of the experience spoken of in stanzas IX and X of 'The Ship of Death' is deliberately unclear, indeed necessarily so. It may be that there is a 'dawn' (633) after the 'dark' (632) into which the ship of death sails, it may be that there is a 'coming back to life' after 'oblivion' (633). But the nature thereof is and can be couched only in poetic imagery. What does it mean to say 'the whole thing starts again' or that the 'soul steps out, into her house again' (633)? The mode of the stanzas is somewhere between faith and imagination, and partakes of both. There is nothing so strong as an affirmation of faith in an after-life here, yet the poet who, as Gilbert says, is imagining what might be after death, is imagining in such a personally involved way as to approximate a kind of faith. It may be, these poems say, that there is a new dawn, a new life after death, and they say no more than that. Lawrence had quoted from *Hamlet* in 'The Ship of Death', and he plays with Shakespeare's analogy between death and sleep in 'Sleep and waking' (638–9). If death, as Hamlet had speculated, is like nothing so much as sleep, then it may be that there is a waking from it, as there is from sleep. It may be; these poems know or ask for no more.

Lawrence has believed since the war in a dark God, absolutely unknowable to us. The last of the 'Notebook' poems are his final way of affirming this belief. The key concept of these poems is that of 'oblivion'. In 'Forget', Lawrence writes of 'god who dwells in deep oblivion', and that 'Only in sheer oblivion are we with God' (639). Lawrence's thinking about the darkness of God culminates in the oblivion in which God dwells in the last poems of the 'Notebook' and in which, in death, one meets him. This divine oblivion is a source of great consolation to the poet, who is facing death with precisely the courage and faith he had said was necessary in 'The Ship of Death'. In 'Song of Death', Lawrence writes that the soul, in death,

> . . . enters fold after fold of deepening darkness
> for the cosmos even in death is like a dark whorled shell
> whose whorls fold round to the core of soundless silence
> and pivotal oblivion
> where the soul comes at last, and has utter peace. (637)

The oblivion of death, in which alone one meets God, who cannot be known in this life, is an experience of peace, the poet believes. As the image of the whorled shell suggests, it is a natural experience, and therefore a good one. As Lawrence writes at the beginning of the poem, 'without the song of death, the song of life / becomes pointless and silly' (637). Death, that is, is an integral part of life. Gilbert writes of 'Bavarian Gentians' that 'insofar as the dead man is *en soi*, he has a paradoxical fullness of being the living can never have' (*Acts* 296). This is not the case in 'Song of Death'. There, death is not a fullness of being but rather a natural and integral part of life, which whole constitutes a fullness in itself, and which the poet can contemplate with a deep sense of peace.

The circular images in this and subsequent poems suggest that the wheel, which symbolized evil in earlier poems, is a kind of fallen version of the true centre of human life, the central silence of God, around which the world moves. In 'What then is Evil?' the wheel is dialectically related to 'the soul of man, when it pivots upon the ego' (626), which is the essence of evil. In 'Song of Death', by contrast, death takes us to 'pivotal oblivion' (637), which is where the poet finds the peace of being without himself in God. In the next poem, 'The End, The Beginning', silence and oblivion are 'at the core of everything', such that 'the very sun himself is pivoted / upon a core of oblivion' (637). There are two circular structures at work in 'The Last Poems Notebook', the circle of consciousness and the circle of unconsciousness. The centre of the former is the ego, living by which constitutes a fall away from the God who is the centre of the latter, travelling towards which constitutes pure peace. It is the last place in which Lawrence finds what he has been writing about since *The Rainbow*, being 'consummated' (639).

Bibliography

Adorno, Rolena. *The Polemics of Possession in Spanish American Narrative*. New Haven, CT: Yale University Press, 2007.
—. 'Bernal Díaz del Castillo: Soldier, Eyewitness, Polemicist'. Bernal Díaz del Castillo, *The History of the Conquest of New Spain*. Ed. Davíd Carrasco. Albuquerque: University of New Mexico Press, 2008, pp. 389–98.
Balbert, Peter. 'Snake's Eye and Obsidian Knife: Art, Ideology and "The Woman Who Rode Away"'. *D. H. Lawrence Review* 18 (1985–86): 255–73.
Bandelier, Adolf. *The Delight Makers*. 2nd edn. New York: Dodd, Mead and Company, 1916.
Bell, Michael. *D. H. Lawrence: Language and Being*. Cambridge and New York: Cambridge University Press, 1992.
Berrin, Kathleen and Esther Pasztory. *Teotihuacan: Art from the City of the Gods*. New York: Thames and Hudson, 1993.
Black, Michael. *D. H. Lawrence: The Early Philosophical Works: A Commentary*. Cambridge and New York: Cambridge University Press, 1992.
Blavatsky, Helena P. *The Secret Doctrine: The Synthesis of Science, Religion and Philosophy*. 2 vols. Pasadena: Theosophical University Press [1888], 1952.
Booth, Howard J. 'Lawrence in Doubt: A Theory of the "Other" and Its Collapse'. *Modernism and Empire*. Eds. Howard J. Booth and Nigel Rigby. Manchester: Manchester University Press, 2000, pp. 197–223.
Brault, Élise. 'Frictional Encounters: D. H. Lawrence and Native Americans'. *Études britanniques contemporaines* 37 (2009): 41–56.
Brett, Dorothy. *Lawrence and Brett: A Friendship*. Santa Fe: Sunstone Press, 2006.
Brewster, Earl and Achsah, ed. *D. H. Lawrence: Reminiscences and Correspondence*. London: Secker, 1934.
Bricout, Shirley. *L'itinéraire d'un prophète en fuite, ou, Le texte biblique et la réflexion politique dans* Aaron's Rod, Kangaroo *et* The Plumed Serpent *de D. H. Lawrence*. Montpellier: Presses Universitaires de la Méditerranée, 2008.

—. 'From Babel to Eden: D. H. Lawrence's Quest Abroad'. *Études britanniques contemporaines* 37 (2009): 27–39.

Brown, Keith. 'Welsh Red Indians: D. H. Lawrence and *St. Mawr*'. *Essays in Criticism* 32 (1982): 158–79.

Burack, Charles Michael. *D. H. Lawrence's Language of Sacred Experience: The Transfiguration of the Reader*. Basingstoke and New York: Palgrave Macmillan, 2005.

Burnet, John. *Early Greek Philosophy*. 2nd edn. London: A. & C. Black, 1908.

—. *Early Greek Philosophy*. 3rd edn. London: A. & C. Black, 1920.

Bynner, Witter. *Journey with Genius: Recollections and Reflections concerning the D. H. Lawrences*. New York: The John Day Company, 1951.

Carpenter, Rebecca. '"Bottom-Dog Insolence" and "The Harem Mentality": Race and Gender in The Plumed Serpent'. *D. H. Lawrence Review* 25 (1993–94): 119–29.

Carter, Frederick. *The Dragon of the Alchemists*. London: Elkin Matthews, 1926.

—. *D. H. Lawrence and the Body Mystical*. London: Denis Archer, 1932.

Chambers, Jessie [E. T.]. *D. H. Lawrence: A Personal Record, by E. T.* Cambridge and New York: Cambridge University Press [1935], 1980.

Charles, R. H. *The Revelation of St. John*. 2 vols. Edinburgh: T. & T. Clark, 1920.

Clark, L. D. *Dark Night of the Body: D. H. Lawrence's* The Plumed Serpent. Austin: University of Texas Press, 1964.

—. 'D. H. Lawrence and the American Indian'. *D. H. Lawrence Review* 9 (1976): 305–72.

—. *The Minoan Distance: The Symbolism of Travel in D. H. Lawrence*. Tucson: University of Arizona Press, 1980.

Cobau, William W. 'A View from Eastwood: Conversations with Mrs. O. L. Hopkin'. *D. H. Lawrence Review* 9 (1976): 126–36.

Contreras, Sheila. '"They Were Just Natives to Her": Chilchui Indians and "The Woman Who Rode Away"'. *D. H. Lawrence Review* 25 (1993–94): 91–107.

Courlander, Harold. *The Fourth World of the Hopis: The Epic Story of the Hopi Indians as Preserved in Their Legends and Traditions*. Albuquerque: University of New Mexico Press, 1971.

Cowan, James. *D. H. Lawrence's American Journey: A Study in Literature and Myth*. Cleveland and London: The Press of the Case Western Reserve University, 1970.

Crunfli, Edina Pereira. 'Representing the "Primitive" in Mexico: Lawrence's Endeavor in The Plumed Serpent. *'Terra Incognita': D. H. Lawrence at the Frontiers*. Eds. Virginia Crosswhite Hyde and Earl G. Ingersoll. Madison and Teaneck, NJ: Fairleigh Dickinson University Press, 2010, pp. 56–71.

Cushman, Keith. 'Indians, an Englishman, and an Englishwoman: Lawrence's and Dorothy Brett's Representations of Indian Ceremonial Dancing'. *'Terra Incognita': D. H. Lawrence at the Frontiers*. Eds. Virginia Crosswhite Hyde and Earl G. Ingersoll. Madison and Teaneck, NJ: Fairleigh Dickinson University Press, 2010, pp. 112–30.

Delavenay, Emile. *D. H. Lawrence and Edward Carpenter: A Study in Edwardian Transition*. London: Heinemann, 1971.

—. *D. H. Lawrence: The Man and His Work. The Formative Years: 1885–1919*. trans. Katherine M. Delavenay. London: Heinemann, 1972.

Dennis, George. *The Cities and Cemeteries of Etruria*. 2 vols. London: J. M. Dent, 1907.

Díaz del Castillo, Bernal. *The History of the Conquest of New Spain*. Ed. David Carrasco. Albuquerque: University of New Mexico Press, 2008.

Dix, Carol. *D. H. Lawrence and Women*. Totowa, NJ: Rowman and Littlefield, 1980.

Doherty, Gerald. 'Connie and the Chakras: Yogic Patterns in D. H. Lawrence's *Lady Chatterley's Lover*', *D. H. Lawrence Review* 13 (1980): 79–93.

—. 'The Salvator Mundi Touch: Messianic Typology in D. H. Lawrence's "Women in Love"'. *Ariel* 13 (1982): 53–71.

—. 'The Darkest Source: D. H. Lawrence, Tantric Yoga, and "Women in Love"'. *Essays in Literature* 11 (1984): 211–22.

—. *Oriental Lawrence: The Quest for the Secrets of Sex*. New York and Oxford: Peter Lang, 2001.

Durkheim, Émile. *The Elementary Forms of Religious Life*, trans. Carol Cosman. Oxford and New York: Oxford University Press [1912], 2001.

Eggert, Paul. 'Comedy and Provisionality: Lawrence's Address to His Audience and Material in His Australian Novels'. *Lawrence and Comedy*. Eds. Paul Eggert and John Worthen. Cambridge and New York: Cambridge University Press, 1996, pp. 131–57.

Eliade, Mircea. *The Sacred and the Profane: The Nature of Religion*, trans. Willard R. Trask. Orlando and London: Harcourt [1957], 1959.

Ellis, David. *D. H. Lawrence: Dying Game: 1922–1930*. Cambridge and New York: Cambridge University Press, 1998.

Fell, R. A. L. *Etruria and Rome*. Cambridge: Cambridge University Press, 1924.

Fernihough, Anne. *D. H. Lawrence: Aesthetics and Ideology*. Oxford and New York: Clarendon Press, 1993.

Fewkes, Jesse Walter. *Hopi Snake Ceremonies: An Eyewitness Account by Jesse Walter Fewkes. Selections from Bureau of American Ethnology Annual Reports Nos. 16 and 19 for the Years 1894–95 and*

1897–98. Albuquerque, NM: Avanyu Publishing, Inc. [1897, 1900], 2000.

Filippis, Simonetta de. '"Is There a Great Secret? D. H. Lawrence and the Etruscans'. *D. H. Lawrence: Critical Assessments*. Eds. David Ellis and Ornella de Zordo, Vol. IV. Mountfield, East Sussex: Helm Information, 1992, pp. 131–44.

Fjågesund, Peter. *The Apocalyptic World of D. H. Lawrence*. Oslo: Norwegian University Press, 1991.

Frazer, Sir James George. *The Golden Bough: A Study in Magic and Religion. A New Abridgement from the Second and Third Editions*. Ed. Robert Fraser. Oxford and New York: Oxford University Press, 1994.

—. *The Golden Bough: A Study in Magic and Religion*. Abridged edn. New York: Macmillan, 1922.

Gellhaus, V. 'Maurus of Subiaco, St.' *New Catholic Encyclopedia*. Eds. Berard L. Marthaler et al. 2nd edn. Vol. 9. Detroit, MI: Gale, 2003, p. 375.

Gilbert, Sandra M. *Acts of Attention: The Poems of D. H. Lawrence*. 2nd edn. Carbondale and Edwardsville: Southern Illinois University Press, 1990.

—. 'D. H. Lawrence's Mexican Hat Dance: Rereading The Plumed Serpent'. *Rereading Texts, Rethinking Critical Presuppositions: Essays in Honour of H. M. Daleski*. Eds. Shlomith Rimmon-Kenan, Leona Toker and Shuli Barzilai. Frankfurt and New York: Peter Lang, 1997, pp. 291–304.

—. 'Some Notes toward a Vindication of the Rites of D. H. Lawrence'. *Approaches to Teaching the Works of D. H. Lawrence*. Eds. M. Elizabeth Sargent and Garry Watson. New York: The Modern Language Association of America, 2001, pp. 41–7.

Griffin, Roger, ed. *Fascism*. Oxford and New York: Oxford University Press, 1995.

Grandsen, K. W. 'Rananim: D. H. Lawrence's Letters to S. S. Koteliansky'. *Twentieth Century* 159 (1955): 22–32.

Harris, Janice J. 'The Many Faces of Lazarus: *The Man Who Died* and Its Context'. *D. H. Lawrence Review* 16 (1983): 291–311.

Harrison, Jane. *Ancient Art and Ritual*. London: Thornton Butterworth, 1913.

Hinz, Evelyn J. and John J. Teunissen. 'Savior and Cock: Allusion and Icon in Lawrence's *The Man Who Died*'. *Journal of Modern Literature* 5 (1976): 279–96.

Hyde, Virginia. *The Risen Adam: D. H. Lawrence's Revisionist Typology*. University Park, PA: Pennsylvania State University Press, 1992.

—. 'Kate and the Goddess: Subtexts in *The Plumed Serpent*'. *D. H. Lawrence Review* 26 (1995–96): 249–74.

—. 'Picking Up "Life-Threads" in Lawrence's Mexico: Dialogism and Multiculturalism in the Plumed Serpent'. *Approaches to Teaching the Works of D. H. Lawrence*. Eds. M. Elizabeth Sargent and Garry Watson. New York: The Modern Language Association of America, 2001, pp. 172–82.

—. 'Mexican Cypresses: Multiculturalism in Lawrence's "Novel of America"'. *D. H. Lawrence: New Worlds*. Eds. Keith Cushman and Earl G. Ingersoll. Madison and Teaneck, NJ: Fairleigh Dickinson University Press and London: Associated University Presses, 2003, pp. 195–215.

Hyde, Virginia and L. D. Clark. 'The Sense of an Ending in *The Plumed Serpent*'. *D. H. Lawrence Review* 25 (1993–94): 140–8.

Iida, Takeo. 'On a Topos Called the Sun Shining at Midnight in D. H. Lawrence's Poetry'. *D. H. Lawrence Review* 15 (1982): 271–90.

Inge, William Ralph. *The Philosophy of Plotinus*. 3rd edn. 2 vols. London and New York: Longmans, Green and Co., 1929.

James, Eric. *A Life of Bishop John A. T. Robinson: Scholar, Pastor, Prophet*. Grand Rapids, MI: William B. Eerdmans, 1987.

James, William. *The Varieties of Religious Experience: A Study in Human Nature*. London and New York: Penguin [1902], 1982.

Janik, Del Ivan. 'D. H. Lawrence's "Future Religion": The Unity of *Last Poems*'. *The Critical Response to D. H. Lawrence*. Ed. Jan Pilditch. Westport, CT and London: Greenwood Press, 2001.

Jarrett-Kerr, Martin. *D. H. Lawrence and Human Existence*. 2nd edn. London: SCM Press, 1961.

—. 'The Demise of Father Tiverton'. *D. H. Lawrence Review* 20 (1988): 61–3.

Jenner, Kathleen [Mrs Henry Jenner]. *Christian Symbolism*. London: Methuen, 1910.

Jones, Bethan. *The Last Poems of D. H. Lawrence: Shaping a Late Style*. Farnham and Burlington, VT: Ashgate, 2010.

Kalnins, Mara. 'Symbolic Seeing: Lawrence and Heraclitus'. *D. H. Lawrence: Centenary Essays*. Ed. Mara Kalnins. Bristol: Bristol Classical Press, 1986, pp. 173–90.

Kermode, Frank. 'Lawrence and the Apocalyptic Types'. *Critical Quarterly* 10 (1968): 14–38.

Kinkead-Weekes, Mark. 'The Gringo Señora who Rode Away'. *D. H. Lawrence Review* 22 (1990): 251–65.

—. *D. H. Lawrence: Triumph to Exile: 1912-1922*. Cambridge and New York: Cambridge University Press, 1996.

Kondo, Kyoko Kay. 'The Influence of Eastern Initiatory Rites in *Women in Love*'. *Études lawrenciennes* 38 (2008): 63-73.

Krockel, Carl. *D. H. Lawrence and Germany: The Politics of Influence*. Amsterdam and New York: Rodopi, 2007.

Lawrence, Frieda. 'Not I, But the Wind . . .'. New York: Viking Press, 1934.
Laird, Holly A. Self and Sequence: The Poetry of D. H. Lawrence.
    Charlottesville: University Press of Virginia, 1988.
Leavis, F. R. 'Mr. Eliot and Lawrence'. Scrutiny XVIII (1951): 66–73.
LeDoux, Larry V. 'Christ and Isis: The Function of the Dying and Reviving
    God in The Man Who Died'. D. H. Lawrence Review 5 (1972): 132–47.
Lockwood, M. J. A Study of the Poems of D. H. Lawrence: Thinking in
    Poetry. New York: St Martin's Press, 1987.
Loftin, John. Religion and Hopi Life. 2nd edn. Bloomington: University of
    Indiana Press, 2003.
Loisy, Alfred. L'apocalypse de Jean. Paris: Émile Nourry, 1923.
Luhan, Mabel Dodge. Lorenzo in Taos. New York: Alfred A. Knopf, 1932.
MacLeod, Sheila. Lawrence's Men and Women. London: William
    Heinemann, Ltd., 1985.
Magnus, Maurice. 'Holy Week at Monte Cassino'. Land and Water, 29
    April 1920: 14–15.
Marcus, Phillip. 'Lawrence, Yeats, and "The Resurrection of the Body"'.
    D. H. Lawrence: A Centenary Consideration. Eds. Peter Balbert and
    Phillip L. Marcus. Ithaca and London: Cornell University Press, 1985,
    pp. 210–36.
McCollum, Laurie. 'Ritual Sacrifice in "The Woman Who Rode Away"'.
    D. H. Lawrence: New Worlds. Eds. Keith Cushman and Earl G.
    Ingersoll. Madison and Teaneck, NJ: Fairleigh Dickinson University
    Press and London: Associated University Presses, 2003, pp. 230–42.
Mensch, Barbara. D. H. Lawrence and the Authoritarian Personality.
    New York: St. Martin's Press, 1991.
Mershman, Francis. 'St Maurus'. The Catholic Encyclopedia. Vol. 10.
    New York: Robert Appleton, 1911. 17 December 2011. < http://www.
    newadvent.org/cathen/10072a.htm > .
Michelucci, Stefania. 'D. H. Lawrence's Discovery of the Etruscans:
    A Pacific Challenge against Imperialism'. Moving the Borders. Eds.
    Marialuisa Bignami and Caroline Patey. Milan, Italy: Unicopli, 1996,
    pp. 374–81.
Miles, Thomas H. 'Birkin's Electro-Mystical Body of Reality: D. H.
    Lawrence's Use of Kundalini'. D. H. Lawrence Review 9 (1976):
    194–212.
Millett, Kate. Sexual Politics. London: Virago, 1970.
Montgomery, Robert. The Visionary D. H. Lawrence: Beyond Philosophy
    and Art. Cambridge and New York: Cambridge University Press, 1994.
Morgan, Philip. Fascism in Europe, 1919-1945. London and New York:
    Routledge, 2003.
Murray, Gilbert. Five Stages of Greek Religion. 2nd edn. Oxford: Oxford
    University Press, 1925.
Nehls, Edward, ed. D. H. Lawrence: A Composite Biography. 3 vols.
    Madison: University of Wisconsin Press, 1957–59.

Nixon, Cornelia. *Lawrence's Leadership Politics and the Turn against Women*. Berkeley and London: University of California Press, 1986.

Nuttall, Zelia. *The Fundamental Principles of Old and New World Civilizations*. Cambridge, MA: Peabody Museum of American Archaeology and Ethnology, 1901.

Odio, Arnold. 'D. H. Lawrence among the Mexicans'. *The Reception of D. H. Lawrence around the World*. Ed. Takeo Iida. Fukuoka: Kyushu University Press, 1999, pp. 165–92.

Oman, John. *Book of Revelation*. Cambridge: Cambridge University Press, 1923.

Otto, Rudolf. *The Idea of the Holy*, trans. John W. Harvey. Oxford and New York: Oxford University Press [1917], 1958.

Panichas, George A. *Adventure in Consciousness: The Meaning of D. H. Lawrence's Religious Quest*. The Hague and London: Mouton, 1964.

Parmenter, Ross. *Lawrence in Oaxaca: A Quest for the Novelist in Mexico*. Salt Lake City: Peregrine Smith Books, 1984.

Pasztory, Esther. *Teotihuacan: An Experiment in Living*. Norman and London: University of Oklahoma Press, 1997.

Pichardie, Jean-Paul. *D. H. Lawrence: la tentation utopique: de Rananim au Serpent à Plumes*. Rouen: Publications de l'université de Rouen, 1988.

Pitre, David. 'The Mystical Lawrence: Rupert Birkin's Taoist Quest'. *Studies in Mystical Literature* 3 (1983): 13–21.

Poplawski, Paul. *Promptings of Desire: Creativity and the Religious Impulse in the Works of D. H. Lawrence*. Westport, CT and London: Greenwood Press, 1993.

—. '*St. Mawr* and the Ironic Art of Realization'. *Writing the Body in D. H. Lawrence: Essays on Language, Representation, and Sexuality*. Ed. Paul Poplawski. Westport, CT and London: Greenwood Press, 2001, pp. 93–104.

Radford, Andrew. 'Strange Gods Beneath the Post-War Rubble in Kangaroo'. *D. H. Lawrence Review* 30 (2002): 51–65.

Reid, Robert. 'The Virtue of Faith'. *Eastwood and Kimberley Advertiser*. 26 July 1907: 2.

Roberts, Neil. *D. H. Lawrence, Travel and Cultural Difference*. Basingstoke and New York: Palgrave Macmillan, 2004.

Rolph, C. H., ed. *The Trial of Lady Chatterley: Regina v. Penguin Books Ltd.* London: Penguin, 1990.

Roodhouse, Mark. 'Lady Chatterley and the Monk: Anglican Radicals and the Lady Chatterley Trial of 1960', *Journal of Ecclesiastical History* 59 (2008): 475–500.

Rossman, Charles. 'D. H. Lawrence and Mexico'. *D. H. Lawrence: A Centenary Consideration*. Eds. Peter Balbert and Phillip L. Marcus. Ithaca and London: Cornell University Press, 1985, pp. 180–209.

Ruderman, Judith. *D. H. Lawrence and the Devouring Mother: The Search for a Patriarchal Ideal of Leadership.* Durham, NC: Duke University Press, 1984.

—. 'Lawrence as Ethnographer and Artist: Apprehending "Culture" in the American Southwest'. *'Terra Incognita': D. H. Lawrence at the Frontiers.* Eds. Virginia Crosswhite Hyde and Earl G. Ingersoll. Madison and Teaneck, NJ: Fairleigh Dickinson University Press, 2010, pp. 37–55.

Russell, Bertrand. *The Autobiography of Bertrand Russell.* 3 vols. Boston, MA: Little, Brown and Co., 1967–69.

—. *The Selected Letters of Bertrand Russell: The Public Years, 1914-1970.* Ed. Nicholas Griffin. London and New York: Routledge, 2001.

Sagar, Keith. *D. H. Lawrence: Life into Art.* Athens: The University of Georgia Press, 1985.

—. 'The Resurrection of Pan: Teaching Biocentric Consciousness and Deep Ecology in Lawrence's Poetry and Late Nonfiction'. *Approaches to Teaching the Works of D. H. Lawrence.* Eds. M. Elizabeth Sargent and Garry Watson. New York: The Modern Language Association of America, 2001, pp. 146–56.

—. *D. H. Lawrence: Poet.* Penrith: Humanities-Ebooks LLP, 2007.

Schapiro, Barbara. 'Sadomasochism as Intersubjective Breakdown in D. H. Lawrence's "The Woman Who Rode Away"'. *Psychoanalyses/Feminisms.* Eds. Peter Rudynytsky and Andrew Gordon. Albany: State University of New York Press, 2000, pp. 123–33.

Schneider, Daniel. *The Consciousness of D. H. Lawrence: An Intellectual Biography.* Lawrence, KS: University Press of Kansas, 1986.

Sheerin, Daniel. 'John Thomas and the King of Glory: Two Analogues to D. H. Lawrence's Use of Psalm 24:7 in Chapter XIV of *Lady Chatterley's Lover'*. *D. H. Lawrence Review* 11 (1978), 297–300.

Siegel, Carol. *Lawrence among the Women: Wavering Boundaries in Women's Literary Traditions.* Charlottesville and London: University Press of Virginia, 1991.

Simpson, Hilary. *D. H. Lawrence and Feminism.* DeKalb, IL: Northern Illinois University Press, 1980.

Smith, Bob L. 'D. H. Lawrence's *St. Mawr:* Transposition of Myth'. *Arizona Quarterly* 24 (1968): 197–208.

Smith, Jad. '*Völkisch* Organicism and the Use of Primitivism in Lawrence's *The Plumed Serpent'*. *D. H. Lawrence Review* 30 (2002): 7–24.

Snyder, Carey. '"When the Indian was in Vogue": D. H. Lawrence, Aldous Huxley, and Ethnological Tourism in the Southwest'. *Modern Fiction Studies* 53 (2007): 662–96.

Spencer, Herbert. *First Principles.* 6th edn. London: Watts and Co. [1900], 1945.

Steven, Laurence. '"The Woman Who Rode Away": D. H. Lawrence's Cul-de-Sac'. *English Studies in Canada* 10 (1984): 209–20.

Storch, Margaret. *Sons and Adversaries: Women in William Blake and D. H. Lawrence*. Knoxville: University of Tennessee Press, 1990.

—. '"But Not the America of the Whites": Lawrence's Pursuit of the True Primitive'. *D. H. Lawrence Review* 25 (1993–94): 48–62.

Talayesva, Don. *Sun Chief: The Autobiography of a Hopi Indian*. Ed. Leo Simmons. New Haven and London: Yale University Press, 1942.

Templeton, Wayne. '"Indians and an Englishman": Lawrence in the American Southwest'. *D. H. Lawrence Review* 25 (1993–94): 14–34.

Terry, T. Philip. *Terry's Guide to Mexico: The New Standard Guidebook to the Mexican Republic*. Rev. ed. Boston and New York: Houghton Mifflin Company, 1923.

Thompson, Theresa Mae. 'Unlearning Europe: Postcolonial Questions for Teaching *The Plumed Serpent*': *Approaches to Teaching the Works of D. H. Lawrence*. Eds. M. Elizabeth Sargent and Garry Watson. New York: The Modern Language Association of America, 2001: 221–5.

Tindall, William York. *D. H. Lawrence and Susan His Cow*. New York: Columbia University Press, 1939.

Torgovnick, Marianna. *Gone Primitive: Savage Intellects: Modern Lives*. Chicago and London: University of Chicago Press, 1990.

Tracy, Billy T. '"Reading up the Ancient Etruscans": Lawrence's Debt to George Dennis'. *Twentieth Century Literature* 23 (1977): 437–50.

Tylor, E. B. *Primitive Culture: Researches into the Development of Mythology, Philosophy, Religion, Language, Art, and Custom*. 6th edn. London: John Murray, 1920.

VanHoosier-Carey, Kimberly. 'Struggling with the Master: The Position of Kate and the Reader in Lawrence's "Quetzalcoatl" and *The Plumed Serpent*'. *D. H. Lawrence Review* 25 (1993–94): 104–18.

Whelan, P. T. *D. H. Lawrence: Myth and Metaphysic in* The Rainbow *and* Women in Love. Ann Arbor and London: UMI Research Press, 1984.

Wilding, Michael. *Political Fictions*. London and Boston: Routledge and Kegan Paul, 1980.

Wright, T. R. *D. H. Lawrence and the Bible*. Cambridge and New York: Cambridge University Press, 2000.

—. 'Holiness in the Modern World: Durkeim, Otto, Bataille and Lawrence'. *Transforming Holiness: Representations of Holiness in English and American Literary Texts*. Eds. Irene Visser and Helen Wilcox. Leuven and Dudley, MA: Peeters, 2006, pp. 161–79.

Zytaruk, George J. 'Rananim: D. H. Lawrence's Failed Utopia'. *The Spirit of D. H. Lawrence: Centenary Studies*. Eds. Gāmini Salgado and G. K. Das. Totowa, NJ: Barnes and Noble, 1988, pp. 266–94.

Index

Adam and Eve 126, 128
Adelphi 102–4, 110
animism 55–7, 59–61, 67
Apache, the 52, 54
apophatic discourse 9–10, 39,
   44, 78–9, 87, 103, 105
Asquith, Lady Cynthia 19–20
Aztecs, the 51, 53, 56, 68–9, 89,
   92, 94

Balbert, Peter 72, 90
Bandelier, Adolf 60–1, 63–4
Bell, Michael 124
Belt, Thomas 39
Bible, the 31–2, 91, 93, 103–4,
   123–6, 130, 133–4,
   153–5 *see also* Genesis;
   Revelation
Black, Michael 23
Blavatsky, Helena 27, 31–6,
   46, 48, 153 *see also*
   theosophy
Brett, Dorothy 55, 69, 92
Brewster, Achsah 305
Brewster, Earl 30, 51, 131, 147
Brown, Keith 78
Burack, Charles 47
Bynner, Witter 53
Burnet, John 17–23, 25, 34,
   143–4, 148–9

Campbell, Gordon 12
Carswell, Catherine 14
Carter, Frederick 64–5, 76, 100,
   101–2, 106–7, 141–3

Catholic Church, the 52–3,
   97–100, 102, 105–9,
   126–7, 134
Charles, R. H. 142
Christianity 1, 6–8, 12, 14, 17, 19,
   24–5, 28, 32, 38, 40–2,
   44, 53–4, 77–8, 82–3, 85,
   97–9, 101–5, 110, 122–33,
   135–6, 138–9, 141–3,
   145, 147, 149, 152–3, 155
   see also Adam and Eve;
   Bible; Catholic Church;
   Congregationalism; Holy
   Ghost; marriage; Trinity;
   Revelation
Clark, L. D. 57, 61, 74, 104–5, 116
Communism 13–14, 82, 126
Contreras, Sheila 72
Cooper, James Fenimore 51
Cornwall 14, 27–8, 59
Courlander, Harold 63
Cowan, James 76
Cushman, Keith 61–2

de Sola Pinto, Vivian 130
Delavenay, Émile 27, 48
Dennis, George 136–8, 140
Díaz del Castillo, Bernal 97–8
Dix, Carol 71
Doherty, Gerald 47–9
Durkheim, Émile 4–5

Eder, David 27–8
Eggert, Paul 86–8
Eliade, Mircea 4–6, 44

Fascism   81–2, 146
Fell, R. A. L.   137–8, 140
Fewkes, Jesse   61
Fjågesund, Peter   14
Forster, E. M.   79
Frazer, Sir James   69–71,
      134–6, 144

Garnett, Edward   2
Genesis, Book of   31–5, 47, 103
      see also Bible
Gilbert, Sandra   95–6, 147, 156–7
Girard, René   73–4
The Golden Bough see Frazer,
      Sir James
gramophone, symbol of   9–10
Grandsen, K. W.   11–12

Harrison, Jane   54
Heraclitus   17–18, 22, 25–6, 34,
      112 see also pre-Socratic
      philosophers
Heseltine, Philip   27–8
Hinduism   31, 33, 61
Hinz Evelyn   131–2
Holy Ghost, Lawrence's concept
      of   25, 29, 40, 103
Hopi, the   55–65, 92
Hopkin, Olive   27
Hough, Graham   119
Huitzilopochtli   89, 95, 98
Hyde, Virginia   89, 113, 115,
      119–20, 130

Iida, Takeo   90
Inge, Dean W. R.   147, 151–4

James, William   2–4, 9, 42, 44
Janik, Del Ivan   147
Jarrett-Kerr, Martin   129–30
Jenner, Katherine   12–13

Kabala   31
Kalnins, Mara   17

Kinkead-Weekes, Mark   27–8, 48,
      58, 72
Kermode, Frank   40
Kiowa ranch   65–7, 69, 75
Kondo, Kyoko Kay   47
Koteliansky, Samuel   2, 11–12
kundalini   28–9, 45–7, 49

Lady Chatterley's Lover trial see
      Regina v Penguin Books
Lawrence, D. H.,
      authoritarian politics of   18,
            20, 112–6, 140–1, 146
      belief in living cosmos of
            33, 35–6, 56–7, 60–1,
            65–7, 77–9, 112, 139–41,
            143–5
      belief in soul of   38, 40, 84–6,
            121–2, 132, 146
      belief in unknown God
            of   7–10, 32, 39, 43–5,
            81–92, 98–100, 102–6,
            111, 114, 116, 126, 132,
            146, 149–54, 156–7
      feminist criticism of   71–5,
            113–20
      heterodox Christian language
            of   19–20, 25, 40, 47,
            123–30, 133–4
      post-colonial criticism
            of   58–9, 71–2, 113
      works by
            PROSE
            'A Propos of "Lady
                  Chatterley's Lover"'
                  126–7, 131–2, 136
            Aaron's Rod   116
            Apocalypse   2–3, 44, 64–5,
                  141–6
            'Au Revoir, U. S. A.'   53
            'Books'   102–4
            'Certain Indians and an
                  Englishman'   52
            'The Crown'   20–6

'The Dance of the Sprouting
    Corn' 54, 74
The Escaped Cock 3, 130–6
Fantasia of the
    Unconscious 38–40, 76,
    84, 146
'Foreword to Sons and
    Lovers' 147
'The Future of the
    Novel' 104
'The Georgian
    Renaissance' 2
'Henry St. John de
    Crêvecoeur' 30–1, 37–8
'The Hopi Snake Dance'
    55–65, 67, 78–9, 96
'Hymns in a Man's Life' 1
'Indians and an
    Englishman' 52, 74
'Indians and Entertainment'
    54–5, 74
'Just Back from the Snake
    Dance' 55–6, 61–2
Kangaroo 9, 75, 79, 81–9,
    98–9, 104, 114–16
Lady Chatterley's
    Lover 121–30, 133–4
'Morality and the
    Novel' 116
Movements in European
    History 81
'New Mexico' 2–3, 74
'Nottingham and the Mining
    Countryside' 90–1
'On Being Religious'
    8, 102–3
'On Human Destiny'
    103–4
'Pan in America' 65–7, 75,
    78–9
The Plumed Serpent 76,
    89–100, 104–20, 140
'The Princess' 67
'The Proper Study' 103–4

Psychoanalysis of the
    Unconscious 38–40,
    51, 84, 146
Quetzalcoatl 92–101,
    104–7
The Rainbow 8, 19, 47, 49,
    123, 130, 154, 157
'Review of Art-Nonsense
    and Other Essays, by
    Eric Gill' 8
'The Risen Lord' 3, 133
Signature 19–21
Sketches of Etruscan
    Places 136–41
Sons and Lovers 21
St Mawr 67, 76–9
Studies in Classic American
    Literature 30–9, 51–2
Study of Thomas Hardy
    19, 21
Twilight in Italy 23–5, 29
'The Two Principles' 31–8
'There is no real
    battle...' 102
Women in Love 40–9, 75,
    79, 115
'The Woman Who Rode
    Away' 67–76, 78–9
POETRY
'The Argonauts' 148
'The Body of God' 152–4
'Demiurge' 3, 152
'The End, The Begin-
    ning' 157
'For the heroes are dipped
    in scarlet' 148–9
'Forget' 156–7
'The Hands of God' 154–5
'The Last Poems Note-
    book' 3, 147–57
'Let us be men—' 9
'Middle of the
    World' 148–9
'The Man of Tyre' 151

'Maximus'   150–1
'Pax'   155
'Red Geranium and Godly
    Mignonette'   153
'The Ship of Death'   155–7
'Sleep and waking'   156
'Song of Death'   157
'What then is Evil?'   157
'The work of Creation'   153
Lawrence, Frieda   4, 11, 89, 116
Leavis. F. R.   130
LeDoux, Larry   135
Loisy, Alfred   142
Luhan, Mabel Dodge Sterne
    51, 55–6, 61, 68–9
Luhan, Tony   55

Magnus, Maurice   77
Mansfield, Katherine   14–15, 20
Marcus, Philip   135
marriage, sacrament of   122–30,
    133–4, 136
Martz, Louis   107
McCollum, Laurie   73–4
McLeod, Sheila   72–3, 115
Mensch, Barbara   108
Mexico, indigenous peoples
    of   51, 53, 56, 59,
    69–71, 98–9, 111
Miles, Thomas   47, 49
Millett, Kate   71
Monte Cassino   77
Montgomery, Robert   17
morning star, symbol of   93–4, 96,
    104–6, 112–3, 115, 118
Morrell, Lady Ottoline
    13, 15–16, 19
Mountsier, Robert   85
Murray, Gilbert   147–51
Murry, John Middleton   14–15,
    20, 55, 102

Native Americans   51–68, 71, 76–7,
    98, 137, 139–40 see also
    Apache; Hopi; Pueblo Indians

negative theology see apophatic
    discourse
Neoplatonism   148–54
The New Age   27
Nietzsche, Friedrich   145
Nixon, Cornelia   81–2, 115
Nuttall, Zelia   88–92

occultism   27, 48 see also
    theosophy
Oman, John   142
Otto, Rudolf   8

Pan   65–7, 75–9
Panichas, George   147
Pitre, David   47
Plato   35, 101, 121–2, 144, 149,
    152–3
Poplawski, Paul   8
pre-Socratic philosophers,
    the   17–19, 21–3, 25,
    34, 143–4, 149 see also
    Heraclitus
Pryse, James   28–31, 36–8,
    45–9, 101 see also
    kundalini; theosophy
psychoanalysis   38–40, 72
Pueblo Indians   52, 54–7, 59–61,
    63–8, 91–2, 110, 140
    see also Hopi; Native
    Americans; Santo
    Domingo Pueblo; Taos

Quetzalcoatl   52–3, 70, 90,
    92–101, 105–6
Temple of   52–3

Rananim   11–15
Regina v Penguin Books
    129–30
Reid, Rev Robert   1–2, 8
Revelation, Book of   28–9, 37,
    47–8, 64, 83, 141–6 see
    also Bible; Pryse, James
Robinson, Bishop John   129–30

Roberts, Neil   55, 58, 65, 72, 113, 116
Rosicrucianism   34–5, 100
Rossman, Charles   51
Ruderman, Judith   58, 114
Russell, Bertrand   13–20, 112
   'Philosophy of Social
      Reconstruction'   16–17

Sagar, Keith   41, 43, 77, 156
Santo Domingo Pueblo   54, 74
Schapiro, Barbara   72
Schneider, Daniel   14, 17
Sheerin, Daniel   124
Siegel, Carol   71, 114–15
Simpson, Hilary   115–16
Smith, Bob   76
Snyder, Carey   58–9
Spence, Lewis   92–6
Spencer, Herbert   6–8, 21
Starr, Meredith   27
Steven, Laurence   71–2
Storch, Margaret   58, 114

Talayesva, Don   62, 64, 67
Tantrism   47–9

Taos   51–2, 54–5
Templeton, Wayne   58
Teotihuacan   52–3
Terry's Guide to Mexico   53, 92
Teunissen, John   131–2
theosophy   27–40, 45–9, 52, 100–1, 117–18 see also Blavatsky, Helena; kundalini; Pryse, James
Thompson, Theresa Mae   92
Tindall, William   48
Tracy, Billy   136–7
trial of Lady Chatterley's Lover see Regina v Penguin Books
Trinity, the   23–5, 29, 40, 103
Tylor, E. B.   59–61

Whelan, P. T.   27, 48
Wilding, Michael   88
Wright, T. R.   40, 45, 47, 123–5

yoga see Tantrism

Zennor see Cornwall
Zytaruk, George   13–14